14725

VERDI

and His Operas

VERDI

and His Operas

EDITED BY STANLEY SADIE
Compiled by Roger Parker

MACMILLAN REFERENCE LIMITED, LONDON
ST. MARTIN'S PRESS, INC, NEW YORK, NY

Published in Great Britain by
MACMILLAN REFERENCE LTD
25 Eccleston Place, London, SW1W 9NF

Basingstoke and Oxford
Companies and representatives throughout the world

British Library Cataloguing in Publication Data
Verdi and his operas - (Composers and their operas)
1. Verdi, Giuseppe, 1813—1901. 2. Operas. 3. Composers - Italy - Biography
I. Sadie, Stanley, 1930—
782.1´092
ISBN 0-333-790200

Published in the United States and Canada by
ST. MARTIN'S PRESS, INC
175 Fifth Avenue, New York, NY 10010

ISBN 0-312-244312

A catalog record for this book is available from the Library of Congress

Typesetting by The Florence Group, Stoodleigh, Devon, UK

Printed and bound in Britain by Cambridge University Press, Cambridge.

CONTENTS

PREFACE

This volume is one of a series drawn from *The New Grove Dictionary of Opera* (1992). That dictionary, in four volumes, includes articles on all significant composers of opera and on their individual operas (as well as many other topics). We felt that it would serve the use of a wider readership to make this material available in a format more convenient for the lover of opera and also at a price that would make it accessible to a much larger number of readers.

The most loved, and most performed, of opera composers are (in chronological order) Mozart, Verdi, Wagner and Puccini, who form the central topics of these volumes. The volumes each include chapters on the composer's life (with particular emphasis on his operatic activities) and a chapter on each of his operas. In some cases, the availability of additional space has made it possible for us to include, additionally, information that provides a fuller context for the composer and his work. Not for Verdi, who (perhaps unfortunately) composed so many operas that space did not permit any additions. And in the case of Wagner, whose operas demand quite extensive discussion, it was possible to add material only on his original singers and of course on Bayreuth.

For the Mozart volume, however, in which only a relatively modest number of operas call for extensive treatment, we were able to include material on virtually all his singers (excluding only those on whom we are almost totally ignorant) and on his interesting array of librettists, as well as some background on cities in which his music was heard. And for Puccini, there is material not only on librettists and singers but also on the most important composers among his Italian contemporaries, men whose music is still in the repertory (for instance the composers of *Cavalleria rusticana* and *Pagliacci*).

The authors of the chapters in these books are leading authorities on their subjects. The Mozart volume is chiefly the work of Julian Rushton, the Verdi of Roger Parker and the Wagner of Barry Millington, while the Puccini principal author is Julian Budden. Writers of the shorter sections are individually acknowledged within the book. We are grateful to all of them for permitting the re-use of their work.

STANLEY SADIE
London, 1999

ILLUSTRATIONS

Plate 1 – Title-page of the first edition of the vocal score of *Rigoletto* (Milan: Ricordi, 1851), with a vignette showing the opening scene of Act 3; the costumes are identical with those in Ricordi's published 'figurini' for the opera [Richard Macnutt]

Plate 2 – *Rigoletto*: design by Giuseppe and Pietro Bertoja for Act 1 scene ii (the most deserted corner of a blind alley) of the original production at La Fenice, Venice, 11 March 1851 [Museo Correr (photo Civici Musei Veneziani d'Arte e di Storia)]

Plate 3 – Scene from Colonello's production of *I Lombardi alla prima crociata* in the Verona Arena 1984 [Arena di Verona Press Office Archive (photo Franco Fainello)]

Plate 4 – *Aida*, Act 2 scene ii (one of the city gates of Thebes): engraving showing the first production at the Paris Opéra (Salle Garnier), 22 March 1880 [Civica Raccolta delle Stampe 'Achille Bertarelli', Castello Sforzesco]

Plate 5 – Giuseppe Verdi: photograph by Nadar, 1860s [Museo Teatrale alla Scala, Milan]

Plate 6 – Tito Gobbi in the title role of *Simon Boccanegra* [Stuart-Liff Collection]

Plate 7 – Verdi's preliminary sketches (possibly from late 1852) for Violetta's double aria at the end of Act 1 of *La traviata*: 'Ah fors'è lui' (top four systems) and 'Sempre libera degg'io' (central system); the passage marked 'Gran Duetto' was not used in the definitive version. The fact that there is no text underlay, and that the melodies are connected by a prose commentary, suggests that Verdi had not yet received the final version of the libretto [C. Gatti, Verdi nelle immagini (Milan, 1941)]

Plate 8 – Amelita Galli-Curci as Violetta in *La traviata* [Stuart-Liff Collection]

CHRONOLOGY OF VERDI'S LIFE AND OPERAS

1813

9/10 October   Born at Rancole, near Busseto, in the Duchy of Parma, northern Italy, to Carlo and Liugia Uttini Verdi

11 October   Baptized Giuseppe Fortunino Francesco

1825   Sponsored by the merchant Antonio Barezzi; begins studies with Ferdinando Provesi, director of the municipal music school in Busseto

1836   After studies in Milan with Vincenzo Lavigna, *maestro concertatore* at La Scala, returns to Busseto to become *maestro di musica*

4 May   Marries Margherita Barezzi

1839

17 November   Première of *Oberto, conte di San Bonifacio*, Milan, Scala

1840

5 September   Disastrous première of comic opera *Un giorno di regno*, Milan, Scala

Death of Margherita, predeceased by their two infant sons

1842

9 March   *Nabucco*, Milan, Scala

Giuseppina Strepponi (1815—97) creates the role of Abigaille and becomes Verdi's lifelong companion

1843

11 February   *I Lombardi alla prima crociata*, Milan, Scala

1844

9 March   *Ernani*, Venice, La Fenice

3 November   *I due Foscari*, Rome, Teatro Argentina

1845

15 February   *Giovanna d'Arco*, Milan, Scala

12 August   *Alzira*, Naples, San Carlo

1846

17 March   *Attila*, Venice, Fenice

1847

14 March   *Macbeth*, Florence, Pergola

22 July   *I masnadieri*, London, Her Majesty's Theatre

26 November   *Jérusalem*, Paris, Opéra

1848	Returns from Paris to Milan to support rising against Austrian rule
25 October	*Il corsaro*, Trieste, Grande
1849	Returns to Busetto
27 January	*La battaglia di Legano*, Rome, Argentina
8 December	*Luisa Miller*, Naples, San Carlo
1850	
16 November	*Stifellio*, Trieste, Grande
1851	Establishes permanent home with Strepponi at Sant'Agata, near Busetto
11 March	*Rigoletto*, Venice, Fenice
1853	
19 January	*Il trovatore*, Rome, Apollo
6 March	*La traviata*, Venice, Fenice
1855	
13 June	*Les vêpres siciliennes*, Paris, Opéra
1857	
12 March	*Simon Boccanegra*, Venice, Fenice
16 August	*Aroldo*, Rimini, Nuovo
1859	Verdi and Giuseppina Strepponi marry
17 February	*Un ballo in maschera*, Rome, Apollo
1860	Risorgimento culminates in war to expel Austria from Italy
1861	At the invitation of the Prime Minister, Camilio Cavour, Verdi becomes a member of the first parliament of an independent Italy
1862	
10 November	*La forza del destino*, St Petersburg, Imperial
1865	
21 April	*Macbeth* (revised version), Paris, Lyrique
1867	
11 March	*Don Carlos*, Paris, Opéra
1868	Verdi returns to Milan after a twenty-year absence; on the death of Rossini, proposes to Ricordi a *Messa per Rossini* to be written by leading Italian composers of the day; composes the 'Libera me'
1870	Unification of Italy, incorporating Naples, Sicily and the Papal States
1871	
24 December	*Aida*, Cairo, Opera; composed to celebrate the opening of the Suez Canal

1874	Elected to the Italian Senate
May	*Messa da Requiem* in honour of Alessandro Manzoni, Milan, San Marco
1884	
10 January	*Don Carlo* (revised version of *Don Carlos*), Milan, Scala
1887	
5 February	*Otello*, Milan, Scala
1893	
9 February	*Falstaff*, Milan, Scala
1897	
14 November	death of Giuseppina
1901	
27 January	Verdi dies in Milan, aged 87

Biography

Giuseppe Verdi

A month after Verdi's death, a solemn procession through Milan accompanied by hundreds of thousands of mourners assisted the transfer of his remains to their final resting place. At one point during this procession the crowd, aided by the chorus and orchestra of La Scala, apparently sang a moving rendition of 'Va pensiero', the chorus of Hebrew slaves from one of Verdi's earliest operas, *Nabucco*.

It is easy to see why this event has captured the imagination and assumed significance. By the time of his death, Verdi had established a unique position among his fellow countrymen: although many of his operas had disappeared from the repertory, he had nevertheless become a profound artistic symbol of the nation's achievement of statehood. Parts of his operatic legacy had entered into a kind of empyrean, divorced from the checks and balances of context and passing fashion. The fact that 'Va pensiero', written some 60 years earlier, could express contemporary Italians' feelings for their departed hero demonstrated the extent to which Verdi's music had been assimilated into the national consciousness.

However, nearly a hundred years after Verdi's death, such an event is likely to take on other meanings, and it can serve here as a cautionary note on which to introduce an account of the life and works. To begin at the end of Verdi's long life is a timely reminder of our present perspective: Verdi's story has continually been written backwards, the early events and achievements accruing narrative force and meaning through the powerful attraction of our sense of their ending. Such is of course true of all critical biography, but the extent to which it has influenced our perception of Verdi makes his an exceptional case. In an attempt to revalue (rather than evade) that perspective, the present survey will follow much recent scholarship in attempting to place Verdi's operas more firmly in the context of their time; and, perhaps more important, it will treat their reception as a separate historical phenomenon, so far as is possible disentangled from present-day critical opinion.

After an outline of Verdi's early years, his life and operas will be discussed within three unequal periods. This particular grouping of works is unusual, though as defensible as any other on artistic grounds; it is, however, made primarily for practical reasons and should not be taken to imply the kind of hierarchy of value traditionally signalled by subheadings such as 'youth' or 'maturity'. The first period takes in the 19 operas from *Oberto* (1839) to *La traviata* (1853). Claims are frequently made for a qualitative leap to a 'second period', beginning some time in the late 1840s or early 1850s, with *Macbeth*, *Luisa Miller* or *Rigoletto* as the watershed; but the entire period is probably best seen as a gradual unfolding within the Italian operatic tradition. A second period, during which the influence of French grand opera is of great importance, includes the seven operas from *Les vêpres siciliennes* (1855) to *Aida* (1871). After the compositional hiatus of the 1870s, a final period, that of Verdi's last style, includes the revisions to *Simon Boccanegra* and *Don Carlos*, and the operas *Otello* (1887) and *Falstaff* (1893).

1813–39 Verdi was born in Roncole, a small village near Busseto in the Duchy of Parma. His exact birth date is uncertain. The baptismal register of 11 October records him as 'born yesterday', but as days were sometimes counted as beginning at sunset, that could mean either 9 or 10 October. The birth register describes his father Carlo (1785–1867) as an 'inn-keeper', his mother Luigia Uttini (1787–1851) as a 'spinner'; both belonged to families of small landowners and traders, certainly not the illiterate peasant class from which Verdi later liked to present himself as having emerged.

In typically middle-class fashion, Carlo Verdi was energetic in furthering his son's education. Before the age of four, Verdi began instruction with the local priests, probably in music as well as other subjects; his father bought him an old spinet when he was seven, and he was soon substituting as organist at the local church of San Michele, taking the position permanently at the age of nine. In 1823 he moved to Busseto, and at the age of 11 he entered the *ginnasio* there, receiving training in Italian, Latin, humanities and rhetoric. In 1825 he began lessons with Ferdinando Provesi, *maestro di cappella* at San Bartolomeo, Busseto, and director of the municipal music school and local Philharmonic Society. The picture emerges of youthful precocity eagerly nurtured by an ambitious father and of a sustained, sophisticated and elaborate formal education – again something Verdi tended to hide in later life, giving the impression of a largely self-taught and obscure youth.

In 1829 Verdi applied unsuccessfully for the post of organist at nearby Soragna. He was becoming increasingly involved in Busseto's musical life, both as a composer and as a performer. As he later recalled:

From the ages of 13 to 18 I wrote a motley assortment of pieces: marches for band by the hundred, perhaps as many little *sinfonie* that were used in church, in the theatre and at concerts, five or six concertos and sets of variations for pianoforte, which I played myself at concerts, many serenades, cantatas (arias, duets, very many trios) and various pieces of church music, of which I remember only a *Stabat mater*.

In May 1831 he moved into the house of Antonio Barezzi, a prominent merchant in Busseto and a keen amateur musician. Verdi gave singing and piano lessons to Barezzi's daughter Margherita (born 4 May 1814; died 18 June 1840) and the young couple became unofficially engaged.

At about the same time it became clear that the musical world of Busseto was too small, and Carlo Verdi applied to a Bussetan charitable institution (the Monte di Pietà e d'Abbondanza) for a scholarship to allow his son to study in Milan, then the cultural capital of northern Italy. The application, bolstered by glowing references from Provesi and others, was successful; but no scholarship was available until late 1833. However, Barezzi guaranteed financial support for the first year and in May 1832, at the age of 18, Verdi travelled to Milan and applied for permission to study at the conservatory. He was refused entry, partly for bureaucratic reasons (he was four years above the usual entering age and was not resident in Lombardy-Venetia), partly on account of his unorthodox piano technique. It was an 'official' rejection that Verdi felt keenly until the end of his life. Barezzi agreed to the added expense of private study in Milan, and Verdi became the pupil of Vincenzo Lavigna, who had for many years been *maestro concertatore* at La Scala.

According to Verdi's later recollections, lessons with Lavigna involved little but strict counterpoint: 'in the three years spent with him I did nothing but canons and fugues, fugues and canons of all sorts. No one taught me orchestration or how to treat dramatic music.' This insistence was probably a further attempt to fashion his own image as a 'self-taught' composer. Contemporary evidence suggests that Lavigna encouraged Verdi to attend the theatre regularly, and his letters of recommendation specify study in 'composizione ideale' (free composition) as well as in counterpoint. Lavigna also helped his pupil into Milanese musical society; in 1834 Verdi assisted at the keyboard in performances of Haydn's *Creation* given by the Milan Philharmonic Society directed by Pietro Massini, and a year later co-directed with Massini performances of Rossini's *La Cenerentola*.

By the time Verdi had completed his studies with Lavigna, in mid-1835, Busseto had again claimed his attention. Provesi had died in 1833, leaving open the post of musical director there; by June 1834 one Giovanni Ferrari had been appointed organist at San Bartolomeo but, encouraged by Barezzi, Verdi was eventually appointed to the post of *maestro di musica* (that is, to the secular portion of Provesi's post) in March 1836, though not before a prolonged struggle between rival factions in the town. On 4 May 1836 Verdi married Margherita Barezzi and settled in Busseto, directing and composing for the local Philharmonic Society and giving private lessons. He held the post for nearly three years, during which time he and Margherita had two children, Virginia (born 26 March 1837; died 12 Aug 1838) and Icilio Romano (born 11 July 1838; died 22 Oct 1839).

Verdi's provincial existence is best seen as an irritating delay in his professional career, and there is evidence that he was actively pursuing more ambitious plans. In April 1836 he renewed his contact with Massini's Milanese society by composing for them a cantata, to words by Count Renato Borromeo, in honour of the Austrian Emperor Ferdinand I. A series of letters to Massini informs us that during 1836 Verdi composed an opera entitled *Rocester*, to a libretto by the Milanese journalist and man of letters, Antonio Piazza. During

1837 he tried unsuccessfully to have the opera staged at the Teatro Ducale in Parma. But eventually, again with Massini's help, Verdi arranged for a revised version of the opera, now entitled *Oberto, conte di San Bonifacio*, to be performed at La Scala. In October 1838 he resigned as *maestro di musica* of Busseto and in February 1839 left for Milan. Nine months later his first opera received its première in the Lombard capital's most famous theatre.

1839–53   From the première of *Oberto* until at least the midpoint of his long career, the outward progress of Verdi's life is inseparable from that of his professional activities: a continual round of negotiations with theatres and librettists, of intense periods of composition and of exhausting preparations for and direction of premières and revivals. Much of this activity is summarized in the introductory sections to the entries in this dictionary on individual operas; certain general matters, however, are best mentioned here.

The success of *Oberto* apparently encouraged Bartolomeo Merelli, impresario at La Scala, to offer Verdi a contract for three more operas, to be composed over two years. The first was the comic opera *Un giorno di regno*, which failed disastrously on its first night in September 1840. Verdi's later autobiographical glosses (which are notoriously unreliable) state that this professional failure, together with the tragic loss of his young family (his wife Margherita died in June 1840; they had lost their two children in the previous two years), caused him to renounce composition. This may be partly true: his next opera, *Nabucco*, appeared some 18 months later, an unusually long delay. However, Verdi certainly continued a level of professional activity by writing new music for, and supervising revivals of, *Oberto*.

After *Nabucco*, whose public success in Milan was unprecedented, the round of new operas was virtually unremitting: in the 11 years from March 1842 (the première of *Nabucco*) to March 1853 (the première of *La traviata*), Verdi wrote 16 operas, an average of one every nine months. He also supervised numerous revivals, on occasion writing new music to accommodate a star performer. During the first part of this period he moved almost continually from one operatic centre to another, dividing what little time remained between Milan and Busseto. The years 1844–7 were particularly arduous (eight operas appearing in less than four years); his health broke down frequently and more than once he vowed to renounce operatic composition once he had achieved financial security and fulfilled outstanding contracts. His gathering fame did, however, have its advantages. The success of *Nabucco* opened doors in Milanese society and Verdi soon made some longstanding friendships, notably with Clara Maffei, whose artistic salon he frequently attended. It is likely that during these early years of success he formed a lasting attachment to the soprano Giuseppina Strepponi, who was to become his lifelong companion.

Apart from a brief visit to Vienna in 1843, Verdi remained within the Italian peninsula until March 1847 when he undertook a long foreign expedition, initially to supervise the premières of *I masnadieri* in London and *Jérusalem* in Paris. He then set up house with Strepponi in Paris, staying there about two years, although with a visit to Milan during the 1848 uprisings and a trip to the short-lived Roman Republic to supervise the première of *La battaglia di Legnano* in early 1849. Verdi returned with Strepponi to Busseto in mid-1849, and in 1851 they moved to a permanent home at the nearby farm of Sant'Agata, land once owned by Verdi's ancestors.

OPERAS: 'OBERTO' (1839) TO 'LA TRAVIATA' (1853)

Composition   The genesis of a Verdian opera of this period follows a fairly predictable pattern, one that can teach us a good deal about the composer's artistic priorities and aims. The first step almost always involved negotiations with a theatre, an agreement of terms and deadlines. Unlike most of his Italian predecessors, Verdi was reluctant to deal through theatrical agents, preferring to negotiate fees for the première performance directly with the theatre management. Even though copyright protection was not fully established, he would supplement this income with rental fees and sales of printed materials; indeed, as his career progressed, Verdi's publishers (almost always the Milan firm of Ricordi) took a more active part in commissioning new works. The eventual contract with the theatre often included stipulations about the cast of the première, and Verdi chose operatic subjects with a direct eye to the available performers. The subject itself was then decided upon either by Verdi or his librettist, although – as success brought a new level of artistic freedom – Verdi became increasingly likely to reserve for himself this crucial decision. He favoured works that had already proved their worth as spoken dramas, and he had a fondness for foreign subjects, in particular Romantic melodramas set in the Middle Ages, by famous authors such as Byron, Schiller and Hugo, or by their more obscure contemporaries. In searching for new subjects he constantly stressed the need for unusual, gripping characters and for what he called 'strong' situations: scenes in which these characters could be placed in dramatic confrontation.

The first stage in fashioning an opera from the source text would typically involve a parcelling of the action into musical numbers such as arias, duets and ensembles. This was often done by annotating a prose summary of the source, and would typically be a collaborative effort between Verdi and his librettist. Once the work's essential formal outlines had been fixed, the librettist would prepare a poetic text in which the configuration of verse forms would reflect in detail the various musical forms agreed upon. Verdi frequently played an active part in this stage, particularly when working with his most common librettist of this period, Francesco Maria Piave. He might, for example, require certain sections to be cut down (Verdi was in general anxious to avoid long passages of recitative), might ask for changes of poetic metre in fixed forms, or even for line by line rewording to clarify the dramatic effect.

Finally came composition of the score, which typically occurred in at least three stages. First Verdi drafted the opera in short score, usually on just two staves (only one of these drafts, for *Rigoletto*, is currently available, although we can infer from the structure of Verdi's autographs that similar documents existed from at least the time of *Nabucco*). In writing this short-score draft, Verdi differed from predecessors such as Rossini and Donizetti, who typically composed straight on to the autograph; the practice gives an indication of the care and time he was willing to spend on each new work. The second stage of composition involved transferring the draft version to the autograph, adding essential instrumental lines (usually the first violin and bass) to create what has been termed a 'skeleton score'. From this skeleton score, vocal parts would be extracted by copyists and given to the singers of the première. Pressure of time dictated that only when Verdi arrived at the venue of the first performance, and had heard his singers in the theatre, would he complete (often in extreme haste) the orchestration.

Dramatic forms   It is clear from the preceding summary that various fixed forms were at the basis of Verdian musical drama; and these forms, geared as they mostly were to the individual expression and patterned confrontation of the major characters, arose from an awareness of the overwhelming importance of the principal performers in the success of an opera. The basic forms, inherited by Verdi from his Italian predecessors, are fairly simple to outline. The normative structure was the solo aria, called 'cavatina' if it marked the first entrance of a character, and typically made up of an introductory scena or recitative followed by three 'movements': a lyrical first movement, usually slow in tempo, called 'cantabile' or (preferably) 'adagio'; a connecting passage, often stimulated by some stage event – the entrance of new characters or the revelation of new information – and called the 'tempo di mezzo'; and a concluding cabaletta, usually faster than the first movement. The grand duet was identically structured, though with an opening movement before the Adagio, commonly employing patterned exchanges between the characters and called the 'tempo d'attacco'. Large-scale internal finales followed the pattern of the grand duet, though often with a more elaborate *tempo d'attacco*; the Adagio in ensembles was often called 'largo' or 'largo concertato', and the final movement was called a 'stretta'. Ranged around these large, multi-sectional units were shorter, connecting pieces, notably various purely choral movements and shorter, one-movement arias, often called 'romanza'. There is a close parallel between musical and poetic forms, each 'movement' tending to be in a different type of *versi lirici* (rhyming stanzas of fixed line length and syllable count). Given the nature of an opera's genesis, this parallel is of course unremarkable; the fact that it has occasioned so much detailed discussion of late is perhaps as much due to the possibilities it furnishes for formal abstraction as to the dramatic insights it occasionally offers.

In discussing Verdi's individual approach to these fixed forms, there has been a tendency to paint a romantic picture, one that equates release from formal 'constraints' with 'progress', and that celebrates the composer's gradual emancipation from formal 'tyranny'. According to this interpretation Verdi is a formal revolutionary, constantly striving towards a more naturalistic mode of musical drama. There is some truth in this image: as the 19th century progressed, opera in all countries turned to looser, less predictable musical forms. However, Verdi is perhaps better seen as a conservative influence within this broad trend, especially when viewed in the context of his immediate predecessors in Italy. The operas up to *La traviata* are at least as easy to codify in formal terms as those, for example, of Donizetti.

True, Verdi sometimes radically altered or ignored traditional forms. There are classic examples: the introduction of Macbeth by means of an understated duettino, 'Due vaticini', rather than a full-scale cavatina; the curious Act 1 duet between Rigoletto and Sparafucile, which is a kind of free conversation over an instrumental melody; the stretta-less grand finales of *Nabucco* Act 2, *I due Foscari* Act 2, *Attila* Act 1, *Luisa Miller* Act 1 and *Il trovatore* Act 2; the complete absence of a concertato finale in *I masnadieri* and *Rigoletto*. Other moments are less often mentioned: the grand duets of *La battaglia di Legnano* Act 1 and *Stiffelio* Act 3 follow the fluctuations of character confrontation so minutely that they are extremely difficult to parcel out into the traditional four 'movements'; the Act 1 duet in *Alzira* moves from *tempo d'attacco* straight to cabaletta, a process repeated in the Act 1 trio finale of *Il trovatore*.

However, much more often Verdi chose to manipulate forms from within, preserving their boundaries but expanding or condensing individual movements as the drama dictated. Famous examples include the Violetta-Germont duet in *La traviata* Act 2, which boasts a vastly expanded and lyrically enriched *tempo d'attacco*; or Leonora's aria in *Il trovatore* Act 4, in which the usually fugitive *tempo di mezzo* expands to become the famous 'Miserere' scene. Equally important

11

in this enrichment is Verdi's tendency to focus musical weight on ensemble numbers and to concentrate in these numbers on the opposition between characters. In this respect the almost complete absence in his works of the 'rondò finale' (a favourite Donizettian form in which a soloist, usually the soprano, closes the opera with an elaborate, two-movement aria) is significant, as is its replacement by ensemble finales such as those of *Ernani* and *Il trovatore*. The lyrical movements of Verdi's ensembles, particularly of the grand duets, tend to establish at the outset a vivid sense of vocal difference and often retain that sense until the last possible moment. The extended passages of parallel 3rds or 6ths so well-known in Donizetti and Bellini are rare and are usually reserved as coda material.

Certain operas, particularly those written in collaboration with temistocle Solera, are notable for a dynamic new use of the chorus. While choruses in the earlier 19th century had typically served a neutral, scene-setting function, Verdi's chorus frequently appears in the vocal forefront, offering powerful sonic enrichment to ensemble numbers and even intruding into the soloist's domain. *Nabucco* offers many early examples: the dramatic incursion of the chorus in both the slow movement and the cabaletta of Zaccaria's Act 1 aria; their climactic appearance in the Act 2 canonic ensemble, 'S'appressan gl'istanti'; and of course 'Va pensiero' in Act 3, where the chorus sings mostly in unison, with a directness and simplicity of emotional appeal that had traditionally been heard only from soloists.

Lyric prototype   In attempting to summarize the smaller-scale level of Verdi's lyrical movements, many critics have again appealed to a traditional norm, though one more abstractly analytical than the set-piece forms and one whose limitations and partiality need to be remembered. This is the 'lyric prototype', a four-phrase pattern usually represented by the scheme $AA'BA''$ or (its common variant) $AA'BC$. Such a model could also include subscript numbers to indicate phrase length – the normative phrase would be four bars – and poetic lines can also be incorporated, as the usual consumption of text exactly parallels the musical periodicity, with two poetic lines matching one four-bar period. The prototype does, however, ignore harmonic movement, which can vary significantly within pieces that would have an identical letter scheme. What is more, in its 'pure' form the scheme appears only rarely, usually as one character's solo statement in an ensemble movement; in solo arias, some level of expansion, typically in coda material, is clearly necessary to achieve adequate length. These limitations notwithstanding, the prototype has proved the most reliable and flexible method of codifying Verdi's basic lyric shapes.

A very early example of the model, close to its basic form, comes in the cabaletta of the protagonist's aria in Act 2 of *Oberto* (ex.1). Even at this early stage, a Verdian novelty can be discerned in the comparative restriction of the formal scheme. In the hands of Verdi's predecessors, the prototype tended to dissolve after the *B* section into looser periods of ornamental vocal writing and word repetition, especially in a solo aria. Verdi did occasionally write arias of that kind: for Riccardo in Act 1 of *Oberto*, or – significantly, as the part was expressly written for the 'old-fashioned' virtuosa Jenny Lind – for Amalia in both Acts 1 and 3 of *I masnadieri*. However, his typical

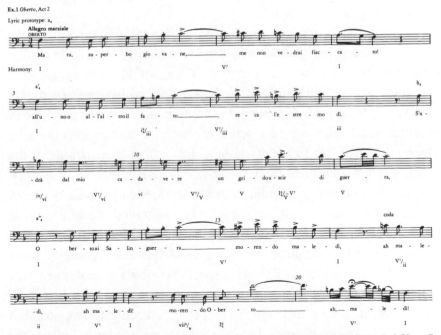

Ex.1 *Oberto*, Act 2

['But you, proud youth, you will not exhaust me! For one of us, this day will be the last. From my corpse, a war-like cry will be heard: the dying Oberto, cursing the Salinguerra!']

13

Ex.2 *Ernani*, Act 1

['Ernani!... Ernani, spirit me away from this horrible embrace. Let us fly... if love allows me to live with you, I will follow you through caves and barren lands. Those caves will be for me an Eden of delights.']

practice, even when writing a bravura aria, was to bind the ornamentation strictly within a periodic structure, even as the aria reached
its final stages.

As with his conservatism in larger formal matters, this self-
imposed restriction had the effect of channelling Verdi's invention
into manipulations of the prototype from within, into expansions,
contractions and enrichments of the lyric form. Elvira's *Andantino*
in Act 1 of *Ernani*, for example, contains an expansion of the *B*
section which injects a new sense of dialectic tension into the aria.
More than that: far from 'dissolving' into ornamental writing at the
end, the aria continues to subordinate, or rather harness, the ornamentation, containing it within a strictly controlled periodicity (ex.2).
Such an example, which could easily be multiplied, demonstrates at
least a part of how the energy so typical of Verdi's music is created.

As the 1840s unfolded, Verdi's lyrical forms increasingly show
the influence of French models, especially after his prolonged stay
in Paris in 1847–9. *Il corsaro*, for example, opens with two slow
arias that, if in very different ways, are organized into two strophes
(a typically French design). Later, more famous examples include the

couplet forms (so called because of the shorter, refrain line that ends each stanza) found in Rodolfo's 'Quando le sere al placido' (*Luisa Miller* Act 2) and Germont's 'Di Provenza il mar, il suol' (*La traviata* Act 2). However, none of these examples entirely abandons the lyric prototype; indeed, in one sense it is more pervasive, tending to appear in miniature in each stanza. As we move to the early 1850s, the variety of internal structures that can be generated proliferates, giving rise to such startling experiments as Gilda's 'Caro nome' (*Rigoletto* Act 1), in which the second half of an initial *AA'BA"* form, remarkable for its simplicity, is subjected to an elaborate series of surface variations.

Harmony, tinta, local colour Verdi's small-scale harmonic language is for the most part simple and direct, following general patterns that can easily be summarized within the lyric prototype. The opening *A* sections concentrate on tonic and dominant harmonies, sometimes ending with a modulation to a near-related key; the *B* section is comparatively unstable; the final *A* (or *C*) section returns to a stable tonic. Secondary modulations within an aria are frequently to keys a 3rd apart, thus allowing a new harmonic underpinning for important vocal sonorities. In large set pieces, notably in the Largo concertato, there is often a dramatic plunge into a distant key area near the end, a gesture from which Verdi occasionally found some difficulty in extricating himself. A few pieces show that Verdi was fully capable of an advanced, colouristic chromaticism – the Act 1 'Salve Maria' from *I Lombardi* is an early example, the prelude to Act 3 of *La traviata* a later, more persuasive one; but for the most part his liking for strict periodic structures made elaborate chromatic effects difficult to employ except at moments of high relief.

The extent to which organized, directed tonality may be traced at a larger level of structure is still a matter for debate. Unlike most of his Italian predecessors, Verdi seemed indifferent to tonal closure at levels larger than the single 'movement': most arias, duets and ensembles begin in one key and end in another; nor do individual acts, let alone entire operas, often display any obvious tonal plan. It seems likely that Verdi chose the tonality of movements within set pieces primarily with a view to the vocal tessituras he wished to exploit, and various last-minute transpositions he effected to aid individual singers would seem to support this theory. There is, though, evidence in some operas of an association between certain keys and certain characters or groups of characters. *Il trovatore* is an obvious example: the flat keys are linked with the aristocratic world of Leonora and Count di Luna, while sharp keys tend to accompany Manrico, Azucena and the world of the gypsies. *Macbeth* shows a similar binary divide (Macbeth and Lady Macbeth on the flat side, the witches on the sharp side). Such associations may also attend other harmonic recurrences, such as the occasional repetition of large-scale tonal progressions. But these rather loose juxtapositions – by no means rigidly maintained – probably represent the ultimate point of tonal organization in Verdi: there have been no convincing demonstrations of 'tonal motion' across large spans of Verdian musical drama.

More important than harmony as a means of establishing what Verdi called the *tinta* or *tinte* (identifying colour or colours) of a given opera are various recurring melodic shapes. These should not be confused with recurring motifs, which Verdi occasionally used to great effect by association with an important element of the drama (the horn-call in *Ernani* is a classic early example), and which gain their effect by means of straightforward semantic identification and a sense of isolation from the basic musical fabric. Nor are they connected with the proto-leitmotivic experiment of *I due Foscari*, in which the main entrances of certain characters or groups are marked by the repetition of a 'personal' instrumental theme (an interesting case in that the curiously undramatic tone of these recollections illustrates, as Carl Dahlhaus has suggested, that leitmotivic technique is basically incompatible with Italian opera's constant tendency to create a vivid sense of the affective present). On the contrary, these recurring shapes will tend to hover on the edge of obvious reminiscence, thus contributing to a sense of musical cohesion without accruing semantic weight. The rising 6th that begins so many lyric pieces in *Ernani*, the 'bow shape' of *Attila*, perhaps even the stepwise rising line of *Oberto* are possible examples, ones that could cautiously be multiplied.

At least until the later part of this period, the fixing of an opera within a specific ambience, the use of what is often called 'local colour', was sporadic and often routine. The single gesture towards the exotic ambience of *Nabucco*, for example (the chorus that opens Act 3), is probably the opera's least inspired number, and one reason why *Nabucco* is more successful than *I Lombardi* (Verdi's next opera, and one that resembles *Nabucco* in many ways) is that the later opera's frequent changes of locale and ambience necessitate a larger amount of this rather pallid, 'colouristic' music. By the end of the 1840s, however, particularly after his exposure to the French stage, Verdi's attitude changed. In *Luisa Miller*, the rustic ambience is an important element of the opera's *tinta*, joining with the recurring shapes (in this case as much rhythmic ideas as melodic ones) to give the work a pronounced individuality. This merging of local colour with other recurring elements is also evident in *Il trovatore*, where the 'Spanish' atmosphere is intimately bound to the musical sphere inhabited by Azucena. It reaches a pinnacle with *La traviata*, in which much of the drama unfolds against telling refractions of the waltz-laden social world so vividly depicted in the opening scene.

Reception and politics   By the early 1850s, Verdi had become the most famous and frequently performed Italian opera composer in Europe, having wrested the former epithet from Rossini, the latter from Donizetti. He commanded unprecedented fees for new operas (although he lagged some way behind the most famous singers in earning potential), could choose more-or-less freely which theatres were to launch his latest works, and had begun to acquire substantial assets in farm land and buildings. Admittedly, Verdi's 'noisy' instrumentation (perhaps in particular his favouring of the middle to low register of the orchestra), his often extreme demands on singers and his taste for extravagant melodramatic plots had on occasions brought him criticism in the press during the 1840s; and several of his operas failed to find a place in the 'repertory' that was rapidly forming during this period. However, despite the occasional critical attack, and the occasional public failure such as that which initially greeted *La traviata*, opponents of Verdi (at least within Italy) were becoming an eccentric minority.

On occasion it seemed that the composer's most serious opposition came from those elaborate and multifarious organs of state censorship which controlled artistic expression in most parts of Italy. Librettos could be subject to modification on religious, moral or political grounds; and in Milan and Naples (perhaps elsewhere) the censor would also attend the dress rehearsal, to ensure that the music and staging produced no improprieties. However, severity varied greatly from state to state, and because censorship in the northern states (in which Verdi concentrated his early career) was far more easygoing than that in Rome or Naples, the composer encountered few difficulties with his early operas. The Zaccaria of *Nabucco*, for example, ended his Act 1 cabaletta with the words 'Che dia morte allo stranier' ('That gives death to the foreigner') without censorial interference in a huge number of early productions, and even the 'revolutionary' *Ernani* encountered only minor obstacles in the north. After 1848 the situation worsened, and it is significant that Verdi's most severe bouts with the censor occurred in the austere, counter-revolutionary atmosphere of the late 1840s and 50s, over the religious subject matter of *Stiffelio* and over many aspects of *Rigoletto* and *Un ballo in maschera*.

The business of government censorship, imposed by foreign nations and the local governments that controlled Italy, inevitably leads to a consideration of Verdi's political status during this period and of the extent to which his operas served to heighten the Italian people's national consciousness. Verdi was undoubtedly a staunch patriot, as can be seen from many of his letters, from his return to Milan during the 1848 uprising, and from his one unambiguously 'patriotic' opera, *La battaglia di Legnano* (1849, Rome). However, before 1846 there is hardly any evidence that his operas were regarded as especially dangerous politically or that they excited patriotic enthusiasm in their audiences. In the period between the liberal reforms of Pius IX in 1846 and the revolutions of 1848, the theatre increasingly became a focus of political demonstrations, but Verdi's operas seem to have accompanied such outbursts no more often than those of other composers. It is also significant that, during the months of mid-1848 in which the Milanese governed their own city, neither the newly-liberated theatrical press nor the public seemed especially interested in Verdi or his music. This is not to deny the stirring force of Verdi's early music, in particular his treatment of the chorus as a dynamic new expressive power; but connections between his music and political events were for the most part made later in the century, some time after the revolutionary atmosphere had cooled.

1853–71   After the première of *La traviata* in March 1853, the pace of Verdi's operatic production slowed considerably. The 11 years up to *Traviata* had produced 16 operas; the 18 years that followed saw only six new works: *Les vêpres siciliennes, Simon Boccanegra, Un ballo in maschera, La forza del destino, Don Carlos* and *Aida*. Admittedly, such a comparison gives a slightly exaggerated picture. Two of the operas (*Vêpres* and *Don Carlos*) were written for the Paris Opéra: they are thus both considerably longer than any other of Verdi's scores and required the composer's presence in Paris during extended rehearsal periods. Furthermore, Verdi devoted much time and creative energy to revising various works: there were relatively minor adjustments to *La traviata* and *Simon Boccanegra* after unsuccessful first performances, and to *Il trovatore* for its Paris version; a thorough overhaul of *Macbeth*, again for Paris; the refashioning of *Stiffelio* as *Aroldo*; and substantial revisions to *La forza del destino* for its La Scala première. Such efforts notwithstanding, however, Verdi now spent an increasing amount of time away from the theatre, and on at least one occasion – in the more than three-year gap between finishing *Un ballo in maschera* (early 1858) and starting *La forza del destino* (mid-1861) – he seems to have decided to stop composing altogether.

His three most extensive foreign expeditions were all related to professional engagements: a two-year period in Paris (1854–5) saw the completion and performance of *Les vêpres siciliennes*; *La forza del destino* required two trips to Russia, with visits en route to Paris, London and Madrid (1862–3); and the production of *Don Carlos* kept him in Paris for nearly a year (1866–7). When not travelling, Verdi divided his time between periods of intense activity on his farmlands at Sant'Agata and visits to friends in other cities, notably Naples and Venice. In 1859, after more than ten years together, Verdi and Giuseppina Strepponi were finally married; in 1866 they set up permanent winter quarters in Genoa, finding the climate of Sant'Agata too hostile. As early as 1845, Verdi had quarrelled with the directors of La Scala over what he considered the unacceptable production standards. Not long after, he broke completely with Milan, which had been his centre of operations in the early to mid-1840s; after his dramatic return during the 1848 revolutions, he did not enter the city again for 20 years, losing touch with most of his Milanese friends. But the late 1860s saw a rapprochement. In 1868 he returned to the city to visit Clara Maffei and to meet for the first time Alessandro Manzoni, whom he had long revered. A year later he re-established contacts with La Scala, supervising there the première of the revised *Forza del destino*. On hearing of the death of Rossini (in November 1868), Verdi suggested to Ricordi that a *Messa per Rossini* be written jointly by the most famous Italian composers of the day. The Mass was duly completed, Verdi supplying the 'Libera me', but there was much bitter wrangling over administrative problems and the work was never performed.

OPERAS: 'LES VÊPRES SICILIENNES' (1855) TO 'AIDA' (1871)

Composition   The genesis, and thus to a certain extent the aesthetic premises, of a Verdi opera of this period had changed a little from those operating earlier in his career, the principal difference being that the composer's burgeoning reputation allowed him greater artistic freedom. He was besieged by offers from the major theatres of Italy, Europe and beyond, and could choose the venue and the subject of any new opera. He was also free to refuse commissions much more often than he had in the hectic 1840s, as he could live from accumulated wealth for long periods. However, when he did work the old patterns remained. Verdi was still wary of committing himself to a subject before the principal singers had been engaged, refusing, for example, to sign a contract for *La forza del destino* until the company had been fixed. He still composed by way of a prose scenario to clarify the musical forms, a libretto to reflect those forms, a draft and then a 'skeleton score', and finally an orchestration of that score. He continued to compose with great facility and, allowing for the vastly increased length of several of these operas, probably took no longer drafting music than he had when writing his earliest works.

On the surface, at least, the types of subject he chose were also unchanged: he remained loyal to Schiller and also to the lesser lights of romantic melodrama. Towards the end of the period, however, there is evidence of a decisive move away from melodramatic extremes. In revising *Macbeth* in 1865, for example, he replaced the final, onstage death scene with a Victory Chorus; more telling still, in the 1869 revision of *La forza del destino* he replaced the bloody denouement with an ensemble of religious consolation. This move towards a broader canvas is part of a larger change, a gradual expansion in the stylistic and dramatic scope of his operas. Verdi now repeatedly called for more variety in his operatic subjects and he castigated his earlier operas as one-dimensional. He strove to blend or boldly juxtapose comic and tragic scenes and genres (notably in *Un ballo in maschera* and *La forza del destino*) and to explore greater extremes of musical and dramatic ambience, sacrificing the dramatic cohesion of his best earlier work in an effort to bring Italian opera into line with an increasingly dominant French fashion.

Dramatic forms   Were we to judge solely from Verdi's correspondence, it would seem that this period saw the composer seeking radical alternatives to the fixed dramatic forms that had characterized his early operas. In negotiations over a possible setting of *King Lear*, for example, he more than once voiced his need for entirely new structures, and in discussing *Un ballo in maschera* he warned the Neapolitan impresario Torelli that Scribe's libretto 'has the conventional modes of all operas, a thing that I have always disliked and now find insufferable'. However, these radical epistolary statements are better taken as hortatory rather than prescriptive: a way of encouraging his librettists not to lapse into the merely routine. When it came to the discussion of concrete detail, Verdi continued to think along traditional lines, and the eventual librettos for both *Re Lear* and *Ballo* are largely constructed in the conventional manner. As in the earlier period, the bulk of Verdi's operatic music remains definable within traditional formal types, although his tendency to manipulate these types according to the dramatic situation became ever more extreme.

The most fragile unit of the old, multi-movement structure was the cabaletta (which, in its ensemble form as stretta, had already disappeared from certain finales of the 1840s). Verdi was inclined to shorten it, sometimes (for example in the Henri-Montfort duet of *Les vêpres siciliennes* Act 3) making it nothing more than a fast coda section with no independent thematic ideas, or even to omit it entirely, ending the number with some stage action or portentous utterance (as in the Boccanegra-Fiesco duet in the prologue of *Simon Boccanegra*), or with a final, climactic melody (as in Riccardo's aria in Act 3 of *Un ballo in maschera)*. But, in particular with the earlier movements of set pieces, his usual practice was to continue those complex expansions and manipulations found in the Germont-Violetta duet from *La traviata* Act 2; the multi-movement form became extremely flexible, but could nevertheless articulate important stages in the dramatic development. The classic illustration of this internal renewal of form is in the last opera of this period, *Aida*, which boasts a magnificent series of grand duets, each traceable to traditional patterns but each offering a profoundly individual solution to the dramatic situation it underpins.

It is entirely in keeping with Verdi's ambivalent position towards formal conventions that, even as the various 'movements' of set pieces became less and less predictable, he sought ever more vivid ways of using the moment of transition between one movement and the next to articulate dramatic turning points. One outward manifestation of this search was his coining of the term 'parola scenica', which, as he wrote to Antonio Ghislanzoni, the librettist of *Aida*, 'sculpts and renders clear and evident the situation'. 'Parole sceniche', utterances such as Amonasro's 'Dei Faraoni tu sei la schiava!' in his Act 3 duet with Aida, typically occur immediately before the start of a new movement, signalling with a violent injection of musical prose that a new stage of the dramatic conflict, and a new lyrical stage of the set piece, is about to ensue.

Although examples in which traditional structures can still be found constitute the main stylistic line there are, especially in the French operas, passages where we see an emerging new aesthetic. Arias such as Philip II's 'Elle me n'aime pas' (*Don Carlos* Act 4) show comparatively little tendency to formal partition, and are better regarded as descendants of the great ariosos of Verdi's youth, especially those for Macbeth and Rigoletto. In numbers such as the Don Carlos-Elisabeth de Valois duet in Act 2 of *Don Carlos* it may even be nugatory to search for the remnants of traditional forms: the musical discourse follows in minute and constantly changing configuration the ebb and flow of the confrontation, creating the kind of 'musical prose' (or, as Verdi would call it, musical *dramma*) that was rapidly becoming the norm in European opera.

Lyric prototype The proliferation of lyrical types towards the end of the previous period continues into this one, with the influence of French operatic forms increasingly evident. While solo statements within duets and ensembles frequently retain the old *AA'BA''* form, full-scale aria movements commonly show a typically French ternary form, with larger *A* sections (often themselves based on the old 'lyric prototype') flanking a looser, declamatory *B* section. Amelia's 'Come in quest'ora bruna' (*Simon Boccanegra* Act 1) is a fine example of this form at its most extended; the classic condensed example is Radames' 'Celeste Aida' (*Aida* Act 1), which brings back elements of the *B* material to fashion a delicate coda.

When Verdi chose to retain the old-fashioned Italian model, he usually did so for characters in old-fashioned melodramatic situations: Posa's 'C'est mon jour' in *Don Carlos* Act 4 is an obvious example. And frequently he made telling changes, ones indicative of a general shift in his lyric language. In Don Carlo's 'Urna fatal' (*La forza del destino* Act 3) the harmonic openness at the start of each lyric segment undermines the *AA'BC* form, encouraging us to hear the first two sections as one limb, and thus as the first part of a larger structure.

While the move towards larger, looser periods underlies much of Verdi's music during this period, he also continued to experiment in the opposite direction: following the example of 'Caro nome', he was occasionally encouraged by the dramatic situation to construct lyric movements of extreme formal simplicity. The final section of the Aida-Radames duet (*Aida* Act 4) is a most telling example (ex.3). This passage, first sung by Aida, is repeated literally by Radames and then repeated again by both characters in unison. The energy is, as it were, turned inwards, the extreme angularity and sheer difficulty of the vocal line forming an uncanny complement to the wellnigh obsessive formal repetition.

Ex.3 *Aida*, Act 4

['Farewell, earth; farewell valley of tears, dream of joy that vanished in sorrow. Heaven opens to us, and our wandering spirits to the beams of eternal day.']

Harmony, tinta, local colour   In comparison with that of his French and German contemporaries, Verdi's harmonic language remained for the most part within a simple diatonic framework. However, the musical surface of his operas became increasingly complex. Devices seen only exceptionally in the early operas – passages of rootless chromaticism, sudden shifts into remote keys (notably by way of unprepared 6–4 chords), a tendency to add surprising harmonic colour to much-used vocal sonorities – now become the norm. Nor are such devices so frequently subordinate to a firmly diatonic melody. Even in conventional arias such as Posa's 'C'est mon jour', the voice part may now be co-opted into a colouristic chromatic shift, creating a melodic line that makes little sense without its harmonic underpinning (ex.4). The effect, out of context, may sound wildly empirical; but, unlike some parallel moments in the earlier operas, these daring harmonic shifts are often carefully prepared (in the present case by a tonicization of G minor in the preceding *B* section). What is more, as set pieces expanded so too did the extent of chromatic interruption: in many arias and ensembles, the chromatic shifts expand to control entire phrases or even sections.

['Death has its attractions, oh my Carlos, for one who dies for you.']

There remains little evidence of control over spans larger than a single number, whether harmonic or motivic; indeed, the relative broadness of dramatic scope and looseness of construction among these operas work against even that patterned juxtaposition of tonal regions or melodic types found in operas such as *Il trovatore*. Occasionally a key centre or motif may briefly shoulder the burden of semantic weight (the 'death associations' of $D^\flat$ in *Ballo*, for example, or certain recurring motifs in *Don Carlos* or *Aida*), but – as he had learnt much earlier, in the experiment of *I due Foscari* – the continuing formal fixity of Verdi's musical language militates against the sustained use of such techniques, and they never approach a level of 'structural' significance.

On the other hand, local colour becomes an ever more important connecting device, perhaps as a necessary corrective to the expansion of dramatic scope and mood. Each of the operas is shot through with particular colours intimately associated with its setting: the sea images of *Simon Boccanegra*, the Gallic poise of *Un ballo in maschera*, the Spanishness of *La forza del destino* and *Don Carlos*. And with the musical orientalism of *Aida* local colour takes up a central position it will nearly always occupy in *fin-de-siècle* opera. Clearly this added dimension is intimately bound up with Verdi's increasingly sophisticated use of the orchestra. By the time of *Aida*, Verdi was capable of setting up a classic 'nature' scene such as the prelude to Act 3, in which the elements of harmony, melody and rhythm are all subsumed under a mantle of evocative orchestral colour.

Reception and politics As the 1850s unfolded, Verdi's pre-eminence in Italian music, and his international reputation, became ever more secure; although many of the early operas had been forgotten, *Rigoletto*, *Il trovatore* and *La traviata* quickly became cornerstones of the newly-emerging Italian operatic repertory. Each new Verdian opera generated enormous interest both in the national and the foreign press.

It gradually became clear, however, that Verdi's more recent works were not duplicating his successes of the early 1850s. Neither *Les vêpres siciliennes* nor *Don Carlos* established themselves at the

Opéra, and both had difficulties in transplanting to the Italian stage. *Simon Boccanegra* was poorly received and *Un ballo in maschera* and *La forza del destino* made their way comparatively slowly. Part of the problem undoubtedly lay in the seeming conservatism of Verdi's new creations. Although operas such as *Il trovatore* had quickly attained 'classic' status, a new generation of Italians was emerging, with young artistic revolutionaries such as Arrigo Boito calling for an end to the insular, 'formulaic' musical dramas of the past. Italian intellectuals began to read Wagner, and Italian theatres began to open their doors to French (and later to German) operas.

The paradox of this uncertain Italian reaction to Verdi's 'new manner' was that it went hand-in-hand with his institution as a national figure beyond the operatic world. In 1859, his name was apparently taken up as an acrostic message of Italian nationalistic aspirations ('Viva VERDI' standing for 'Viva *V*ittorio *E*manuele *R*e *D*' *I*talia); in 1861, during the first shaky months of Italian statehood, he agreed, at the personal insistence of Cavour, to serve as a member of the newly-formed Italian parliament. And it was precisely during these years that Verdi's early music began to be consistently associated with the revolutionary struggles of the 1840s. The famous choruses of his first operas, in particular 'Va pensiero' from *Nabucco*, gradually assumed something like iconic status, all the more so as the economic collapses and social tensions of the new Italian state engendered nostalgia for a past age in which Italians had been united against a foreign enemy.

In the face of these momentous cultural and political developments, and despite periodic bursts of professional and social activity, Verdi chose strategic withdrawal: physically behind the walls of Sant'Agata, mentally into an image of himself as a rough, untutored man of the soil, the peasant from Roncole, an 'authentic' Italian willing to set himself against the tide of cosmopolitan sophistication he saw washing around him. It was overwhelmingly this image that he offered to those first biographers who now began to pester him for information on his early life, and the resulting self-portrait was one he sedulously cultivated (along with his farm lands) for the rest of his long life.

1871–1901   After *Aida* in 1871, there was to be no Verdi operatic première for 16 years: in the 30 years that were left him, he composed just two more dramatic works, *Otello* and *Falstaff*. The creative tally was not, of course, quite so modest. In 1874 came the *Messa da Requiem*, composed in honour of Alessandro Manzoni; in the early 1880s Verdi made important revisions to *Simon Boccanegra* and, a little later, to *Don Carlos*; there are various sacred vocal pieces, some of them later collected under the title *Quattro pezzi sacri*. But the fact remains that the 1870s and early 80s, years in which we might imagine Verdi to have been at the height of his creative powers, saw no new operas.

The 1870s did, though, see an increase in what might be called Verdi's 'social' energy. He travelled widely to supervise and direct performances of *Aida* and the *Requiem*, in 1875 undertaking a veritable European tour with the latter work, conducting in Paris, London and Vienna. Perhaps not incidental to this new burst of energy was a close attachment to the soprano Teresa Stolz, who was to remain a lifelong friend. More direct creative encouragement came later in the decade from Giulio Ricordi and Boito, whose careful planning and extreme diplomacy seem largely responsible for tempting Verdi back to operatic composition.

Apart from professional tours, Verdi divided his life mostly between Milan, Genoa and Sant'Agata, continuing to oversee his lands and add to his property. In his last years he devoted a considerable amount of money and energy to two philanthropic projects, the building of a hospital at Villanova sull'Arda Piacenza and the founding of a home for retired musicians, the Casa di Riposo, in Milan. Giuseppina Strepponi died in 1897. In December 1900 Verdi made arrangements for his youthful compositions (including, one assumes, those 'marches for band by the hundred') to be burnt after his death. He died in Milan a month later, and was buried next to his wife in the Casa di Riposo.

THE LAST STYLE: 'OTELLO' (1887) AND 'FALSTAFF' (1893)

In spite of the chronological gap, critics have tended to see Verdi's last two operas as a logical continuation (and almost always as the 'culmination') of his previous work, thus stressing stylistic continuity across his entire career. There is much to be said for such an approach. Although Verdi was now firmly established as an international figure who could – and did – dictate his own terms, he continued to compose in the old manner, carefully tailoring his music to the singers at his disposal, for example, and altering or transposing passages that were not suited to them. In choosing to work with Boito, he secured librettos of unprecedented linguistic and prosodic sophistication; but he nevertheless continued an unshakeable allegiance to certain operatic conventions, fashioning for *Otello*, *Falstaff* and the revised *Boccanegra* magnificent examples of the grandest of the traditional set pieces, the Largo concertato.

However, the strain and difficulty with which a suitable concertato was eventually accommodated into *Otello* indicates a fundamental change in Verdian dramaturgy. At some time between *Aida* and *Otello* we might hazard that Verdi passed an intangible divide, and now saw the basis of his musical drama residing in continuous 'action' rather than in a patterned juxtaposition of 'action' and 'reflection'. (It was precisely the difficulty of embedding comprehensible 'action' into the Act 3 concertato of *Otello* that continued to pose problems, even causing Verdi to revise the piece for the opera's Parisian première in 1894.) The long Act 2 duet between Otello and Iago is a good example of how the new hierarchy worked. The duet itself cannot usefully be parsed as a central set piece of contrasting 'movements'; and the true set pieces – the Credo, Homage Chorus, quartet and *racconto* – are embedded within the larger structure.

This tendency for the music to react minutely and spontaneously to the constant changes typical of spoken dialogue brought about an inevitable decrease in periodic structures and a loosening of some of the traditional links between prosody and music. On rare occasions, Verdi may have sought to replace these losses with purely musical structures (the sonata-form subtext of the opening scene in *Falstaff*, or its closing comic figure, are likely examples). The necessary level of purely musical coherence (always less important in opera than in music without text) was, however, usually supplied by local increases in harmonic, motivic and orchestral activity. Passages such as the Act 3 orchestral prelude to the revised *Don Carlos* (1884) show how a short motivic fragment is now sufficient to construct large spans of music, so extensive is Verdi's control over orchestral nuance and chromatic detail. But such moments are strictly local. The occasions on which Verdi used musical recurrence to make long-range connections between dramatic events are rare and, as anyone who has experienced the final minutes of *Otello* will know, such moments gain their extraordinary power from the distinctiveness and simplicity of the musical material involved. Verdi's music, here as ever, continues to serve the drama, never to usurp it.

Reputation, scholarship   By the time Verdi wrote his last operas, he had become a national monument: the premières of *Otello* and *Falstaff* were cultural events of almost unprecedented importance, occasioning a flood of publicity all over Europe. Both works, inevitably in the circumstances, were heralded as brilliant successes, but – like so many of the operas after *La traviata* – neither established a place at the centre of the Italian repertory. The operatic times had changed and, in an era when Wagner and the Italian *veristi* were making the headlines, *Otello* and *Falstaff*, for all their 'modernity', were seen as *sui generis*, unsuitable for the common round of smaller theatres in particular. (It is a strange fact that, despite his pre-eminent position in our present operatic repertory, Verdi's influence on the next generation of composers was very slight.)

Far more important in the development of Verdi's reputation was the consolidation of his national status: as 'vate del Risorgimento' (bard of Italy's struggle towards national unity) and as the self-made man, the 'authentic' product of an emerging nation. As mentioned earlier, this image was encouraged by Verdi himself, whose press interviews and autobiographical statements exaggerated the lowliness of his upbringing and the trials of his early life, and also fashioned for particular musical numbers (notably the chorus 'Va pensiero') an iconic significance within the unfolding of his career. As mentioned at the start of this survey, the singing of that chorus at his burial procession in 1901 was a confirmation that, by the time of his death,

Verdi's preferred self-image was firmly embedded in the minds of the Italian people.

So far as performances and purely musical reputation were concerned, the years around the turn of the century represented a low point in Verdi's fortunes. In the sophisticated, cosmopolitan atmosphere of *fin-de-siècle* Italy, it became commonplace to find Verdi's musical personality too simple and direct, and although *Rigoletto*, *Il trovatore* and *La traviata* remained staples of smaller opera houses, they were rarely granted the prestige of important revivals.

Signs of a general change in attitude began in the 1920s, during which a Verdi Renaissance was fostered in Germany by Franz Werfel (who wrote a novel based on the composer's life) and by several notable revivals, in particular a 1926 Dresden production of *La forza del destino*. By the 1930s, performances of 'forgotten' works such as *Nabucco* and *Ernani* were springing up all over Europe and the USA. Appropriated by fascists and anti-fascists alike, Verdi's music survived World War II relatively untarnished. Since then the boom has shown no signs of losing momentum, and more of Verdi's operas are in the repertory today than ever before. The works continue to provoke fresh interpretations and renewed energies. It is hard to imagine an operatic world in which they will cease to enrich and inspire.

Verdi scholarship and editions Although there continue to be lingering pockets of resistance, it is rare these days to meet with easy dismissals of Verdi's art. One reflection of this new standing is that scholarly attention to his music is now fully respectable. The first 60 years of our century saw an indispensable series of biographical and epistolary publications: the *Copialettere* of 1913, and books by Gatti, Luzio, Abbiati and Walker. Since the 1960s, the most important stimulus has come from the Istituto Nazionale di Studi Verdiani in Parma, which has assembled a considerable archive and has published a vast amount of biographical and critical writing. In the 1970s, an American Institute of Verdi Studies was formed at New York University. Much of this activity was brought to a larger audience, and magnificently synthesized, by Julian Budden's three-volume commentary on the operas. The inauguration of a complete edition of Verdi's correspondence (by the Istituto Nazionale) and of a critical edition of his complete works (by the University of Chicago Press and Ricordi) is new testimony to the seriousness with which the man and his music are now treated.

No critical edition of Verdi's librettos exists, and the most satisfactory editions remain those published by Ricordi. Most modern printings of the texts obscure important information by ignoring the lineation, verse forms and indentations of the original. *Tutti i libretti di Verdi* (ed. L. Baldacci, Milan, 1975), which contains Italian librettos of all the operas except *Stiffelio*, has some useful facsimile pages and other illustrations, but also ignores details of the verse layout.

Vocal scores usually appeared near the time of the operas' first performances (an exception is that of *Un giorno di regno*, issued *c*1845). Most were first published by Ricordi, the exceptions being *Attila*, *I masnadieri* and *Il corsaro* (by Lucca), *Stiffelio* (by Blanchet, Paris, 1850; by Ricordi, 1852) and the French operas *Jérusalem*, *Les vêpres siciliennes* and *Don Carlos* (by the Bureau Central de la Musique/Escudier, Paris, and, often almost simultaneously and in Italian translation, by Ricordi). Vocal scores of most of the Italian operas up to *La forza del destino* were also published in Paris (*Nabucco* by Schonenberger, *Il corsaro* by Chabal and the rest by the Bureau Central de la Musique/Escudier or by Blanchet), often within a year of the Italian editions. In 1981 Ricordi published a vocal score of *Don Carlos* containing all versions of the opera.

Full scores at first circulated in manuscript copies. Ricordi printed (for hire only) *La traviata* (*c*1855) and (later in the century or during the first half of this century) all the operas except *Oberto*, *Un giorno di regno*, *Alzira*, *I masnadieri*, *Jérusalem*, *Il corsaro*, *Stiffelio* and the first versions of *Macbeth*, *Simon Boccanegra* and *Don Carlos*. The first printed full score on public sale was Del Monaco's *La traviata* (Naples, *c*1882). In 1913–14 Ricordi published 'study scores' of *Rigoletto*, *Il trovatore*, *La traviata*, *Un ballo in maschera*, *Aida*, *Otello* and *Falstaff*; in the 1950s, revised editions of these; and in the 1980s a study score of *La forza del destino*. All but three (*I Lombardi*, *I due Foscari* and *Attila*) of the full scores printed by Ricordi have been reprinted by Kalmus (New York). Ricordi published a facsimile of the *Falstaff* autograph in 1951. The complete critical edition, published jointly by the University of Chicago Press and Ricordi under the general editorship of Philip Gossett, is in progress.

Operas

Oberto, conte di San Bonifacio
('Oberto, Count of San Bonifacio')

Dramma in two acts set to a libretto by Antonio Piazza and Temistocle Solera; first performed in Milan, at the Teatro alla Scala, on 17 November 1839.

Verdi's first opera has a chequered history. As we first hear of it in 1836, it was entitled *Rocester*, with a libretto by Antonio Piazza. After unsuccessful attempts to have the work put on in Milan and Parma, and after a lengthy hiatus during which the composer was employed in his home town of Busseto, Verdi – with the help of the librettist Temistocle Solera – revised and renamed the opera for its La Scala première. *Oberto* was moderately successful and was revived a number of times during the next three years, Verdi taking the opportunity to add various new numbers to the score. For Milan (1840) he supplied a new cavatina for Cuniza and a replacement duet for Cuniza and Riccardo, and adapted the role of Oberto for baritone; for Genoa (1841) he wrote a replacement duet for Leonora and Oberto and new music for the chorus 'Fidanzata avventurosa'; and for Barcelona (1841–2) he supplied a new first-act aria for Oberto, the cabaletta of which ('Ma fin che un brando vindice') later became associated with *Ernani*.

*

The action takes place in Bassano during the 13th century. Act 1 opens as Riccardo (tenor), Count of Salinguerra, is about to be married to Cuniza (mezzo-soprano), the sister of Ezzelino da Romano. Riccardo has previously seduced Leonora (soprano), the daughter of Oberto (bass), Count of San Bonifacio and Ezzelino's defeated enemy. Leonora and Oberto arrive in Bassano and enlist the sympathy of Cuniza. In a grand finale to the act, father and daughter confront Riccardo; Oberto challenges him to a duel. The second act begins as Cuniza resolves to make Riccardo take back Leonora. Oberto, however, continues to swear revenge. After a further confrontation between the four principals, the men withdraw to fight their duel; Riccardo emerges victorious but, guilt-ridden at causing

37

Oberto's death, he departs abroad. Leonora, desolate at her father's death, decides to enter a convent.

*

Although Verdi was 26 when *Oberto* was first produced, the opera is in some ways an apprentice work, not typical of his early manner. Some of the lyrical pieces have a formal looseness reminiscent of Bellini (clearly, with Rossini, the main stylistic influence), and connecting passages between or within set pieces are often curiously perfunctory or non-existent. On the other hand, there are strong hints of the future: in powerful unison writing for the chorus, in some dramatically striking ensemble pieces and, perhaps most of all, in the brash rhythmic vitality of many episodes. The Adagio movement of the Act 2 quartet, 'La vergogna', probably the last piece to be written, is in many ways the most impressive. Although, as elsewhere in the opera, the daring chromaticism of the opening is rather shakily deployed, the large-scale control of musical rhythm, in particular the dynamic use of triplet figures, offers compelling testimony to what was to be one of the young Verdi's great strengths. However, such successes notwithstanding, it is unlikely that *Oberto* will become anything more than an occasional curiosity in the operatic repertory.

Un giorno di regno
[*Il finto Stanislao* ('The False Stanislaus')]
('King for a Day')

Melodramma giocoso in two acts set to a libretto by Felice Romani (probably revised by Temistocle Solera) after Alexandre Vincent Pineu-Duval's play *Le faux Stanislas*; first performed in Milan, at the Teatro alla Scala, on 5 September 1840.

Verdi's second opera, his only outright comic work until the end of his long career, was written at great speed. It is likely that Bartolomeo Merelli (impresario at La Scala) assigned him the libretto only in late June 1840; Romani's old *melodramma giocoso* (originally set by Adalbert Gyrowetz in 1818 under the title *Il finto Stanislao*) then had to be substantially revised to bring it some way up to date. (Although no direct evidence survives, the reviser was probably Temistocle Solera, who had helped with revisions of Verdi's first opera and seems then to have been a 'house poet' at La Scala.) The opera was a complete fiasco, removed from the stage after only one performance. To judge from contemporary reviews, and from Verdi's later recollections, its failure had as much to do with the performance as with the music. *Un giorno di regno* (which has occasionally reassumed the original title of *Il finto Stanislao*) enjoyed a few revivals in Verdi's lifetime, and has occasionally been staged in modern times.

*

The action takes place near Brest, in the castle of Kelbar, during the early 18th century. Belfiore (baritone) is an officer posing as King Stanislaus of Poland in order to protect the king from harm. But he is in love with a young widow, the Marchesa del Poggio (mezzo-soprano), who is about to marry another. Secondary romantic interest comes from a pair of young lovers, Edoardo (tenor) and Giulietta (soprano); comic scenes are supplied by a pair of *buffo* basses, the Baron Kelbar (Giulietta's father) and La Rocca, the state treasurer (Edoardo's uncle), who wishes to marry Giulietta. After several farcical intrigues, Belfiore uses his disguise to effect the marriage of the young lovers and then reveals his true identity in time to claim the Marchesa as his own.

*

The opera is curiously uneven and, not surprisingly given the rushed circumstances of its creation, tends to peter out in the second act. It is heavily influenced by Rossini, but there are moments – particularly those passages that were altered from the old Romani libretto – in which we find a more up-to-date, Donizettian conception of sentimental comedy. The opera's most interesting vocal character is the Marchesa, whose role was written for Antonietta Ranieri-Marini, the singer who had earlier created Leonora in Verdi's first opera, *Oberto, conte di San Bonifacio*. The lovelorn tenor Edoardo shows early signs of Verdian robustness (particularly in his Act 1 duet with Belfiore), but later reverts to the lighter, higher style associated with the Rossinian tenor. *Un giorno di regno* must, by and large, be judged an unfortunate interlude in Verdi's progress; but even through the barrier of its alien style there are glimpses of the vital individuality that was to emerge so decisively in his next opera, *Nabucco*.

Nabucco
[Nabucodonosor]

Dramma lirico in four parts set to a libretto by Temistocle Solera
after Antonio Cortesi's ballet *Nabuccodonosor* and Auguste Anicet-
Bourgeois' and Francis Cornu's play *Nabuchodonosor*; first
performed in Milan, at the Teatro alla Scala, on 9 March 1842.

At the première the cast included Prosper Dérivis (Zaccaria),
Giuseppina Strepponi (Abigaille), Giorgio Ronconi (Nabucco),
Corrado Miraglia (Ismaele) and Giovannina Bellinzaghi (Fenena).

Nabucodonosor [Nabucco; Nebuchadnezzar]	
King of Babylon	baritone
Ismaele *nephew of Sedecia, King of Jerusalem*	tenor
Zaccaria *High Priest of the Hebrews*	bass
Abigaille *slave, presumed to be the first daughter*	
of Nabucodonosor	soprano
Fenena *daughter of Nabucodonosor*	soprano
The High Priest of Baal	bass
Abdallo *elderly officer of the King of Babylon*	tenor
Anna *Zaccaria's sister*	soprano

Babylonian and Hebrew soldiers, Levites, Hebrew virgins,
Babylonian women, magi, Lords of the Kingdom of Babylon,
populace etc.

Setting Jerusalem and Babylon, 587 BC

The story of *Nabucco* began some 18 months before its first performance, soon after the successful première of Verdi's first opera,
Oberto, conte di San Bonifacio. A contract was drawn up between
Verdi and Bartolomeo Merelli, impresario at La Scala, according to
which Verdi would write three further operas. The first of these, the
comic work *Un giorno di regno* (1840), was a disastrous failure and
(at least according to Verdi's own later memories) the humiliation
of public rejection caused the composer to give up his professional

41

calling. However, in the winter of 1840–41, Merelli persuaded Verdi to take on Temistocle Solera's libretto of *Nabucco*, which had been turned down by the young Prussian composer Otto Nicolai.

The background of *Nabucco* (or *Nabucodonosor* as it was originally called) derives from biblical sources, most extensively from *Jeremiah*; and although Nabucco (Nebuchadnezzar) is the only biblical character to appear, the part of the prophet Zaccaria has strong overtones of Jeremiah. Solera's main source was a French play, first performed in 1836, although some of his alterations can be traced to the scenario of a ballet also derived from the play, given at La Scala in 1838. The lack of documentation concerning the genesis of the opera can be put down to a number of factors: Verdi was relatively unknown at the time, and few of his letters were preserved; he and Solera were together in Milan, and had little need of correspondence; and Solera – unlike some of Verdi's future librettists – was an experienced man of the theatre who apparently needed little help in constructing a dramatically convincing text.

After a number of delays, *Nabucco* was first performed at La Scala in March 1842. Strepponi, with whom Verdi formed a permanent attachment probably beginning around this time, was in poor voice (and her final scene was cut after two performances), but the opera was nevertheless a great success. It was revived at La Scala for the autumn season of 1842 and ran for a record 57 performances. For this revival Verdi made a number of small changes to suit the new Abigaille, Teresa De Giuli Borsi, and added some adjustments to the vocal line of Fenena's preghiera in Part 4. For a Venice revival in the Carnival season 1842–3, he replaced this preghiera with a *romanza* for Fenena. It seems that Verdi wrote ballet music for a revival of *Nabucco* in Brussels in 1848, although no trace of it has survived.

*

The overture, except for the chorale-like opening, is made up of themes from the opera: the main, recurring idea is from the 'Maledetto' chorus in Part 2; there is also a compound-time, pastoral version of 'Va pensiero' and several more martial inspirations.

Part 1: 'Jerusalem'

Inside the temple of Solomon The Babylonian army has reached Jerusalem and is at the gates of the temple. The Israelites lament their fate, but the prophet Zaccaria rallies them: he has as a hostage Fenena, daughter of Nabucco, the Babylonian king, and God will assist them. The people follow Zaccaria into battle. The two numbers that encompass this action are linked and in many ways comprise a single unit. The opening chorus, 'Gli arredi festivi', is fashioned on a large scale and draws its effect from the juxtaposition of contrasting blocks: a terrified populace, a group of praying Levites, another of supplicant virgins. Zaccaria's response is set in the usual cavatina form of a double aria. The Andante, 'D'Egitto là sui lidi', has an unusual two-stanza structure in which the opening of the second stanza is sustained by unison chorus. The cabaletta, 'Come notte al sol fulgente', also features a unison choral interruption.

The stage clears, leaving Fenena and Ismaele alone. We learn in recitative that Ismaele and Fenena fell in love while Ismaele was imprisoned in Babylon, and that Fenena has helped him escape to Israel. They are interrupted by Abigaille, who has stolen into the temple at the head of a band of disguised Assyrian warriors. She had also fallen in love with Ismaele during his captivity and now taunts him with her victory. The accompanied recitative that introduces Abigaille immediately fixes her unusual vocal character, which requires power in the lower register, agility above the staff and a forceful dramatic presence throughout. The ensuing terzetto, 'Io t'amava', is a moment of lyrical relaxation graced with much vocal ornamentation, somewhat out of character with the rest of the score.

The finale of Part 1 begins with a pseudo-fugal chorus, 'Lo vedeste?', as the Israelites panic in defeat. Nabucco arrives on horseback to the triumphant strains of a *banda* march, but Zaccaria threatens to kill Fenena if Nabucco profanes the temple. This tableau precipitates the central, static moment of the finale, 'Tremin gl'insani', which is led off by Nabucco and which characterizes by turn the conflicting attitudes of the principals. When the stage action resumes Ismaele, fearful for Fenena, disarms Zaccaria. Nabucco is now free to act and, in a furious stretta, orders the destruction of the temple.

Part 2: 'The Impious One'

ACT 2 Scene i   *The royal apartments in Babylon*   While Nabucco is away Fenena has been appointed regent. The act opens with a full-scale double aria for Abigaille, who, it turns out, is the daughter of a slave, not the king. After an intense recitative her thoughts turn to Ismaele in the Andante 'Anch'io dischiuso un giorno'. The aria is highly ornamental, with each two-bar phrase rounded by a vocal flourish; but the ornaments, typically for Verdi, are strictly contained, giving their proliferation at the climax a compelling energy. The High Priest of Baal arrives with news that Fenena has freed the Israelites; urged on by a warlike chorus, Abigaille decides to assume power herself. Her cabaletta, 'Salgo già del trono aurato', returns to the forceful tone of the recitative and, although in a far more dynamic context, again succeeds in wedding ornamental gestures to a rigorously controlled structure.

ACT 2 Scene ii   *A room in the palace, giving on to other rooms* Zaccaria's recitativo and preghiera, 'Vieni o Levita', is an oasis of calm in this generally hectic opera, its accompaniment of six solo cellos deployed with great variety of texture. As Zaccaria leaves by one door, Ismaele arrives by another, only to be shunned by the Levites in the chorus 'Il maledetto'. Then follows another grand finale, similar in its opening sections to that of the first part. Abigaille is declared queen and is about to crown herself when Nabucco, whose death had been falsely reported, reappears to snatch the crown for himself. This precipitates the centrepiece of the finale, 'S'appressan gl'istanti', a quasi-canonic movement that gains its effect not from individual characterization (each of the principals sings the same melody) but from an inexorable increase in textural complexity and sonic power. Nabucco then faces the crowd and declares himself not only their king but their God. A thunderbolt strikes him down for this blasphemy and the crowd murmurs in shocked response. Italian operatic convention would now suggest a fast concluding movement, but instead Solera and Verdi decided on a mad scene for Nabucco during which his discourse distractedly moves between fast and slow tempos before he faints. A triumphant cry from Abigaille brings down the curtain.

Part 3: 'The Prophecy'

ACT 3 Scene i   *The hanging gardens of Babylon*   The routinely cheerful opening chorus, complete with stage-band interpolations borrowed from Part 1 ('E l'Assiria una regina'), is in its orchestration perhaps an early Verdian effort at depicting local colour. It leads to one of the opera's best numbers: the Abigaille-Nabucco duet, in which Abigaille dupes her father into signing Fenena's death sentence. After an opening recitative, the duet unfolds in the traditional four-movement pattern. A fast-paced dialogue movement ('Donna, chi sei?'), in which repeated orchestral motifs supply the continuity, leads to a movement of lyrical repose in which the characters develop their opposing attitudes in greater detail ('Oh di qual'onta aggravasi'). The third movement reimposes the outside world, as offstage trumpets announce the death sentence; and then in the final cabaletta ('Deh perdona') Nabucco and Abigaille restate their fixed positions: he begging her to show mercy, she inflexibly maintaining her dominance.

ACT 3 Scene ii   *The banks of the Euphrates*   The closing scene of Part 3 is entitled 'Coro e Profezia'. The Hebrews' sighs for their lost homeland are violently countered by Zaccaria, who presents a vision of the future in which Babylon will be reduced to ruins. The Hebrews' choral lament ('Va pensiero') is the most famous piece in *Nabucco*, perhaps in all Verdi. It is deliberately simple, almost incantatory in its rhythmic tread, unvaried phrase pattern and primarily unison texture; and by these means it creates that powerful sense of nostalgia which, later in the century, gave the chorus its status as a symbol of Italian national aspirations. In the context of the drama, however, the chorus's attitude is cast aside by Zaccaria, whose two-part minor-major prophecy ('Del futuro nel buio') takes up rhythmic and melodic strands from 'Va pensiero' and places them in a fresh dynamic context.

Part 4: 'The Broken Idol'

ACT 4 Scene i *The royal apartments (as in Act 2 Scene i)* The scene opens with Nabucco alone on stage, an orchestral prelude representing the king's distraction through scattered recollections of past themes. He hears a funeral march, sees Fenena on her way to execution, but is powerless to help her. As a last resort, he offers a prayer to the God of Israel; sanity returns and he marshals a band of followers to save his daughter. The scene is structured as a double aria for Nabucco, with his prayer ('Dio di Giuda') as the first part. The ensuing cabaletta ('Cadran, cadranno i perfidi') is highly unusual in beginning with a choral statement of a subsidiary theme.

ACT 4 Scene ii *The hanging gardens* To an extended version of the funeral march heard fleetingly in the previous number, Fenena and the Israelites are led towards their deaths. Fenena offers a brief but touching prayer ('Oh dischiuso è il firmamento'), and then, just in time, Nabucco rushes on to save her. He announces his conversion and is restored as king; Abigaille (we learn) has taken poison. All now join in a triumphant hymn to their new God ('Immenso Jeovha'), a grandiose unaccompanied chorus with which, in most 19th-century performances, the opera came to a close. In the score, however, there is a far more restrained ending: the dying Abigaille enters to ask forgiveness, singing a fragmented melody ('Su me . . . morente') to the accompaniment of solo cello and english horn.

*

There are many ways in which *Nabucco*, as the composer himself said, is the true beginning of Verdi's artistic career, the true emergence of his distinctive voice. It is admittedly an uneven score, with occasional lapses into banality and some unsteady formal experiments that we shall rarely see in future works. But the essential ingredients of Verdi's early style are in place: a new and dynamic use of the chorus, an extraordinary rhythmic vitality and, above all, an acute sense of dramatic pacing. Although, unusually for Verdi, *Nabucco* has no important tenor role, Nabucco and Zaccaria present magnificent opportunities for the baritone and bass, and Abigaille, though always problematic to cast, can prove highly effective for a forceful yet agile soprano. However, as has often been pointed out, the true protagonist of the opera is undoubtedly the chorus, which dominates several of the strongest scenes, and which enters with such stirring effect at climactic points in so many of the solo numbers.

I Lombardi alla prima crociata
('The Lombards on the First Crusade')

Dramma lirico in four acts set to a libretto by Temistocle Solera after Tommaso Grossi's poem *I Lombardi alla prima crociata*; first performed in Milan, at the Teatro alla Scala, on 11 February 1843. *I Lombardi* was revised in French in 1847, as Jérusalem.

The original cast included Giovanni Severi (Arvino), Prosper Dérivis (Pagano), Carlo Guasco (Oronte) and Erminia Frezzolini (Giselda).

Arvino	} *sons of Folco, Lord of Rò*	tenor
Pagano		bass
Viclinda *Arvino's wife*		soprano
Giselda *her daughter*		soprano
Pirro *Arvino's squire*		bass
Prior of the City of Milan		tenor
Acciano *tyrant of Antioch*		bass
Oronte *his son*		tenor
Sofia *Acciano's wife, a secret Christian convert*		soprano

Nuns, priors, populace, hired ruffians, armigers in Folco's palace, ambassadors from Persia, Media, Damascus and Chaldea, harem woman, knights and crusading soldiers, pilgrims, celestial virgins, Lombard women

Setting Milan, in and around Antioch, and near Jerusalem in 1096–7

As with Verdi's previous opera, *Nabucco*, there seems to be hardly any surviving information about the genesis of *I Lombardi*. No records exist of negotiations with La Scala, although popular rumour has it that, after the huge success of *Nabucco*, Bartolomeo Merelli (the impresario there) left to the composer's discretion the fee for the new opera, and that Verdi took advice on a proper sum from his future wife, Giuseppina Strepponi. Nor is there any surviving correspondence between Verdi and his librettist, Temistocle Solera. They were both in Milan during the period of composition (presumably the second half of 1842) and, if we are to trust Verdi's later recollections, he altered very little of Solera's initial draft. The opera was apparently frowned upon by the religious censors in Milan but eventually escaped with only a few unimportant changes. The first night was a wild public success. For a revival in Scnigallia in July 1843, Verdi composed a new cabaletta in Act 2 for Antonio Poggi (as Oronte). His revised, French version of the opera was given as *Jérusalem* in Paris in 1847.

*

The prelude (the first Verdi wrote) is very short and follows the conventional strategy of attempting a kind of radical synopsis of the ensuing action.

ACT 1: 'The Vendetta'

ACT 1 Scene i *The piazza of San Ambrogio, Milan* To a stage-band accompaniment, the opening chorus celebrates new friendship between the brothers Arvino and Pagano ('Oh nobile esempio!'); the two have been enemies ever since Pagano jealously attacked Arvino during the latter's wedding to Viclinda 18 years ago. Pagano and Arvino appear with their family and supporters to announce publicly their reconciliation. This leads to a large-scale concertato movement, 'T'assale un tremito! . . . padre che fia?', which is led off by Giselda, who anxiously asks why her father seems so ill at ease; as the ensemble develops, all the principals are musically differentiated. A Prior of the city announces that Arvino will lead a group to the Crusades. All join in a bellicose chorus, 'All'empio che infrange', and process off to a robust march. An offstage chorus of nuns introduces Pagano, who, in the Andante movement of a double aria, 'Sciagurata! hai tu creduto', informs us that he can never forget Viclinda. A group of supporters enters, swearing to help him against Arvino, and he finishes the scene with a fierce cabaletta of revenge, 'O speranza di vendetta'.

ACT 1 Scene ii *A gallery in the Folco palace* Viclinda and Giselda are still uneasy. Arvino enters to inform Viclinda that his father,

Folco, is in the adjoining room. Giselda offers a prayer for divine assistance, the subtly scored and harmonically bold preghiera 'Salve Maria!'. As the women go off, Pagano and his henchman Pirro appear. Pagano enters Arvino's room, to emerge a little later, bloody dagger in hand, dragging Viclinda after him. But, as flames are seen through the windows, Arvino and his followers intercept the villain. The discovery that Pagano has killed his own father precipitates the central Andante mosso, 'Mostro d'averno orribile'. Arvino demands his brother's death while Giselda counsels mercy; Pagano tries unsuccessfully to kill himself, and all join in pronouncing his banishment in a final stretta, 'Va! sul capo ti grava'.

ACT 2: 'The Man of the Cave'

ACT 2 Scene i   *A room in Acciano's palace in Antioch*   Months have passed; Vielinda has died and the Crusaders are at the gates of Antioch. Acciano and his supporters remain defiant in the chorus 'È dunque vero?'. The stage empties to leave Acciano's wife Sofia (who has converted to Christianity) and their son Oronte. Oronte has fallen in love with Giselda, who has been taken prisoner, and recalls her in an Andante ('La mia letizia infondere') remarkable for its motivic economy. With his mother's prompting, Oronte agrees to convert, celebrating his decision in the gentle cabaletta, 'Come poteva un angelo'.

ACT 2 Scene ii   *The mouth of a cave at a mountain peak*   A suitably sombre orchestral prelude introduces Pagano (now called 'The Hermit'), who emphasizes his new-found faith in the minor-major *romanza* 'Ma quando un suon terribile'. Pirro enters and, failing to recognize his old accomplice, confesses his sins and seeks to atone by revealing to the Crusaders Antioch's defences. A distant stage-band march heralds the Crusaders, who appear with Arvino at their head. Arvino tells 'The Hermit' that Giselda has been captured, and Pagano swears to aid them in battle. The scene closes with a brash, warlike chorus, 'Stolto Allhà!'.

ACT 2 Scene iii   *Inside the harem at Antioch*   A female chorus, complete with rather bland musical gestures towards 'eastern' local colour, introduces Giselda, who closes the act with a full-scale double aria billed as a 'Rondò-Finale'. In the first movement, 'Se vano è il pregare', she prays to her dead mother. The middle-section sees the stage suddenly filled with fleeing women and pursuing Crusaders. Sofia tells Giselda that Arvino has killed her husband and son, and in the closing cabaletta, 'No! . . . giusta causa non è d'Iddio', Giselda turns on her father for his ungodly violence.

ACT 3: 'The Conversion'

ACT 3 Scene i   *The valley of Jehoshaphat*   A group of Crusaders and their followers cross the stage, singing the noble chorus, 'Gerusalem!', one of the simplest but most effective pieces in the opera. Giselda appears and is soon joined by Oronte, whom she had believed dead. The lovers' decision to run off together is played out in a traditional four-movement duet, notable for its second movement, 'Oh belle, a questa misera', in which the couple bid farewell to their homelands; and for an unusually curtailed cabaletta, 'Ah, vieni, sol morte', punctuated by offstage warlike cries from the Lombard soldiers.

ACT 3 Scene ii   *Arvino's tent*   Arvino has discovered the disappearance of his daughter and calls down a curse on her. A group of Crusaders reports that Pagano has been seen nearby and in a driving aria with chorus, 'Sì! del ciel che non punisce', Arvino vows to search Pagano out and kill him.

ACT 3 Scene iii   *Inside a cave*   An elaborate orchestral prelude with solo violin, divided into three contrasting sections, begins the scene. Giselda helps on Oronte, wounded by the Crusaders. Railing against God, she launches the first movement of an ensemble, 'Tu la madre mi togliesti'; but she is interrupted by Pagano (still 'The Hermit'), who brings holy water with which to bless the dying Oronte. The solo violin is still much in evidence (a sure sign that

Oronte is destined for heaven) in the second, lyrical movement, the richly melodic Andantino 'Qual voluttà trascorrere'.

ACT 4: 'The Holy Sepulchre'

ACT 4 Scene i *A cave near Jerusalem* A brief dialogue in the original printed libretto, not set to music, explains that Giselda has been brought back to her father by 'The Hermit', and that Arvino has forgiven his daughter. The scene then opens with Giselda, overtaken in sleep by a chorus of celestial spirits. A vision of Oronte appears to sing the Andante 'In cielo benedetto', in which he tells his beloved that the Crusaders will find much-needed water at Siloim. When the vision vanishes, Giselda breaks into a brilliant cabaletta of joy, 'Non fu sogno!'– apparently one of the most popular numbers in the opera with contemporary audiences.

ACT 4 Scene ii *The Lombard camp near Rachel's tomb* The Lombards, dying of thirst, conjure up visions of their distant homeland in the famous chorus 'O Signore, dal tetto natio', a number whose hymn-like slowness and predominantly unison texture suggest it was modelled on 'Va pensiero' from *Nabucco*. Giselda announces that the Lombards can find water at Siloim, and they prepare for battle with the warlike chorus 'Guerra! guerra!', first heard in Act 2 as 'Stolto Allhà!'.

ACT 4 Scene iii *Arvino's tents* 'The Hermit', gravely wounded, is supported on by Giselda and Arvino. Pagano reveals his true identity and, on the point of death, leads off the final ensemble, 'Un breve istante'. The tent is thrown open to reveal Jerusalem, now in the hands of the Crusaders, and the opera ends with a grand choral hymn, 'Te lodiamo, gran Dio di vittoria'.

*

I Lombardi has often been compared to *Nabucco*, the immensely successful opera that preceded it in the Verdi canon. It is easy to see how such comparisons usually find the later opera less satisfactory. *I Lombardi* has a wider-ranging action than *Nabucco*, but Verdi, at this stage of his career, was less able or willing to depict various sharply contrasting locales, and many of the opera's choral sections (which traditionally carried the weight of such depictions) are pallid and routine. The great exception is the chorus 'O Signore, dal tetto natio', which rightly stands beside 'Va pensiero' as representative of Verdi's new voice in Italian opera. The opera's musical characterization is strangely uneven: the presence of two leading tenors seems to divide attention where it might usefully have been focussed, but the leading soprano, Giselda, stamps her personality on the drama at a very early stage and succeeds in emerging with impressive effect.

Ernani

Dramma lirico in four parts set to a libretto by Francesco Maria Piave after victor Hugo's play *Hernani*; first performed in Venice, at the Teatro La Fenice, on 9 March 1844.

The cast at the première included Carlo Guasco (Ernani), Antonio Superchi (Don Carlo), Antonio Selva (Silva) and Sophie Loewe (Elvira).

Ernani *the bandit*	tenor
Don Carlo *King of Spain*	baritone
Don Ruy Gomez de Silva *a Spanish grandee*	bass
Elvira *his niece and betrothed*	soprano
Giovanna *her nurse*	soprano
Don Riccardo *the king's equerry*	tenor
Jago *Silva's equerry*	bass

Rebel mountaineers and bandits, knights and members of Silva's household, Elvira's maids-in-waiting, the king's knights, members of the *Lega*, Spanish and German nobles, Spanish and German ladies

Walk-on parts: Mountaineers and bandits, electors and nobles of the imperial court, pages of the imperial court, German soldiers, ladies and male and female followers

Setting The Pyrenees, at Aix-la-Chapelle and at Saragossa, in 1519

Verdi's fifth opera was commissioned by the Teatro La Fenice, Venice, and was the first he wrote for a theatre other than La Scala. The Venetian authorities, impressed by the recent reception of *Nabucco* at La Fenice and of *I Lombardi* at La Scala, allowed the young composer to negotiate a sizable fee, and to make various unusual conditions, notably that he would have the right to choose from that season's company the singers for his new opera. A contract was signed in June 1843, and various subjects and librettists were mulled over; Verdi made it clear that he intended to break with the format of his previous two Milanese successes. A subject attributed to Sir Walter Scott and entitled *Cromvello* (or, sometimes, *Allan Cameron*) was initially decided upon, the librettist to be an unknown poet called Francesco Maria Piave; but Verdi became enthusiastic about Victor Hugo's *Hernani* and, in spite of worries that its political plot would create difficulties with the censor, persuaded Piave to switch course.

During autumn 1843 the correspondence between Verdi, Piave and the theatre management makes it clear that the composer took an unusually active interest in shaping the libretto, and intervened on several important points, insisting for example that the role of Ernani be sung by a tenor (rather than by a contralto, as had originally been planned). At least in part, this new concern for the poetic text was necessitated by his working with Piave, who was inexperienced in theatrical matters and occasionally made what Verdi deemed errors in broad dramatic planning. Last-minute alterations to the cast caused Verdi to make various late changes to his score, notably in adding a cantabile for Silva to the Act 1 finale. The première run of performances was an enormous success.

Ernani quickly became immensely popular, and was revived countless times during its early years. In general, Verdi was adamant that no changes be made to the score; but he did allow at least one exception. At the request of Rossini, who was acting on behalf of the tenor Nicola Ivanoff, he supplied an aria with chorus for Ernani as an alternative ending to the Act 2 finale. The piece was first performed in Parma on 26 December 1844. Although there is no direct evidence, it is possible that Verdi also sanctioned the addition of a cabaletta for Silva in Act 1. This piece, originally written for the bass Ignazio Marini as part of an additional aria in *Oberto* (1841–2, Barcelona), was inserted by Marini into performances of *Ernani* at La Scala in the autumn of 1844.

*

The prelude economically sets forth musical ideas connected with the two main dramatic issues of the opera: first, intoned on solo trumpet and trombone, the theme associated with Ernani's fatal oath to Silva; and then a lyrical theme whose initial rising 6th might plausibly be thought to suggest the love between Ernani and Elvira in its purest state.

ACT 1: 'The Bandit'

ACT 1. Scene i *The Pyrenees; Silva's castle is seen in the distance*
A simple opening chorus ('Evviva! beviam!') sets the scene by introducing the boisterous, carefree world of 'mountaineers and bandits'. Their leader Ernani (in reality Don Giovanni of Aragon) has been proscribed by the King, his enemy. He enters to tell of his love for Elvira; all agree to help him steal her away from Don Ruy Gomez de Silva, her uncle, guardian and fiancé. Ernani's cavatina is in the conventional double-aria format, but the first movement, 'Come rugiada al cespite', shows an expansion of the usual lyrical period as Ernani dwells on his hatred of his rival Silva. The cabaletta, 'O tu, che l'alma adora', makes prominent use of syncopation to suggest Ernani's impatience for action.

ACT 1 Scene ii *Elvira's richly furnished apartments in Silva's castle* Elvira's cavatina, during which she meditates on her beloved Ernani, repeats the double-aria formal outline of Ernani's, though the entire scene is more expansively developed musically. The Andantino, 'Ernani! . . . Ernani involami', has the expanded but still highly schematic form that was becoming common in Verdi's early works and, again characteristically, shows a rigorous control of the soprano's ornamental gestures. A jaunty, Spanish-sounding middle section, during which Elvira's entourage compliment her on her forthcoming marriage to Silva, leads to a forceful cabaletta, 'Tutto sprezzo che d'Ernani', in which the opening phrase's vocal and expressive range gives some indication of the new demands that Verdi was placing on his principal interpreters. Elvira and her women sweep out and the stage is taken by a disguised Don Carlo, King of Spain. Carlo, also in love with Elvira and outraged that he has been passed over, sends Giovanna, Elvira's nurse, to fetch his beloved. Elvira enters to express outrage at the King's audacity and they settle into one of Verdi's most successful formal vehicles, the so-called 'dissimilar' duet between baritone and soprano. The first movement, as usual, is rapid-fire dialogue with continuity preserved by the orchestra, but this soon gives way to a first statement of fixed positions: Carlo leads off with a lyrical outpouring, 'Da quel dì che t'ho veduta'; Elvira counters in the parallel minor with spiky dotted rhythms. The third movement offers a thoroughly Romantic *coup de scène*: Carlo impatiently tries to drag Elvira away, she grabs his knife to defend her honour, and at the peak of the action Ernani himself appears through a secret door. There is a shocked *declamato* from Carlo before Elvira and Ernani launch into the furious stretta of the duet-turned-trio, one that is full (perhaps too full) of syncopations to emphasize the young lovers' defiant energy.

The extended cadences of the stretta are immediately followed by the appearance of Elvira's third suitor, the aged Silva, and the start of the first finale. Silva is of course dismayed at the scene that greets him and, after angrily summoning his followers, engages in a sorrowful, chromatically inflected Andante, 'Infelice! e tu credevi'. (This is sometimes followed by the cabaletta 'Infin che un brando vindice'; see above.) But there are more surprises to come and, soon after Silva has finished, emissaries reveal the true identity of the king. The revelation precipitates the central Adagio of the finale, which begins in utter confusion but gradually finds lyrical voice, notably through the repetition and development of a small cadential motif. As the Adagio ends, Silva kneels to ask the King's forgiveness, which the latter grants, explaining that he is there to canvass support for the forthcoming election of an emperor. In an aside the King offers to help Ernani – wishing to exact revenge himself later rather than leaving it to Silva – and, openly announcing that the bandit is under royal protection, orders him to leave. Ernani's angry aside, in which he threatens to follow Carlo merely to exact revenge, leads off the stretta of the finale, which begins in hushed but pointed minor and progresses to the major mode with a simple but highly effective crescendo.

Act 2: 'The Guest'

A magnificent hall in Silva's castle After a routine, scene-setting chorus praising Silva and Elvira, there occurs an example of the kind of complex articulated scene Verdi often favoured in the middle of an opera. The number is entitled 'Recitativo e Terzetto' but enfolds within its trio a prolonged duet. As the crowd disperses, Silva grants entry to a 'pilgrim' who has asked for shelter. Elvira appears and Silva introduces her as his future bride, at which the 'pilgrim' (who is of course Ernani) throws off his disguise and offers his own head as a wedding present. The ensuing Andante, 'Oro, quant'oro ogn'avido' – Ernani angry at Elvira's apparent betrayal, Elvira miserable, Silva (who has not recognized Ernani) simply confused – is dominated by Ernani, and makes dynamic use of triplet figures. Silva assures his 'guest' of protection and speeds off to arm his castle. As soon as the lovers are alone, Elvira assures Ernani that she had intended to kill herself on the wedding night, and their reconciliation is sealed by a brief Andantino with prominent harp and woodwind. When Silva returns he is horrified to find them in each other's arms. He learns that Don Carlo is waiting for Ernani outside the castle with hostile intent; but he will not give up the bandit, wishing in his turn for a more personal revenge, and in an angry stretta ushers Ernani into a secret hiding place as the lovers voice their despair.

Carlo's entry heralds a long passage of accompanied recitative. The King asks Silva to reveal Ernani's whereabouts and, on being denied, disarms the old man and orders a search of the castle. During the search Carlo sings 'Lo vedremo, o veglio audace', the first movement of what is formally entitled an 'aria', but in which Silva joins freely. The King's anger manifests itself in a wide-ranging, highly declamatory line while Silva denies him with obsessively restricted rhythms and pitches. The middle movement, though often lyrical, is packed with stage action: Carlo's followers return, having found nothing in the castle; the King threatens Silva; Elvira 'enters precipitously' and begs for mercy; Carlo takes her as a hostage. The closing cabaletta, Vieni meco, sol di rose', is a magnificent dramatic stroke: after all the action and conflict, Verdi ends with a passage of pure baritone lyricism, full of gentle ornaments as the King invites Elvira to join him. The stage clears to leave Silva alone. He releases Ernani from hiding and immediately challenges him to a duel. Ernani refuses, and reveals that the King himself is pursuing Elvira. In order to join forces with Silva in taking revenge on Carlo, Ernani offers the old man a hunting-horn – as honour demands, his life is forfeit – and proposes a deadly pact, suitably emphasized with solemn brass chords: when Silva wishes Ernani to kill himself, he must simply sound the horn. The deal is struck; Ernani joins Silva and his followers in an explosive Prestissimo, 'In arcione, in arcion', to close the act.

ACT 3: 'Clemency'

Subterranean vaults confining the tomb of Charlemagne at Aax-la-Chapelle   Dark instrumental colours suitable to the setting begin the act. Carla enters with Riccardo, his equerry. It is the day of the election of the Holy Roman Emperor, and Carlo has heard that conspiracy is afoot. He instructs Riccardo to fire three cannon shots if the election goes in his favour. Left alone 'to converse with the dead', the King bitterly reviews his misspent youth and resolves to rise in stature if he is elected. The aria that illustrates this most important turning point in the drama, 'O de' verd'anni miei', is notable for its extreme change in atmosphere halfway through: from sombre musical recollections of the florid baritone that has characterized the previous acts to a new-found strength and broadness of expression at the words 'e vincitor de, secoli'. Carlo conceals himself in Charlemagne's tomb as the conspirators enter: sombre orchestral colours reassert themselves as the plotters exchange the password and draw lots for the task of assassinating the King. Ernani wins and, with the triplet figures that have been sprinkled through the scene gradually gaining ascendancy in the orchestra, all join in a grand chorus, 'Si ridesti il Leon di Castiglia'. In rhythmic stamp, this piece bears a certain relationship to 'Va pensiero' (*Nabucco*) and 'O Signore, dal tetto natio' (*I Lombardi*), but here the rhythmic vitality and consequent spur to action is far more immediate. The three cannon shots sound, and

Carlo emerges triumphantly from the tomb as the stage fills with his followers. In a magnificent finale to the act, Carlo forgives the conspirators and even consents to the marriage of Ernani and Elvira; his closing peroration to Charlemagne, 'Oh sommo Carlo', eventually draws everyone into his musical orbit.

ACT 4: 'The Mask'

A terrace in the palace of Don Giovanni of Aragon [Ernani] in Saragossa As is common with Verdi and his contemporaries, the final act is by far the shortest. A chorus and a group of dancers tell us that wedding preparations for Ernani and Elvira are under way. The two lovers emerge for a brief but intense affirmation of their happiness, but are cut short by the sound of a distant horn. Ernani attempts to hide the truth from Elvira by complaining of an old wound and sending her for help. Left alone, he momentarily convinces even himself that the horn was an illusion. But Silva appears to demand the life that is owed him. Elvira returns as Ernani takes the proffered dagger; and so begins the final trio, 'Ferma, crudel, estinguere', justly one of the most celebrated pieces in the score, notable above all for its profusion of melodic ideas. The close of the trio is followed immediately by Silva's repetition of the pact music. In spite of Elvira's protests, Ernani takes the dagger and stabs himself. The lovers have time only for a last, desperate affirmation of love before the hero dies, leaving his bride to faint away as the curtain falls.

*

As Verdi himself stated more than once, Ernani represents an important change of direction in his early career. His two earlier successes, *Nabucco* and *I Lombardi*, had both been written for La Scala, one of the largest stages in Italy and well suited to the grandiose choral effects of those works. For the more intimate atmosphere of La Fenice, he created an opera that instead concentrated on personal conflict, carefully controlling the complex sequence of actions necessary to bring characters into intense confrontation. This new format brought about a fresh consideration of the fixed forms of Italian opera, in particular an expansion and enrichment of the solo aria and duet, together with a more flexible approach to the musical sequences that bind together lyrical pieces. Most important, however, was Verdi's gathering sense of a musical drama's larger rhetoric, his increasing control over the dynamics of entire acts rather than merely of entire numbers. In this respect, the third act of *Ernani* sets an imposing standard of coherence, one that is rarely equalled until the operas of the early 1850s.

I due Foscari
('The Two Foscari')

Tragedia lirica in three acts by set to a libretto by Francesco Maria Piave after Byron's play *The Two Foscari*; first performed in Rome, at the Teatro Argentina, on 3 November 1844.

The première cast included Achille De Bassini (Francesco Foscari), Giacomo Roppa (Jacopo) and Marianna Barbieri-Nini (Lucrezia).

Francesco Foscari *Doge of Venice*	baritone
Jacopo Foscari *his son*	tenor
Lucrezia Contarini *Jacopo's wife*	soprano
Jacopo Loredano *member of the Council of Ten*	bass
Barbarigo *senator, member of the Giunta*	tenor
Pisana *Lucrezia's friend and confidante*	soprano
Officer of the Council of Ten	tenor
Servant of the Doge	bass

Members of the Council of Ten and the Giunta, Lucrezia's maids, Venetian women, populace and masked figures of both sexes

Walk-on parts: Il Messer Grande, Jacopo Foscari's two small children, naval commanders, prison guards, gondoliers, sailors, populace, masked figures, pages of the Doge

Setting Venice in 1457

Soon after the première of *Ernani* in Venice, Verdi agreed to write a new opera with Piave for the Teatro Argentina in Rome. The first choice was *Lorenzino de' Medici*, but this proved unacceptable to the Roman censors, and a setting of Byron's *The Two Foscari* was agreed upon. It is clear from Verdi's early descriptions that he conceived of the opera as in the *Ernani* vein (relatively small-scale, concentrating on personal confrontations rather than grand scenic effects), although he did urge Piave to attempt something grandiose for the first-act finale. The correspondence between composer and librettist reveals the extent to which Verdi intervened in the making of the libretto, a good deal of the large-scale structure of the opera being dictated by his increasingly exigent theatrical instincts. The composer was also concerned with matters of ambience and anxious to introduce certain moments in which scenic effects could be exploited.

Composing *I due Foscari* occupied Verdi for about four months (a long time by the standards of most of its predecessors). Its first performance was not a great success, possibly because the expectations of the audience had been driven too high by Verdi's enormous and widespread success with *Ernani*. In 1846 Verdi supplied the famous tenor Mario with a replacement cabaletta for Jacopo in Act 1 (first performed at the Théâtre Italien, Paris).

*

The prelude depicts an atmosphere of stormy conflict before introducing two themes from the opera, the first a mournful clarinet melody to be associated with Jacopo, the second an ethereal flute and string passage from Lucrezia's cavatina.

ACT 1 Scene i *A hall in the Doge's Palace in Venice* The curtain rises as the Council of Ten and the Giunta are gathering. Their opening chorus ('Silenzio ... Mistero') immediately casts over the opera a subdued yet menacing atmosphere, suggested musically by dark instrumental and vocal sonorities and by tortuous chromatic progressions. The prelude's clarinet melody is heard as Jacopo, the Doge's son, falsely accused of murder and exiled from Venice, appears from the prisons to await an audience with the Council. In a delicately scored arioso he salutes his beloved Venice and begins the first section of a two-part cavatina. The first movement, 'Dal più remoto esilio', evokes local colour in its 6/8 rhythm, prominent woodwind sonorities and unusual chromatic excursions. The cabaletta, 'Odio solo, ed odio atroce', is routinely energetic, although it defies convention in allowing the tenor to linger over a high $A^\flat$ as the orchestra undertakes a reprise of the main theme.

ACT 1 Scene ii *A hall in the Foscari Palace* Lucrezia, Jacopo's wife, enters to a rising string theme, associated with her at intervals through the opera. She is determined to confront the Doge in an attempt to save her husband, but first offers a prayer, 'Tu al cui sguardo onnipossente'. This preghiera exhibits a more highly ornamental vocal style than is usual in early Verdi, although ·the decoration is – typically for the composer – strictly controlled within fixed phrase lengths. The ensuing cabaletta, 'O patrizi, tremate l'Eterno', is novel in formal design, beginning with an arioso-like passage in the minor and dissolving into open-structured ornamental writing at the end.

ACT 1 Scene iii *A hall in the Doge's Palace* (as 1.i) The Council has concluded its meeting and, in part with a return to the music of the opening chorus, informs us that Jacopo's 'crime' must be punished with exile.

ACT 1 Scene iv *The Doge's private rooms* The Doge's 'Scena e Romanza' opens with yet another theme that is to recur through the course of the opera, this time a richly harmonized melody for viola and divided cellos. The *romanza* 'O vecchio cor, che batti', in which the Doge apostrophizes his son, is clearly a companion piece to Jacopo's earlier 'Dal più remoto esilio' (notice, for example, the identical opening accompaniment figures), although the baritone father sings with far more direct emotional appeal than his tenor son. The ensuing finale of Act 1 is a lengthy scene between Lucrezia and the Doge, in which Jacopo's wife begs the Doge to show mercy. One of Verdi's finest early soprano-baritone duets, the number falls into the conventional four-movement pattern, but individual sections boast considerable inner contrast, responding closely to the differing emotional attitudes of the principals.

ACT 2 Scene i *The state prisons* A fragmentary, highly chromatic prelude for solo viola and cello introduces Jacopo, alone in prison. He has a terrifying vision of Carmagnola, a past victim of Venetian law, and in the *romanza* 'Non maledirmi, o prode' begs the vision for mercy. 'Non maledirmi' is conventional in its move from minor to major, but has an unusual return to the minor as the vision of

64

Carmagnola reappears to haunt the prisoner and eventually render him unconscious. Lucrezia, accompanied by her rising string theme, enters and, after reviving Jacopo, announces his sentence of exile. There follows one of Verdi's very rare love duets, this one laid out in the usual multi-movement form though without an opening 'action' sequence. The closing portions of the duet see an injection of local colour: gondoliers singing in praise of Venice interrupt husband and wife, giving them fresh hope for the future. The Doge, powerless to affect the decision of the Council, whose ruling he must put into effect, now enters to bid a sad farewell to his son. The first lyrical movement of the ensuing trio, 'Nel tuo paterno amplesso', makes much of the contrast in vocal personalities – declamatory tenor, sustained, controlled baritone, breathless, distraught soprano – while the final stretta (in which the principals are joined by a gloating Loredano) simplifies matters by uniting Jacopo and Lucrezia in syncopated unison.

ACT 2 Scene ii   *The hall of the Council of Ten*   An opening chorus, again partly built on material from Act 1 scene i, explains that Jacopo's crimes are murder and treason against the state. The Doge appears, soon followed by his son, who continues to protest his innocence. The Doge will not listen, but all are dumbfounded by the sudden appearance of Lucrezia, who has brought her children with her in a final plea for mercy. The stage is set for the concertato finale, 'Queste innocenti lagrime', led off by Jacopo, who is seconded by Lucrezia. This grandiose movement develops impressive momentum up to the final peroration (the passage sometimes termed 'groundswell'), but its last cadence is interrupted: Jacopo returns to the minor mode and intimate musical language of his opening phrases, and is in turn interrupted by a further tutti repetition of the 'groundswell' idea. The extreme juxtaposition creates sufficient dramatic charge to close the act without a traditional fast stretta.

ACT 3 Scene i   *The old piazzetta di San Marco*   Local colour in the form of an 'Introduzione e Barcarola' begins the act, with gondoliers offering a more developed reprise of the music that had earlier interrupted the Jacopo-Lucrezia duet. Jacopo is brought forth for the final parting. His 'All'infelice veglio' is *romanza*-like in its progress from minor to major but is enriched by contributions from Lucrezia and, eventually, from the chorus, making the scene a fitting grand climax to the tenor's role.

ACT 3 Scene ii *The Doge's private rooms* (as in Act 1 Scene iv) First comes a scena for the Doge in which he is presented with a deathbed confession revealing that Jacopo is innocent. But the message is too late: Lucrezia rushes on to announce that Jacopo died suddenly on leaving Venice. Lucrezia's aria 'Più non vive!' is, as befits this late stage of the drama, highly condensed, and is perhaps best considered a kind of bipartite cabaletta, allowing (as did her first-act aria) more room than is usual in early Verdi for ornamental flourishes. As she leaves, the Council of Ten appear, led by Loredano, asking the Doge to relinquish his power on account of his great age. He answers in an impassioned aria, 'Questa dunque è l'iniqua mercede'. In many ways the most powerful section of the opera, this 'aria' is really a duet between the Doge and the male chorus: he in declamatory triplets demanding the return of his son; they in inflexible unison. The great bell of St Mark's sounds to mark the election of a new Doge – not Loredano, in spite of his ambitions – and, after a final apostrophe to Jacopo, the Doge falls lifeless to the ground.

*

I due Foscari, as Verdi himself was later to admit, suffers somewhat from being too gloomy in its general tone, in spite of periodic evocations of the Venetian lagoon. But the opera nevertheless offers several interesting experiments. Perhaps most striking is the use of recurring themes to identify the principals. These proto-'leitmotifs' are here perhaps applied too rigidly, serving ultimately to deny any sense of development or progression in the characters; but the experiment itself is significant, suggesting that Verdi was anxious to explore new means of musical and dramatic articulation. The increased importance of local colour is also notable in light of Verdi's future development. Although in *I due Foscar* the sense of a precise ambience seems imposed on the score rather than emerging from it, Verdi's awareness of the potential of this added dimension in musical drama was decisive; from this time onwards he would rarely employ local colour in quite the mechanical way he had in his earliest operas.

Giovanna d'Arco
('Joan of Arc')

Dramma lirico in a prologue and three acts set to a libretto by Temistocle Solera in part after Friedrich von Schiller's play *Die Jungfrau von Orleans*; first performed in Milan, at the Teatro alla Scala, on 15 February 1845.

The cast at the première included Antonio Poggi (King Charles), Filippo Colini (Giacomo) and Erminia Frezzolini in the title role.

Carlo VII [Charles VII] *King of France*	tenor
Giacomo *a shepherd in Dom-Rémy*	baritone
Giovanna [Joan of Arc] *his daughter*	soprano
Delil *an officer of the King*	tenor
Talbot *supreme commander of the English army*	bass

King's officers, villagers, people of Reims, French soldiers, English soldiers, blessed spirits, evil spirits, nobles of the realm, heralds, pages, young girls, marshals, deputies, knights and ladies, magistrates, halberdiers, guards of honour

Setting Dom-Rémy, Reims and near Rouen in 1429

There is virtually no evidence, but it seems that Verdi had arranged to write an opera for the 1844–5 Carnival season at La Scala as early as December 1843, and that soon afterwards he suggested to the impresario Bartolomeo Merelli that Temistocle Solera be engaged as the librettist. Solera was duly hired, and – with typical exaggeration – made much of the fact that his libretto on the life of Joan of Arc was 'original', owing nothing either to Shakespeare or to Schiller. Verdi's correspondence makes no mention of any changes to the libretto, and we must assume that, as with Solera's earlier *Nabucco* and *I Lombardi*, the composer was willing to set the text more or less as it stood. The score was written during the autumn and winter of 1844–5. Its first performance at La Scala (preceded by a revival of *I Lombardi*) was a great public success, but the standards of production were far below Verdi's expectations and caused a rift between him and Merelli that resulted in Verdi's avoiding premières at La Scala for many years.

*

The overture is in three movements. The first is stormy and uncertain; the second is an Andante pastorale featuring solo flute, oboe and clarinet (with more than shades of Rossini's *Guillaume Tell* overture); the last returns to the stormy minor but concludes in a triumphant and bellicose major. It is hardly a masterpiece but is worth its occasional concert-hall revival.

PROLOGUE Scene i *A great hall in Dom-Rémy* The opening scene is a conventional cavatina for the tenor, though with unusually important choral interventions (Verdi and Solera no doubt wished to sustain their image with the Milanese after *Nabucco* and *I Lombardi*). Even before the tenor enters, the unison chorus decries the sad fate of France in 'Maledetti cui spinge rea voglia', and choral forces are again prominent in the soloist's lyrical movements, particularly in an unusually long *tempo di mezzo*. King Charles, after admitting defeat, narrates a dream ('Sotto una quercia'): as he was lying beneath an oak tree, the Madonna told him to place before her his helmet and sword. On hearing that such an oak exists nearby, he decides to visit it, though insisting that he can no longer be king.

PROLOGUE Scene ii *A forest* Giacomo appears for a brief scena, voicing fears that his daughter Joan may be in league with the devil. He retires to be replaced by Joan. In a highly ornamented, Bellinian Andante ('Sempre all'alba ed alla sera'), she prays for weapons in the coming battle. As she falls asleep, a chorus of devils (jauntily recommending sins of the flesh) and of angels (promising her glory as the saviour of her country) jostle for her attention. She awakes to find Charles before her, and immediately declares herself ready for battle. They join in a lively, syncopated cabaletta, during which Giacomo sees them together and concludes that his daughter has in some way bewitched the King.

ACT 1 Scene i *A remote place scattered with rocks* The English soldiers have been routed and feel that supernatural forces are against them. Talbot tries unsuccessfully to allay their fears. Giacomo, still convinced that his daughter is in the grip of evil forces comes on to announce that the woman inspiring the French forces can be their prisoner that evening. In an Andante sostenuto, 'Franco son io', he tells them of his dishonour at the hands of Charles; the ensuing cabaletta, 'So che per via di triboli', explores a father's tender feelings. The usual progression from lachrymose Andante to energetic cabaletta is thus reversed, which allows for a moderate-paced, unusually touching Donizettian cabaletta, quite lacking in characteristic Verdian rhythmic drive.

ACT 1 Scene ii *A garden in the court of Reims* Joan of Arc has fulfilled her mission but is unwilling to leave Charles and the court: the demon voices still torment her. She sings of her simple forest home in 'O fatidica foresta', another delightful example of Verdian pastoral, before Charles arrives to initiate an impressive four-movement duet-finale in which he and Joan admit their love for each other. Particularly notable is the Adagio ('T'arretri e palpiti!'), which includes a remarkable range of emotional attitudes as Joan struggles with her conflicting voices and as Charles swings between unease at her behaviour and attempts to calm her with expressions of love.

ACT 2 *A square in Reims* A somewhat routine 'Grand triumphal march' introduces the victorious troops, prominent among whom are Charles and Joan. Giacomo looks on, giving vent to his religious zeal in a minor-major *romanza*, 'Speme al vecchio era una figlia', which never seems to find its true point of climax. Then comes the grand central finale of the opera, in which Giacomo denounces his daughter. The most interesting movement is the Andante, 'No! forme d'angelo': unaccompanied duet fragments from Charles and Giacomo are juxtaposed with an extended cantabile for Joan; and even in the grand cadential close Verdi finds room to give rein to her fragile musical persona. The remainder of the number offers high drama as Joan refuses three times to deny Giacomo's accusations of sacrilege; she is turned on by the crowd in the stretta, 'Fuggi, o donna maledetta'.

ACT 3 *Inside a fort in the English camp* Joan of Arc, imprisoned, looks on as the English and French do battle, noting with dismay that Charles has been surrounded. Her ardent prayers alert Giacomo to his mistake in accusing her, and they join in a duet of explanation and reconciliation, the most impressive section of which is the slow lyrical movement, 'Amai, ma un solo istante', in which a moving succession of melodic ideas underpins the father's gradual acceptance of his daughter's purity.

Joan is released by her father and rushes to aid the French, and now it is Giacomo's turn to comment on the battle, which with his daughter's help swings decisively against the English. Charles enters victorious, forgives Giacomo, but learns that Joan has been mortally wounded. In the *romanza* 'Quale più fido amico', delicately scored for solo english horn and cello, he bemoans his loss. Joan is brought in to the strains of a funeral march, and has enough strength to salute her father and king and to look forward to a welcome in heaven. She leads off the final ensemble with an elaborately ornamented solo accompanied by obbligato cello before a long-breathed theme for the onlookers carries all before it as she expires.

*

Giovanna d'Arco is unlikely ever to be a mainstream repertory work, but there is nevertheless much to admire. Although the opera was probably intended as a sequel to the grand choral tableau works Verdi and Solera had previously created together, in the end it is dominated by the role of Joan of Arc – Verdi probably being encouraged in this change by the extraordinary skills of his leading soprano, Erminia Frezzolini. And Joan is by no means the typical early Verdian soprano, being entrusted with the kind of delicate ornamentation the youthful composer so rarely saw fit to linger over. The other principals are perhaps less successfully projected, but they are involved in powerfully original ensembles, numbers which again and again make clear that the young Verdi was constantly experimenting with the formal vehicles through which his drama was projected.

Alzira

Tragedia lirica in a prologue and two acts set to a libretto by Salvadore Cammarano after Voltaire's play *Alzire, ou Les Américains*; first performed in Naples, at the Teatro San Carlo, on 12 August 1845.

The cast at the première included Filippo Coletti (Gusmano), Gaetano Fraschini (Zamoro) and Eugenia Tadolini (Alzira).

Alvaro father of Gusmano, initially Governor of Peru	bass
Gusmano Governor of Peru	baritone
Ovando a Spanish Duke	tenor
Zamoro leader of a Peruvian tribe	tenor
Ataliba leader of a Peruvian tribe	tenor
Alzira Ataliba's daughter	soprano
Zuma her maid	mezzo-soprano
Otumbo an American warrior	tenor

Spanish officers and soldiers, Americans of both sexes

Setting Lima and other regions of Peru, about the middle of the 16th century

There were two reasons why *Alzira*, Verdi's eighth opera was something of a special event. It was the first he had written specially for the famous Teatro San Carlo of Naples, and so offered him an opportunity to confront a significant public and theatre with whom he had so far had little success. And it presented a chance to collaborate with Salvadore Cammarano, resident poet at the San Carlo, certainly the most famous librettist still working in Italy, renowned for his string of successes in the previous decade with Gaetano Donizetti. Because of Cammarano's fame, Verdi seems to have taken little active part in the formation of the libretto (this in contrast to the works he prepared with his principal librettist of the period, Piave), being for the most part happy to accept the dictates of Cammarano's highly professional instincts. Work on *Alzira*, begun in the spring of

1845, was delayed by illness and by the fact that Verdi had to add an overture when the work proved too short for a full evening's entertainment. Despite the cast for the première being unusually strong, the first performance was at best only a partial success. Subsequent revivals fared little better, and the opera soon disappeared entirely from the repertory. It has occasionally been revived in modern times, but remains one of the composer's two or three least-performed operas.

*

The overture is in three movements. The first is an Andante mosso in which woodwind and percussion attempt to impose a generic local colour on the exotic ambience; the second juxtaposes warlike calls to arms with a lachrymose clarinet solo; the third is a march-like Allegro brillante.

PROLOGUE ('The Prisoner') *A vast open plain, irrigated by the river Rima* A bloodthirsty tribe of 'Americans' led by Otumbo drag on Alvaro in chains, tie him to a tree and mock him with the driving 6/8 chorus 'Muoia, muoia coverto d'insulti'. They are about to dispatch him horribly when a boat is sighted carrying Zamoro, their leader whom they believed dead. Zamoro, strangely moved by the sight of Alvaro, has him released and orders him returned to his people. With Alvaro gone, Zamoro's unusually extended Andante, 'Un Inca . . . eccesso orribile! ', tells the tribe of his brutal treatment at the hands of the wicked Spaniard Gusmano. The Andante over, Zamoro hears that his beloved Alzira is imprisoned with her father in Lima. Zamoro swears to rescue them, and joins his warriors in a bellicose cabaletta, 'Dio della guerra'.

ACT 1 ('A Life for a Life') Scene i *The main piazza of Lima* A robust choral movement, reinforced by the *banda*, introduces Alvaro, who announces that he is ceding power to his son Gusmano. The latter immediately declares a general peace with the Inca chief Ataliba, reminding him that Ataliba's daughter Alzira has been agreed as Gusmano's reward. But in the Andante of his double aria, 'Eterna la memoria', Gusmano admits that Alzira's feelings for her former lover remain too powerful for him to overcome. Ataliba urges Gusmano to be patient; but the new Governor can brook no delay and, in the forceful cabaletta 'Quanto un mortal può chiedere', declares that he must possess Alzira immediately.

ACT 1 Scene ii *Ataliba's apartments in the Governor's palace*
Tremolando strings introduce a sleeping Alzira, who awakes to utter Zamoro's name and tell her attendants of a strange dream. 'Da Gusman, su fragil barca' narrates how she dreamt of fleeing Gusmano in a boat, being caught in a storm and rescued by her beloved; the aria boldly follows the pattern of the tale rather than duplicating the form of a conventional Italian Andante. Despite the warnings of her entourage, she proudly declares her love for Zamoro in the ornamental cabaletta 'Nell'astro che più fulgido'.

Ataliba comes on, dismisses Zuma and the chorus, and in simple recitative begs Alzira to marry Gusmano. She will have none of it, and asks instead for death. As Ataliba leaves, Zuma announces a 'member of the tribe', and Alzira is ecstatic to see none other than Zamoro. The first movement of their duet, 'Anima mia!', is a rapid exchange of loving words, held together in the traditional manner by a driving orchestral melody. With little else needing to be said, Cammarano and Verdi moved immediately to the sprightly cabaletta, 'Risorge ne' tuoi lumi'.

The lovers are discovered by Gusmano, Ataliba and a host of attendants. Gusmano orders Zamoro to instant execution and, in a fiery Allegro, Zamoro taunts Gusmano with cowardice. The stage is now set for an unusually grand slow concertato, 'Nella polve, genuflesso', one which begins with a freer dialogue structure than usual and, perhaps for this reason, builds to an uncommonly impressive final climax. The concertato over, wild, exotic music is heard in the distance: a messenger reports that a hostile army is without, demanding the return of Zamoro. Gusmano decides to release him, thus offering a life for the life of his father; but in leading off the concluding stretta, 'Trema, trema . . . a ritorti fra l'armi', he warns Zamoro that they will meet again on the battlefield.

ACT 2 ('The Revenge of a Savage') Scene i *Inside the fortifications of Lima* The Incas have again lost the battle; victorious Spanish soldiers indulge in a riotous brindisi 'Mesci, mesci', interrupted only briefly by the mournful sight of Zamoro and his followers trudging across the stage. Gusmano promises his soldiers rich spoils, and loudly pronounces a death sentence on Zamoro. At this Alzira rushes on to beg for clemency, and Gusmano offers her a polite version of Count di Luna's bargain in *Il trovatore*: Zamoro's life for Alzira's hand in marriage. The impasse is explored in an Andante, 'Il pianto ... l'angoscia', Alzira's breathless sobs contrasting with Gusmano's smooth (perhaps too smooth) cantabile. Eventually she agrees, and the pact is sealed by a lively duet cabaletta, 'Colma di gioia ho l'anima'.

ACT 2 Scene ii *A dreary cave* A sombre orchestral introduction, appropriate to the desolate scene, introduces Otumbo, who tells his friends that he has secured the release of Zamoro by bribing his Spanish guards. Zamoro appears, and in the Andante 'Irne lungi ancor dovrei' declares himself desolate without his beloved Alzira. Otumbo makes matters worse by telling him that Alzira is about to marry Gusmano. Nothing can restrain Zamoro's fury, and in the cabaletta 'Non di codarde lagrime' he resolves to take stern revenge.

ACT 2 Scene iii *A great hall in the Governor's residence* A bridal chorus, 'Tergi del pianto America', looks forward to the peace that this marriage will bring, and Gusmano welcomes all to the ceremony. He is about to take Alzira's hand when Zamoro (disguised as a Spanish soldier) bursts upon the scene, plunges a dagger into Gusmano's heart, and awaits bloody retribution. But Gusmano has a surprise in store: he has learnt from Alzira the joys of peace and mercy, and in a final aria accompanied by the chorus ('I numi tuoi'), gives the two lovers his blessing. It is an impressive close, with the chorus gradually taking the lyrical thread as Gusmano loses strength and the mode shifts from minor to major.

*

In later life, Verdi pronounced *Alzira* 'proprio brutta' ('downright ugly'), and the opera is without doubt one of the least likely of his works to be performed, even in today's revival-conscious atmosphere. Perhaps, as happened on other occasions, the esteem in which Verdi held his librettist was a disadvantage, inhibiting him from following freely his dramatic instincts. However, like all Verdi's minor operas, *Alzira* has many fine passages, the large ensembles in particular. Even its moments of comparative failure are interesting, coming as they often do in numbers such as Alzira's Act 1 narration, in which the composer attempted something startlingly new in formal terms. In today's critical atmosphere, when it is commonplace to single out for particular praise those passages that break decisively with tradition, it is at least salutary to observe an opera in which the conventional moments succeed far better than those that challenge accepted norms.

Attila

Dramma lirico in a prologue and three acts set to a libretto by Temistocle Solera (with additional material by Francesco Maria Piave) after Zacharias Werner's play *Attila, König der Hunnen*; first performed in Venice, at the Teatro La Fenice, on 17 March 1846.

The cast at the première included Ignazio Marini (Attila), Natale Costantini (Ezio), Sophie Loewe (Odabella) and Carlo Guasco (Foresto).

Attila *King of the Huns*	bass
Ezio *a Roman general*	baritone
Odabella *the Lord of Aquileia's daughter*	soprano
Foresto *a knight of Aquileia*	tenor
Uldino *a young Breton, Attila's slave*	tenor
Leone *an old Roman*	bass

Leaders, kings and soldiers, Huns, Gepids, Ostrogoths, Heruls, Thuringians, Quadi, Druids, priestesses, men and women of Aquileia, Aquileian maidens in warlike dress, Roman officers and soldiers, Roman virgins and children, hermits, slaves

Setting Aquileia, the Adriatic lagoons and near Rome, in the middle of the 5th century

Verdi had read Werner's ultra-Romantic play as early as 1844, and initially discussed the subject with Piave. However, for his second opera at La Fenice – a highly suitable subject, dealing with the founding of the city of Venice – the composer eventually fixed on Solera, the librettist with whom – at least until then – he seems to have preferred working. Solera set about preparing the text according to his usual format, with plenty of opportunity for grand choral tableaux such as are found in *Nabucco* and *I Lombardi*; but the progress of the opera was beset with difficulties. First Verdi fell seriously ill, and then Solera went off to live permanently in Madrid, leaving the last act as only a sketch and necessitating the calling in of the faithful Piave after all. Verdi instructed Piave to ignore Solera's plans for a large-scale choral finale and to concentrate on the individuals, a change of direction that Solera strongly disapproved of. The première was coolly received, but *Attila* went on to become one of Verdi's most popular operas of the 1850s. After that it lost ground; however, it has recently been more than occasionally revived. In 1846 Verdi twice rewrote the *romanza* for Foresto in Act 3: the first time for Nicola Ivanoff, the second for Napoleone Moriani.

*

The prelude follows a pattern that later became common in Verdi's work: a restrained opening leads to a grand climax, then to the beginnings of melodic continuity that are quickly fragmented. It is the drama encapsulated

PROLOGUE Scene i *The piazza of Aquileia* 'Huns, Heruls and Ostrogoths' celebrate bloody victories and greet their leader Attila who, in an impressive recitative, bids them sing a victory hymn. A group of female warriors is brought on, and their leader Odabella proclaims the valour and patriotic zeal of Italian women. Odabella's double aria is a forceful display of soprano power, its first movement, 'Allor che i forti corrono' showing an unusually extended form which allows Attila to insert admiring comments. Such is the force of this movement that the cabaletta, 'Da te questo', merely continues the musical tone, though with more elaborate ornamentation. Impressed by her bravery, Atilla gives her his sword.

As Odabella leaves, the Roman general Ezio appears for a formal duet with Attila. In the Andante 'Tardo per gli anni, e tremulo', he offers Attila the entire Roman empire if Italy can be left unmolested and in Ezio's hands ('Avrai tu l'universo, resti l'Italia a me': 'For you the world, leave Italy to me' – a phrase with some resonance in the political struggles to come in the 1850s). Attila angrily rejects the proposal, and the warriors end with a cabaletta of mutual defiance, 'Vanitosi! che abbietti e dormenti'.

PROLOGUE Scene ii *The Rio-Alto in the Adriatic lagoons* The scene opens with a sustained passage of local colour (strongly suggesting that Verdi now had his eye on the fashions of the French stage). First comes a violent orchestral storm, then the gradual rising of dawn is portrayed with a passage of ever increasing orchestral colours and sounds. Foresto leads on a group of survivors from Attila's attack on Aquileia; the settlement that they build there will eventually become Venice. In an Andantino which again shows unusual formal extension, 'Ella in poter del barbaro', his thoughts turn to his beloved Odabella, captured by Attila. In the subsequent cabaletta, 'Cara patria, già madre', the soloist is joined by the chorus for a rousing conclusion to the scene.

ACT 1 Scene i *A wood near Attila's camp* A melancholy string solo introduces Odabella, who, refusing a chance to escape, and playing on Atilla's obvious attraction to her, has remained in Attila's camp in order to find an opportunity to murder him. In a delicately scored Andantino, 'Oh! nel fuggente nuvolo', Odabella sees in the clouds the images of her dead father and Foresto. Foresto himself appears: he has seen her with Attila and accuses her of betrayal. Their duet takes on the usual multi-movement pattern: Foresto's accusations remain through the minor-major Andante, 'Sì, quello io son, ravvisami', but Odabella convinces him of her desire to kill Attila, and they lovingly join in a unison cabaletta, 'Oh t'innebria nell'amplesso'.

ACT 1 Scene ii *Attila's tent, later his camp* Attila tells his slave Uldino of a terrible dream in which an old man denied him access to Rome in the name of God ('Mentre gonfiarsi l'anima'). But he dismisses the vision with a warlike cabaletta, 'Oltre quel limite'.

A bellicose vocal blast from Attila's followers is interrupted by a procession of women and children led by Leone, the old man of Attila's dream (he is Pope Leo I, suitably disguised at the behest of the Italian censors). His injunction precipitates the Largo of the concertato finale, 'No! non è sogno', which is led off by a terrified Attila, whose stuttering declamation is answered by a passage of sustained lyricism from Foresto and Odabella. The concertato takes on such impressive proportions that Verdi saw fit to end the act there, without the traditional stretta.

ACT 2 Scene i *Ezio's camp* The scene is no more than a conventional double aria for Ezio. In the Andante, 'Dagl'immortali vertici', he muses on Rome's fallen state. Foresto appears and suggests a plan to destroy Attila by surprising him at his camp. In a brash cabaletta, 'È gettata la mia sorte', Ezio eagerly looks forward to his moment of glory.

ACT 2 Scene ii *Attila's camp* Yet another warlike chorus begins the scene. Attila greets Ezio, the Druids mutter darkly of fatal portents, the priestesses dance and sing. A sudden gust of wind blows out all the candles, an event that precipitates yet another concertato finale, 'Lo spirto de' monti', a complex movement during which Foresto manages to tell Odabella that Attila's cup is poisoned. The formal slow movement concluded, Attila raises the cup to his lips, but is warned of the poison by Odabella (who wishes a more personal vengeance); Foresto admits to the crime, and Odabella claims the right to punish him herself. Attila approves, announces that he will marry Odabella the next day, and launches the concluding stretta, 'Oh miei prodi! un solo giorno'; its dynamism and rhythmic bite prefigure similar moments in *Il trovatore*.

ACT 3 *A wood* Foresto is awaiting news of Odabella's marriage to Attila, and in a minor-major *romanza*, 'Che non avrebbe il misero', bemoans her apparent treachery. Ezio arrives, urging Foresto to speedy battle. A distant chorus heralds the wedding procession, but suddenly Odabella herself appears, unable to go through with the ceremony. Soon all is explained between her and Foresto, and they join Ezio in a lyrical Adagio.

Attila now enters, in search of his bride, and the stage is set for a Quartetto finale. In the Allegro, 'Tu, rea donna', Attila accuses the three conspirators in turn, but in turn they answer, each with a different melodic line. At the climax of the number, offstage cries inform us that the attack has begun. Odabella stabs Attila, embraces Foresto, and the curtain falls.

*

The final act is, as several have pointed out, more than faintly ridiculous in its stage action, and parts of Verdi's setting seem rather perfunctory; perhaps Solera's original plan for a grand choral finale would have been more apt. Perhaps, indeed, the central problem with *Attila* is that it falls uncomfortably between being a drama of individuals (like *Ernani* or *I due Foscari*) and one that is essentially public (like *Nabucco* or *I Lombardi*). It is surely for this reason that two of the principals, Ezio and Foresto, are vague and undefined, never managing to emerge from the surrounding tableaux. On the other hand, Odabella and Attila, both of whom assume vocal prominence early in the opera, are more powerful dramatic presences. As with all of Verdi's early operas, there are impressive individual moments, particularly in those grand ensemble movements that constantly inspired the composer to redefine and hone his dramatic language.

Macbeth

Opera in four acts set to a libretto by Francesco Maria Piave (with additional material by Andrea Maffei) after William Shakespeare's play; first performed in Florence, at the Teatro della Pergola, on 14 March 1847. The revised version, with a libretto translated by Charles-Louis-Etienne Nuitter and Alexandre Beaumont, was first performed in Paris, at the Théâtre Lyrique, on 21 April 1865.

The first Macbeth was Felice Varesi; the first Lady Macbeth, Marianna Barbieri-Nini

Duncano [Duncan] *King of Scotland*	silent
Macbeth	baritone
Banco [Banquo] } *Generals in Duncan's army*	bass
Lady Macbeth *Macbeth's wife*	soprano
Lady-in-waiting to Lady Macbeth	mezzo-soprano
Macduff *a Scottish nobleman, Lord of Fife*	tenor
Malcolm *Duncan's son*	tenor
Fleanzio [Fleance] *Banquo's son*	silent
A Servant of Macbeth	bass
A Doctor	bass
A Murderer	bass
The Ghost of Banco [Banquo]	silent
A Herald	bass

Witches, messengers of the King, Scottish nobles and exiles, murderers, English soldiers, bards, aerial spirits, apparitions

Setting Scotland and the Anglo-Scottish borders

Verdi's contract of 1846 with the impresario Alessandro Lanari and the Teatro delta Pergola of Florence stipulated no particular opera, and in the summer various possibilities, including *I masnadieri* and *Macbeth*, were under consideration. The final decision, Verdi made clear, would depend on the singers available. *Macbeth* would have no tenor lead but needed a first-class baritone and soprano; *I masnadieri*, on the other hand, was dependent on a fine tenor. By late September the cast had been secured, notably with the engagement of Felice Varesi, one of the finest actor-singer baritones of the day; accordingly, the choice fell on *Macbeth*. By this time, Verdi had already drafted the broad dramatic lines of the opera and had written encouraging letters to his librettist, Piave, emphasizing that this, his first Shakespearean subject, was to be a special case: 'This tragedy is one of the greatest creations of man! If we can't do something great with it, let us at least try to do something out of the ordinary . . . I know the general character and the *tinte* as if the libretto were already finished'.

As the première drew near, Verdi again and again demonstrated his particular interest in the opera: by bullying Piave into producing exactly the text he required; by engaging his friend Andrea Maffei to retouch certain passages; by taking unusual time and care in making sure the production was well rehearsed and true to his intentions; and by endlessly coaching the leading singers – in particular Varesi and, Marianna Barbieri-Nini – to ensure that their every nuance was as he wished. The première was a great success and the opera soon began to be performed around Italy; Verdi often advised those responsible for revivals of the special attention that the opera needed.

In 1864 the French publisher and impresario Léon Escudier asked Verdi to add ballet music for a revival of the opera at the Théâtre Lyrique, Paris. The composer agreed but also stated that he wanted to make substantial changes to some numbers that were 'either weak or lacking in character'. As well as the additional ballet and major or minor retouchings to various numbers, this revision eventually included: a new aria for Lady Macbeth in Act 2 ('La luce langue'); substantial alterations to Act 3, including a new duet for Macbeth and Lady Macbeth ('Ora di morte'); a new chorus at the beginning of Act 4 ('Patria oppressa'); and the replacement of Macbeth's death scene with a final 'Inno di vittoria'. The Paris première, which included Jean-Vital Ismael Jammes (Macbeth) and Amélie Rey-Balla (Lady Macbeth), was largely unsuccessful. The reception puzzled

Verdi and, although the original version of the opera continued to be performed for some time in Italy, it is clear that he wished the 'Paris' version to supersede it. In spite of a recent revival of interest in the 1847 version, and in spite of the fact that it is clearly more unified stylistically, the later version is the one generally heard today. In the discussion below, the most substantial revisions will be considered as they appear.

*

The prelude is made up of themes from the opera. First comes a unison woodwind theme from the witches' scene at the start of Act 3, then a passage from the apparition music in the same act. The second half is taken almost entirely from Lady Macbeth's Act 4 'sleepwalking' scene.

ACT 1 Scene i *A wood* The witches' chorus that opens the act divides into two parts, the first ('Che faceste?') in the minor, the second ('Le sorelle vagabonde') in the parallel major. Both partake of the musical 'colour' associated throughout with the witches, among which are prominent woodwind sonorities (both dark and shrill), mercurial string figures and a tendency for rhythmic displacement. Macbeth and Banquo enter and are hailed by the witches with their threefold prophecies (Macbeth shall be thane of Cawdor; he shall be king; Banquo's descendants shall be kings), darkly scored and with prominent tritones in the harmonic progression. A brisk military march then introduces messengers, who inform Macbeth of Cawdor's death and hence the fulfilment of part of the prophecy. As Verdi admitted to his principal baritone, Varesi, this sequence would traditionally have called for a double aria for Macbeth, but instead the composer supplied a one-movement duettino for Macbeth and Banquo, 'Due vaticini', full of broken lines and suppressed exclamations as the two men examine their consciences. The witches' closing stretta, 'S'allontanarono', is far more conventional, though it does find room for yet more 'characteristic' colour.

ACT 1 Scene ii *A room in Macbeth's castle* Lady Macbeth's cavatina generates great dramatic power from a conventional outward form. After a stormy orchestral introduction, she enters to read a letter from her husband describing the events we have just witnessed. The first part of her double aria, 'Vieni! t'affretta!', bids Macbeth hurry home so that she can instil in him her bloody thoughts; it is remarkable for its avoidance of formal repetition and for its tightly controlled but distant harmonic excursions. A messenger announces that Macbeth and Duncan are expected that night, and Lady Macbeth exults in the cabaletta 'Or tutti sorgete', whose moments of agility are tightly woven into the restricted formal structure. The cabaletta over, Macbeth appears and in a brief recitative Lady Macbeth unfolds her plans for Duncan. The couple are interrupted by the arrival of the King himself, whose parade around the stage is accompanied by a 'rustic' march from the stage-band.

The 'Gran Scena e Duetto' that follows begins with Macbeth's extended arioso 'Mi si affaccia un pugnal?!', during which he sees a vision of a dagger and steels himself to murder Duncan. The passage is extremely rich in musical invention, as sliding chromatic figures jostle with distorted 'religious' harmonies and fugitive reminiscences of the witches' music; it will set the tone for the great free recitatives of Verdi's later career. Macbeth enters the king's room, and Lady Macbeth appears, soon to be rejoined by her husband. Macbeth's motif at 'Tutto è finito!' ('All is finished!') furnishes the accompaniment material for the first movement of the four-movement duet, the Allegro 'Fatal mia donna! un murmure'. This first movement involves a rapid exchange between the characters, with musical continuity mostly supplied by the orchestra. As Macbeth describes the inner voice that has forever denied him sleep, the second, more lyrical movement, 'Allor questa voce', begins: the singers again have dissimilar musical material, although they eventually come together for an extended passage. A short transitional movement, 'Il pugnal là riportate', sees Lady Macbeth return the dagger to the King's room and emerge with blood on her hands which she has smeared on his sleeping servants. The duet closes with a short cabaletta, 'Vieni altrove! ogni sospetto', which in the 1847 version quickly turns to the major mode but which in 1865 Verdi revised to keep subdued and in the minor throughout.

The first-act finale begins widh the arrival of Macduff and Banquo, the latter singing a solemn apostrophe to the night. Macduff calls everyone on stage and announces the murder of Duncan. The news launches the Adagio concertato, 'Schiudi, inferno': a tutti outburst of group anguish, a quiet unaccompanied passage in which all pray for God's guidance, and a final soaring melody in which divine vengeance is called down upon the guilty one. Following the pattern of the preceding duet, the final stretta is extremely short, functioning more as a coda than as a movement in its own right.

ACT 2 Scene i *A room in the castle* An orchestral reprise of part of the Act 1 grand duet leads to a recitative between Macbeth and his wife. Malcolm has fled and is suspected of Duncan's murder, but Macbeth, obsessed by the witches' prophet that Banquo's sons will be kings, decides that more blood must flow. In the 1847 version, Lady Macbeth closes the scene with the cabaletta 'Trionfai! securi alfine', a conventional two verse aria in the manner of Elvira's music in *Ernani*. In 1865 Verdi replaced this with 'La luce langue', a multi-sectional aria whose advanced chromaticism is consistently that of his later style.

ACT 2 Scene ii *A park* The quiet, staccato chorus of murderers, 'Sparve il sol', in Verdi's traditional manner of depicting sinister groups, leads to a *romanza* for Banquo, in the coda of which the assassins strike him down but cannot prevent his son Fleance from escaping.

ACT 2 Scene iii *A magnificent hall* Lively festive music underpins the assembling of noble guests, after which Macbeth summons his wife to sing a brindisi. She obliges with 'Si colmi il calice', and (as will happen in Act 1 of *La traviata*) is answered by the unison chorus. The closing strains of the song still echo in the orchestra as Macbeth learns from an assassin of Banquo's death and Fleance's escape. The festive music resumes, but Macbeth has a horrible vision of Banquo at the banquet table (this and the second hallucination were revised and chromatically intensified in the 1865 version). Lady Macbeth calms him and repeats her brindisi, but the vision returns.

The king's terror precipitates the concertato finale, 'Sangue a me', which is led off and dominated by Macbeth, though with frequent interjections from his wife who tries to calm him. There is no formal stretta, the act ending with the general sense of stunned surprise still intact.

Act 3   *A dark cavern*   After a stormy orchestral introduction, the witches' chorus, 'Tre volte miagola', brings back the opening idea of the prelude as the first of a series of increasingly lively, rhythmically bumpy 6/8 melodies, ones clearly intended to depict the 'bizarre' element of the supernatural. The ballet that follows, written for the 1865 Paris version, is broadly in three movements. In the first, various supernatural beings dance around the cauldron to an Allegro vivacissimo. Hecate is called forth and, in an Andante second movement full of the rich chromaticism of Verdi's later style mimes that Macbeth will come to ask of his destiny and should be answered (Verdi insisted that this section be mimed rather than danced). The final movement is a sinister waltz, the spirits dancing even more wildly around the cauldron.

The Apparition Scene, substantially revised in the 1865 version to intensify its harmonic and orchestral effect, has little sustained melodic writing and consists of brief but telling musical episodes. The first introduces the three apparitions, who make their predictions of Macbeth's fate: the armed head is that of Macbeth himself, the bloody child represents Macduff 'from his mother's womb ripp'd', the crowned child holding a bough is Malcolm with the trees of Birnam Wood, with which his soldiers will advance on Macbeth's stronghold. Then, to Macbeth's arioso 'Fuggi, regal fantasima', come the eight kings, the last of whom is in the form of Banquo and precipitates Macbeth's 'Oh! mio terror! dell'ultimo', at the end of which he faints. A gentle chorus and dance of the aerial spirits, 'Ondine e silfidi', precedes the finale, which was completely rewritten for 1865. In the 1847 version the act finished with a fast cabaletta for Macbeth, 'Vada in fiamme', very much in the early Verdi mould though with an unusual minor-major key scheme. In 1865 the composer replaced this with a duettino for Macbeth and Lady Macbeth, 'Ora di morte e di vendetta', in which however, the added subtlety of articulation results in a loss in sheer rhythmic power.

ACT 4 Scene i *A deserted place on the borders of England and Scotland* The original 1847 version of the opening chorus, 'Patria oppressa', not least in its lamenting of the 'lost' homeland, is somewhat reminiscent of the 'patriotic' choruses that became so famous in Verdi's early operas, although the minor mode gives it a different colour. The 1865 replacement is one of the composer's greatest choral movements, with subtle details of harmony and rhythm in almost every bar. Macduff's 'Ah, la paterna mano', which follows, is a conventional minor-major *romanza*, and the scene is rounded off by a cabaletta-like chorus, 'La patria tradita', as Malcolm's troops prepare to descend on Macbeth.

ACT 4 Scene ii *A room in Macbeth's castle* (as in Act 1 Scene ii) Lady Macbeth enters, sleepwalking. Her famous aria,'Una macchia' ('Out, damned spot'), is justly regarded as one of the young Verdi's greatest solo creations. Preceded by an atmospheric instrumental depiction of Lady Macbeth's guilty wandering, the aria itself is distinguished by its expanded formal and harmonic structure and – most important – by a marvellously inventive orchestral contribution.

ACT 4 Scene iii *Another room in the castle* A noisy orchestral introduction leads to Macbeth's confessional Andante sostenuto 'Pietà, rispetto, amore', an effective slow aria with some surprising internal modulations. The aria concluded, soldiers rush on to announce the seeming approach of Birnam Wood; a pseudo-fugal orchestral battle ensues during which Malcolm overcomes Macbeth in single combat. In 1847 the opera ended with a short, melodramatic scene for Macbeth, 'Mel per me' full of declamatory gestures that recall motivic threads from earlier in the drama. For 1865 Verdi replaced this with a Victory Hymn, 'Macbeth, Macbeth ov'è?', a number in his most modern style, with more than a hint of Offenbach in its dotted rhythms, and perhaps even a hint of the *Marseillaise* in its final bars.

*

There is no doubt that Verdi's frequently voiced perception of the 1847 *Macbeth* as an especially important work, ennobled by its Shakespearean theme, was one that he successfully converted into dramatic substance. Much of the opera shows an attention to detail and sureness of effect unprecedented in earlier works. This holds true as much for the 'conventional' numbers, such as Lady Macbeth's opening aria or the subsequent duet with Macbeth, as for formal experiments like the Macbeth-Banquo duettino in Act 1. What is more, the new standard set by *Macbeth* was one that Verdi rarely retreated from in subsequent works.

The 1865 revisions undoubtedly enrich the score, supplying several of its most effective pieces, notably 'La luce langue' and the opening chorus of Act 4. Clearly the sense of stylistic disparity the revisions create did not concern Verdi; indeed, for the most part he made little attempt to match the replacement numbers with the main body of the score, instead producing pieces that are among the most harmonically advanced of his later career. Nor should such disparity unduly concern us: we may well overestimate the importance of stylistic consistency in opera, and the 1865 revision will surely continue to be the most commonly performed version of this magnificent work.

I masnadieri
('The Bandits')

Melodramma in four parts set to a libretto by Andrea Maffei after Friedrich von Schiller's play *Die Räuber*; first performed in London, at Her Majesty's Theatre, on 22 July 1847.

At the première Jenny Lind sang Amelia, Italo Gardoni was Carlo, Filippo Coletti was Francesco, and Luigi Lablache sang Massimiliano.

Massimiliano, Count Moor	bass
Carlo *his son*	tenor
Francesco *brother to Carlo*	baritone
Amalia *orphan, the Count's niece*	soprano
Arminio *the Count's treasurer*	tenor
Moser *a pastor*	bass
Rolla *a companion of Carlo Moor*	tenor

Wayward youths (later bandits), women, children, servants

Setting Germany, at the beginning of the 18th century

The lucrative contract to compose an opera for Her Majesty's Theatre in London was an important sign of Verdi's burgeoning international reputation, and the occasion allowed him to write for some of the most famous singers of the age. More than that, the librettist was his friend Andrea Maffei, a distinguished man of letters with a reputation far above that of Piave or Solera, who had supplied most of Verdi's earlier librettos. However, all this notwithstanding, *I masnadieri* had a troublesome birth: Maffei's lack of experience in theatrical matters was a considerable trial; Verdi quarrelled with the publisher of the opera, Francesco Lucca (with whom he never had the generally cordial relations he enjoyed with the rival firm, Ricordi); and when he arrived in London to supervise the production, he seems to have been oppressed beyond all reason by the detested English weather. The première was a magnificent gala occasion – Queen

Victoria headed the guests of honour – and a triumphant success, aided by the fame of the singers, especially Lind and Lablache, one of the great names of the previous generation of Italian singers, played Massimiliano. But the enthusiastic reception was short-lived, and the opera fared rather badly in Italy. Modern revivals are not uncommon but they remain special occasions: it seems unlikely that the work will find a permanent place in the international repertory.

*

A lachrymose cello solo, written expressly for Piatti principal cellist at Her Majesty's Theatre, forms a brief but effective prelude.

ACT 1 Scene i   *A tavern on the frontier of Saxony*   In a formally conventional carefully crafted double aria with chorus, Carlo muses on his distant homeland and his beloved Amalia (the Andante 'O mio castel paterno') before learning, through a letter from his brother, that he is forbidden to return home. He and his friends decide to become bandits and swear an oath of blood brotherhood (the cabaletta 'Nell'argilla maledetta').

ACT 1 Scene ii   *Franconia: a room in Massimiliano's castle*   A rapid change of locale is effected for a second double aria, this time for Carlo's wicked brother Francesco. In the angular sostenuto, 'La sua lampada vitale', Francesco threatens to hasten the end of his father's life. He then orders that Massimiliano be told of Carlo's death in battle, hoping that shock and grief will finish the old man off. In a forceful cabaletta 'Tremate, o miseri!', he eagerly looks forward to assuming power.

ACT 1 Scene iii   *A bedroom in the castle*   After a prelude in which solo woodwind are prominent, Amalia looks at the sleeping Massimiliano and thinks back over past joys in 'Lo sguardo avea degli angeli'. The aria was clearly written with Jenny Lind in mind: it is far more highly ornamented than the usual Verdian model and to accommodate the free flow of decoration, formally far more discursive. Massimiliano awakes and, in a short duet movement with Amalia, 'Carlo! io muoio', laments that he will die without seeing his favourite son. Arminio and Francesco enter to deliver the false news of Carlo's death, saying that Carlo's dying words accused his father and instructed Amalia to marry Francesco. This revelation precipitates the quartet 'Sul capo mio colpevole': Massimiliano is both repentant and furious with Francesco; Amalia (joined by a reformed Arminio) offers religious consolation, Francesco eagerly looks forward to his triumph. It is a powerfully effective clash of emotions, and ends as Massimiliano, seemingly lifeless, falls to the ground.

Act 2 Scene i   *An enclosure adjoining the castle chapel*   Time has passed, and Francesco is lord of the castle. Amalia visits Massimiliano's grave and in a simple Adagio, 'Tu del mio Carlo al seno', imagines him and Carlo together in heaven. Arminio rushes in to reveal that Carlo and Massimiliano are both alive. Amalia rejoices in a jubilant and distinctly old-fashioned cabaletta, 'Carlo vive?', which again gave ample opportunity for Jenny Lind to demonstrate her famed agility. Francesco enters to declare his love for Amalia and they launch into a four-movement soprano-baritone confrontation duet, a type of dramatic situation at which Verdi almost always succeeded magnificently. But for once the format proves disappointing: the Andantino 'Io t'amo, Amalia' dissolves too quickly into routine rhythmic unison at the 3rd or 6th, and the cabaletta 'Ti scosta, o malnato' in which Amalia defies Francesco's attempts to take her by force, deals unimaginatively with the clash of tessituras that many of Verdi's best examples exploit so powerfully.

Act 2 Scene ii   *The Bohemian forest near Prague*   The 'Scene e Coro' offers a typical slice of bandit life, though the choral writing is more complex than Verdi usually ventured. Rolla, condemned to be hanged, is rescued by Carlo and his followers, who rejoice in their carefree life. They leave Carlo alone to lament his outcast state in a fine minor-major *romanza*, 'Di ladroni attorniato'. His companions return to report that they are under attack and all join in a warlike chorus.

ACT 3 Scene i *A deserted place adjacent to the forest near Massimiliano's castle* Amalia has escaped from Francesco but is now alone and terrified to hear the sound of bandits nearby. She begs for mercy from the first man she sees: miraculously, he turns out to be Carlo, and the lovers are blissfully united in a duet. The first lyrical movement, 'Qual mare, qual terra', is perhaps a trifle dull, although colouristic vocal effects in part make up for a lack of the usual confrontational tension. Amalia tells Carlo of his father's death and of Francesco's attempts on her virtue. They join in a closing cabaletta, 'Lassù risplendere', in which Amalia has yet more opportunity to display her trills and agility.

ACT 3 Scene ii *Inside the forest* A further, rather jaunty bandits' chorus introduces the 'Finale Terzo'. Carlo wrestles with his Byronic soul and even contemplates suicide, but is interrupted by Arminio, whom he sees delivering food to someone imprisoned in a deserted tower. Carlo intervenes, bringing forth from the tower an emaciated old man who reveals himself as Massimiliano. In an impressive minor-major narrative, 'Un ignoto, tre lune or saranno', Massimiliano (who has not recognized his son) tells how Francesco had him confined there after he recovered from his collapse. Carlo is outraged, and calls on his fellow bandits to join him in swearing a solemn oath of vengeance against Francesco.

ACT 4 Scene i *A suite of rooms in Massimiliano's castle* Francesco's 'Pareami che sorto da lauto convito' describes a frightening vision of divine retribution in a movement that prefigures the great soliloquies of Verdi's middle-period operas. He summons Moser and asks forgiveness for his sins: only God can grant forgiveness, the pastor answers. Prompted by signs that the castle is under attack, Francesco rushes off to meet his fate.

ACT 4 Scene ii *The forest* (as in Act 3 scene ii) Carlo will not reveal his identity to Massimiliano but nevertheless asks for 'a father's blessing'. In a gentle duet 'Come il bacio d'un padre amoroso', father and son are vocally united. The robbers appear, having captured Amalia, and very soon Carlo's identity is revealed. In a final trio 'Caduto e il reprobo!', reminiscent of the parallel number in Act 4 of *Ernani*, Carlo rails against his commitment to the life of crime while Amalia offers to stay with him no matter what may befall. But Carlo's robber companions are near at hand, impossible to ignore: in a final declamatory passage, he stabs Amalia and rushes off to the gallows that await him.

*

I masnadieri is one of the most intriguing of Verdi's early works. It should have been a great success: a foreign commission of great prestige, a high Romantic basis in Schiller (one of the composer's favourite sources), a distinguished man of letters as the librettist, a cast of international standing. What is more, Verdi and his librettist consciously tried to break with certain longstanding traditions in order to make their creation more romantically intense: no other early opera dispenses with an opening chorus, for example, or with a concertato finale. But all these ingredients proved problematic. Verdi felt out of touch and out of sympathy with the English environment and may have been unsure of the audience's taste and requirements, the drama proved somewhat unwieldy, particularly in its lack of opportunities for character confrontation; Maffei in spite of his poetic skills and willingness to experiment, was unsure of himself in dramatic pacing; and the cast, Jenny Lind in particular, inspired music which, though distinguished enough on its own, proved difficult to subsume under an overall dramatic colour, the achievement of which was so crucial to Verdian success.

Jérusalem
('Jerusalem')

Opéra in four acts set to a libretto by Alphonse Royer and Gustave Vaëz after Temistocle Solera's and Verdi's earlier opera *I Lombardi alla prima crociata*; first performed in Paris, at the Opéra, on 26 November 1847.

The original cast included Gilbert Duprez (Gaston), Charles Portheaut (the Count), Adolphe-Joseph-Louis Alizard (Roger) and Mme Julian-Van-Gelder (Hélène).

Gaston, Viscount of Béarn	tenor
The Count of Toulouse	baritone
Roger *the Count's brother*	bass
Hélène *the Count's daughter*	soprano
Isaure *her companion*	soprano
Adhemar de Monteil *Papal Legate*	bass
Raymond *Gaston's squire*	tenor
A Soldier	bass
A Herald	bass
The Emir of Ramla	bass
An Officer of the Emir	tenor

Knights, ladies, pages, soldiers, pilgrims, penitents, an executioner, Arab sheiks, women of the harem, people of Ramla

Setting Toulouse and Palestine, in 1095 and 1099

The great Paris opera house, the Académie Royale de Musique (or the Opéra), had been making overtures to Verdi for some two years when, in the summer of 1847, he signed a contract to supply the theatre with a 'new' work by November of that year. As had Rossini and Donizetti, Verdi offered for his début at the Opéra a revision of one of his earlier Italian operas; with the help of Royer and Vaëz, both of whom had considerable experience in such matters, he fashioned a French version from *I Lombardi*, first performed in 1843 and

95

not previously seen in Paris. The librettists retained little of the original plot apart from its basis in a crusade: in vocal terms, the lovers Giselda and Oronte become Hélène and Gaston, the warring brothers Arvino and Pagano become the Count of Toulouse – now a baritone rather than tenor – and Roger. As well as adding the obligatory ballet, Verdi decided on some wide-ranging structural changes, adding much new music, cutting what he considered weak or inappropriate and leaving only a few of the original numbers in their former positions. *Jérusalem* was well received in Paris. However, in spite of being in many ways superior to *I Lombardi*, the opera failed to establish itself in either the French or the Italian repertory and is today only occasionally revived. The following summary will mention musical detail only in passages new to the revised opera.

*

The prelude is new; in contrast with the disparate juxtaposition of musical elements in *I Lombardi*, it sets out to develop in a systematic manner aspects of its opening theme.

ACT 1 *A gallery connecting the Count of Toulouse's palace and his chapel* As the curtain rises, Hélène and Gaston are bidding each other farewell, Gaston assuring his beloved that he will be reconciled to the Count (who killed his father) if permission is granted for their marriage. Their brief duet, 'Adieu, mon bien-aimé', is unaccompanied except for solo horn. As Gaston leaves, Isaure appears and the two ladies kneel in prayer, Hélène offering a French version of 'Salve Maria' from *I Lombardi*, now entitled 'Vierge Marie'.

Hélène and Isaure depart and, as the orchestra depicts a sunrise, the stage fills with lords and ladies who join in a chorus celebrating the end of civil war, 'Enfin voici le jour propice'. The Count and all the other principals appear. They are about to go on a Crusade, and the Count offers peace to Gaston and his family, sealing the pact with his daughter's hand. All rejoice except Roger, who incestuously desires Hélène for himself. The principals explore their individual feelings in the quintet 'Je tremble encor, j'y crois à peine', a number that required some vocal redistribution from its model in *I Lombardi*. In a newly composed linking passage, Gaston swears allegiance to the Count, who is pronounced leader of the crusading army. The scene closes with a grand chorus, 'Cité du Seigneur!'

An organ sounds from inside the chapel; Roger appears and, in the cantabile 'Oh! dans l'ombre, dans le mystère', explores the nature of his incestuous love. The aria over, Roger instructs a soldier to seek out two knights in golden armour and to murder the one not wearing a white cloak. After a warlike chorus looking forward to the Crusade, Roger anticipates the murder of Gaston in a cabaletta new for the French version, 'Ah! viens! démon! esprit du mal!'. The action scene that follows is also new. Cries of 'Murder!' in the chapel precede the appearance of Gaston: it is the Count who has been attacked. Roger's hired assassin accuses Gaston of instigating the violence and all join in an accusatory concertato, 'Monstre, parjure, homicide!'. The Papal Legate sentences Gaston to exile and in a final stretta, 'Sur ton front est lancé l'anathême', all pronounce anathema on him.

ACT 2 Scene i *The mountains of Ramla in Palestine* Four years have passed. At the opening, corresponding with Act 2 scene ii of *I Lombardi*, the disguised Roger is outside his cave, singing the Adagio 'O jour fatal! ô crime!'. Raymond enters, dying of thirst. At the news that others are in a similar plight, Roger hurries to the rescue. Hélène now appears, recognizes Raymond as Gaston's squire and learns that her beloved is alive and imprisoned in Ramla. She breaks into a joyous cabaletta, originally in Act 4 of *I Lombardi* and here retitled 'Quelle ivresse! bonheur suprême!', and leaves to seek out Gaston. A band of pilgrims, weak from lack of water, struggle on to deliver 'O mon Dieu! Ta parole est donc vaine!' (the French version of 'O Signore, dal tetto natio'). As in *I Lombardi*, a lively march introduces the Count (marvellously recovered, he tells us, from the assassination attempt), who asks the hermit's blessing. But Roger (still unrecognized) elects to accompany them into battle. All depart after a lively final chorus, 'Le Seigneur nous promet la victoire', new for the French version.

ACT 2 Scene ii *A room in the Emir's palace at Ramla* Gaston, a prisoner, muses on Hélène in a revised version of his Act 2 Andante from *I Lombardi*, now entitled 'Je veux encor entendre'. The Emir appears, quickly followed by Hélène, who has been captured nearby. The Act 3 lovers' duet from *I Lombardi* then ensues; Hélène and Gaston are about to escape to join the Crusaders but are at the last moment surrounded by guards.

ACT 3 Scene i   *The gardens of the harem at Ramla*   This scene corresponds to Act 2 scene iii of *I Lombardi*, except that the opening chorus is followed by a full-length ballet. By the time the dancing is over, Crusaders are at the gates. Hélène prays for deliverance, Gaston appears at her side. The Crusaders rush in and the Count denounces Hélène for consorting with Gaston, the presumed assassin. Hélène, like her Italian counterpart, responds with a rondò finale, 'Non . . . votre rage', at the close of which the Count drags her away.

ACT 3 Scene ii   *The public square at Ramla*   In an impressive ensemble scene, new for the French version, Gaston is led on to the strains of a funeral dirge. The Legate informs the crowd that he is to be dishonoured and executed; Gaston pleads for mercy in the Andante mosso, 'O mes amis, mes frères d'armes'. But the accusers are unmoved: he will be executed the following day. In a closing stretta, 'Frapper bourreaux!', Gaston asks for immediate death, proud before God of his innocence.

ACT 4 Scene i   *On the edge of the Crusaders' camp in the valley of Jehoshaphat*   The scene is based on the 'Coro della Processione' that opens Act 3 of *I Lombardi*, although the chorus is preceded by a recitative from Roger, looking over the valley at Jerusalem. As the procession moves away, Roger and Hélène remain behind to offer Gaston a final blessing. The tenor appears, and so the new plot links to the famous trio that ends Act 3 of *I Lombardi*: it is now entitled 'Dieu nous sépare, Hélène!', is shorn of its violin solo and boasts an exciting coda in which offstage sounds of battle cause Gaston and Roger to rush off into the fray.

ACT 4 Scene ii   *The Count's tent*   The Count, accompanied by an unknown knight who has distinguished himself in battle, announces victory. The knight reveals himself as Gaston. Roger is now brought on, mortally wounded. The music links into the final scene of *I Lombardi*, with Roger's revelation of his true identity and his pleas that mercy be shown to Gaston, answered by the closing Hymne Général, 'A toi gloire ô Dieu de victoire'.

*

Although *Jérusalem* was soon converted into the Italian *Gerusalemme*, and published in Italy, Verdi's revision failed to oust *I Lombardi* from the Italian stage and gradually disappeared from the repertory. This is in some ways regrettable, as the opera simplifies somewhat the complex action of the Italian original, adds convincing new music (in particular the fine crowd scene of Act 3 scene ii), cuts some of the weaker portions and, by converting Arvino from a tenor to a baritone, solves one of the problems of vocal distribution that occurred in *I Lombardi*. Whatever its ultimate merits, *Jérusalem* serves as a fascinating first document in charting Verdi's relationship with the French stage, a relationship that was to become increasingly important during the next decade.

Il corsaro
('The corsair')

Opera in three acts set to a libretto by Francesco Maria Piave after Byron's poem *The Corsair*; first performed in Trieste, at the Teatro Grande, on 25 October 1848.

The first cast included Gaetano Fraschini (Corrado), Achille De Bassini (Seid) and Marianna Barbieri-Nini (Gulnara).

Corrado *Captain of the corsairs*	tenor
Giovanni *a corsair*	bass
Medora *Corrado's young beloved*	soprano
Seid *Pasha of Coron*	baritone
Gulnara *Seid's favourite slave*	soprano
Selimo *an Aga*	tenor
A Black Eunuch	tenor
A Slave	tenor

Corsairs, guards, Turks, slaves, odalisques, Medora's maids, Anselmo (a corsair)

Setting An island in the Aegean and the city of Coron, at the beginning of the 19th century

Verdi had toyed with setting Byron's poem as early as 1844 and kept the subject in mind during the years immediately following. In 1845 he considered using it to fulfil a commission from Her Majesty's Theatre in London: Piave wrote the libretto, but the London trip was postponed. A year later Verdi showed his continuing enthusiasm for the topic by asking Piave not to give the libretto to any other composer. Eventually, Verdi wrote the opera to fulfil the final part of a long-standing contract with Giovanni Ricordi's rival publisher Francesco Lucca, a man with whom Verdi had had unfortunate dealings ever since Lucca and Ricordi had come to legal blows over the rights to *Nabucco* in 1842. Anxious above all to be rid of his obligation, Verdi set Piave's libretto in the winter of 1847–8, giving the opera to Lucca without any idea of where or when it would first be performed. For a composer who in all previous operas had taken an enormous, often fanatical interest in the details of his creations' first staging, such indifference is suspicious: many have seen it as an indication that Verdi had little faith in his new opera. Lucca eventually placed the opera at the Teatro Grande in Trieste, but Verdi did not even trouble to attend the first performances. The première was poorly received and managed only a few revivals before it disappeared from the repertory. It has rarely been revived in modern times.

*

The prelude, based on material from the opera, is one of extreme contrasts, with the opening orchestral storm music followed by a lyrical subject of great simplicity.

ACT 1 Scene i *The corsairs' island in the Aegean* A boisterous offstage chorus of corsairs introduces Corrado, who bemoans his life of exile and crime in 'Tutto parea sorridere', an aria that delicately hovers between Italian formal convention and the French two-verse variety. A letter containing military intelligence is presented to Corrado, who resolves to set sail, rallying his troops with the cabaletta 'Sì: de' Corsari il fulmine'; in the manner of Verdi's earliest successes, the chorus joins the soloist for the final lines.

ACT 1 Scene ii *Medora's apartments in the old tower* Medora, awaiting Corrado's arrival, takes up her harp and sings a two-verse *romanza*, 'Non so le tetre immagini', full of vague forebodings though not without elaborate vocal ornament. Corrado enters and a conventionally structured duet finale closes the act. The first lyrical movement, 'No, tu non sai', a dissimilar type in which Medora's disturbed chromatic line is settled by Corrado's reassuring melodic stability, is unusual in its progressive deceleration of tempo; the cabaletta, 'Tornerai, ma forse spenta', which sees Corrado about to depart yet again, is more traditionally paced, with a final faster section in which the lovers sing an extended passage in 3rds and 6ths.

ACT 2 Scene i *Luxurious apartments in Seid's harem* A chorus of odalisques, graced with high woodwind local colour, introduces

Gulnara, who hates Seid and seeks to escape from the harem. Her cavatina, 'Vola talor dal carcere', is conventionally scored but has much of that harmonic and orchestral density we expect from post- *Macbeth* Verdi. She agrees to attend a banquet of Seid's and in the cabaletta 'Ah conforto è sol la speme' prays that Heaven will take pity on her.

ACT 2 Scene ii *A magnificent pavilion on the shores of the harbour of Coron* After a brief chorus of greeting, Seid salutes his followers and joins them in a solemn hymn to Allah, 'Salve Allah!', a number whose rhythmic cut is more than a little reminiscent of the famous choruses in *I Lombardi* and *Ernani*. A Dervish appears, asking for protection from the corsairs. He and Seid have time for the brief first movement of a duet, 'Di': que' ribaldi tremano', before flames are seen and offstage cries signal an attack. The Dervish throws off his disguise to reveal himself as Corrado, who calls for his followers. In an extended battle sequence, Corrado and his troops attempt to save the women of the harem, a delay in the attack that causes their defeat and his wounding. In the ensuing Andante of the concertato finale, 'Audace cotanto mostrati pur sai?', Seid derides the fallen hero, Corrado is defiant and Gulnara and the odalisques find their amorous feelings aroused by these handsome would-be saviours. More prisoners are brought on, but Seid is above all happy to have Corrado in his power and leads off the stretta 'Sì, morrai di morte atroce', promising his prisoner an agonizing death.

ACT 3 Scene i *Seid's apartments* The baritone has so far seen little of the vocal limelight, and room is now made for a full-scale double aria. In the Andantino, 'Cento leggiadre vergini', Seid regrets that of all the women available to him, the one whom he loves has spurned him. As in Corrado's Act 1 aria, though even more economically, the aria is notable for its orchestral reprise of the main melody. In the cabaletta 'S'avvicina il tuo momento', a movement more reminiscent of Verdi's first opera *Oberto* than of the post-*Macbeth* style, Seid looks forward to Corrado's grisly death.

Gulnara enters to plead for Corrado's life. The first movement of the ensuing duet, 'Vieni, Gulnara!', is a free dialogue over a complex orchestral melody of a kind later to be made famous in the Rigoletto-Sparafucile duet. But Seid will not be persuaded and eventually concludes that Gulnara must love Corrado. His anger bursts forth in the duet cabaletta, 'Sia l'istante maledetto'.

ACT 3 Scene ii   *Inside a prison tower*   A sombre prelude featuring solo cello and viola introduces Corrado, alone and in chains. He laments his fate in a spare but expressive recitative before falling asleep. Gulnara steals in and awakens him. In the long, expressive and unusually free first movement of their duet, 'Seid la vuole', Gulnara offers Corrado a means of escape, saying that she herself will kill Seid. Corrado's personal honour obliges him to refuse her help, and he further distresses her by admitting his love for Medora. Gulnara departs, and the orchestra sounds a reprise of the stormy music first heard in the prelude to Act 1. As the storm subsides, Gulnara returns to announce that Seid is dead. Corrado now assures her of his protection and in the cabaletta 'La terra, il ciel m'abborrino' they prepare to escape together.

ACT 3 Scene iii   *The corsairs' island* (as 1.i)   An orchestral prelude featuring fragments of Medora's Act 1 *romanza* introduces Corrado's beloved, near death and without hope of seeing him again. But suddenly a ship is sighted, Corrado and Gulnara arrive, and the lovers are in each other's arms. Corrado and Gulnara relate something of their adventures before Medora leads off the concertato, 'O mio Corrado, appressati', whose opening melody appeared in the prelude to the opera. Corrado and Gulnara heighten the emotional temperature by protesting at fate, but Medora's strength fails. In an agony of despair, Corrado flings himself from the cliffs.

*

It is important to recall that the libretto to *Il corsaro* (and therefore its essential dramatic structure) was fixed as early as 1846, some time before Verdi worked on *Macbeth*: much of the opera seems rather old-fashioned in relation to the works that surround it in the Verdian canon. It is also – perhaps for this reason, perhaps (as mentioned earlier) because of Verdi's feud with the publisher Lucca – an uneven work, with an element of the routine in certain passages. On the other hand, there are many moments, particularly in the final act, that stand comparison with the best operas of this period, and some formal experiments – strange and elliptical as they may be in their dramatic context – that were to bear much fruit in the years to come.

La battaglia di Legnano
('The battle of Legnano')

Tragedia lirica in four acts set to a libretto by Salvadore Cammarano after Joseph Méry's play *La bataille de Toulouse*; first performed in Rome, at the Teatro Argentina, 27 January 1849.

The cast at the première included Filippo Colini (Rolando), Teresa De Giuli Borsi (Lida) and Gaetano Fraschini (Arrigo).

Federico Barbarossa	bass
First Consul of Milan	bass
Second Consul of Milan	bass
Mayor of Como	bass
Rolando *a Milanese leader*	baritone
Lida *his wife*	soprano
Arrigo *a soldier from Verona*	tenor
Marcovaldo *a German prisoner*	baritone
Imelda *Lida's maid*	mezzo-soprano
Arrigo's Squire	tenor
A Herald	tenor

Knights of Death, magistrates and leaders of Como, Lida's maids, Milanese people, Milanese senators, soldiers from Verona, Novara, Piacenza and Milan, German army

Setting Milan and Como in 1176

The revolutions that swept through Italy and much of the rest of Europe in 1848 – and in particular Milan's 'cinque giornate', when the Milanese forced the Austrian soldiers from their city – inspired Verdi to attempt an opera in which the theme of patriotism would be overt. Together with his librettist Cammarano, he eventually decided to compose an opera set in 12th-century Italy, the epoch of the Lombard league, adapting for the purpose a recent French drama. Work on *La battaglia di Legnano* took up most of 1848, and by the time it was finished Milan and many other cities were long back in

105

Austrian hands. But Rome was still a beleaguered republic, and the premiére of the opera took place there in what must have been highly charged circumstances. It was a clamorous success, with the entire final act encored. However, the opera was extremely difficult to get past the censors in the repressive, counter-revolutionary atmosphere of the 1850s, and never firmly established itself in the repertory. In the mid-1850s Verdi voiced the intention of rehabilitating *La battaglia* by making a thorough revision of the libretto, but his ideas came to nothing, and the work virtually disappeared from the theatre until its occasional modern revivals.

*

The overture has the usual three-part structure, with the middle section slower and (in the manner of the *Guillaume Tell* overture) dominated by solo woodwind. But its inner workings and its sheer scale far outstrip any of Verdi's previous efforts, and the piece surely deserves revival in today's concert halls.

ACT 1:   'He Lives!'

ACT 1 Scene i   *A part of rebuilt Milan, near the city walls* Soldiers from various parts of northern Italy congregate to an Allegro marziale and sing an unaccompanied patriotic hymn, 'Viva Italia! Sacro un patto' (already heard as the opening subject of the overture). Arrigo emerges from the crowd of soldiers to greet his beloved Milan in 'La pia materna mano', an aria whose subtlety of orchestral detail and distant modulations immediately alert us to the developments taking place in Verdi's musical language. After a brief reprise of the hymn, Rolando joyously greets Arrigo, having thought him killed in battle. His *romanza*, 'Ah! m'abbraccia d'esultanza', functions dramaturgically as a cabaletta but is actually a French-influenced ternary form. The scene is rounded off by a solemn 'giuramento' in which all swear to defend Milan to the last drop of their blood.

ACT 1 Scene ii   *A shady place*   A female chorus celebrating the arrival of the soldiers introduces Lida, who explains in an Andante, 'Quante volte come un dono', that she cannot be happy now that her father and brothers have been slain in battle. Again, unusually detailed orchestration and harmonic excursions underline a new manner in Verdi's style. Marcovaldo pays unwelcome court to Lida, but is interrupted by Imelda, who announces that Rolando has returned, bringing with him Arrigo. Lida's attempts to restrain her joy at the news that Arrigo is alive coalesce into her cabaletta 'A frenarti, o cor nel petto'.

Rolando ushers in Arrigo, saying that his friend must remain in the house as a guest. Left alone, Arrigo and Lida engage in a long, single-movement duet finale, 'Èver? . . . Sei d'altri?', a piece quite unlike the usual multi-movement sequence and gaining its cohesion more from juxtapositions of key than from contrasting formal units.

Act 2: 'Barbarossa!'

A magnificent room in the town hall of Como In the chorus 'Sì, tardi ed invano' the people of Como, ancient enemies of the Milanese, rejoice to hear of their rivals' difficulties with the German Emperor Barbarossa. Arrigo and Rolando enter to request military assistance, urging their cause with a passionate duet, 'Ben vi scorgo'. Hardly has the duet finished than Barbarossa himself appears, his impressive entrance immediately precipitating the concertato finale. The Adagio of the finale, 'A che smarriti e pallidi', is made up of patterned exchanges between Barbarossa and the two Milanese warriors, first in hesitant minor, then in more lyrically extended major, with the chorus firmly on Barbarossa's side. Barbarossa then has the windows thrown open to display the mass of German troops; but Arrigo still trusts the power of the people. In the closing stretta, 'Il destino d'Italia son io!', the fixed opposition between the two sides continues, Verdi lavishing much orchestral and harmonic detail on a section which had traditionally been of the most straightforward.

Act 3: 'Disgrace!'

Act 3 Scene i *A subterranean vault in the basilica of San Ambrogio, Milan* In a sombre opening chorus, 'Fra queste dense tenebre', the Knights of Death celebrate a pact to avenge the deaths

107

of their forefathers. Arrigo is admitted to their ranks before all join in the solemn oath of allegiance, 'Giuriam d'Italia por fine ai danni'. The scene is reminiscent of *Ernani* Act 3, though shot through with French-influenced atmospheric effects.

ACT 3 Scene ii *Apartments in Rolando's castle* Lida has heard of Arrigo's enlistment with the Knights of Death, and has written him a letter which she now gives to Imelda. Her scene is without a formal aria but is full of those lyrical outpourings that will become one of Verdi's greatest strengths. Rolando enters to bid farewell to his wife and child and joins Lida in the tender duet 'Digli ch'è sangue italico'. As Lida and the child leave, Arrigo appears and Rolando confesses his fears for the coming battle. In the gentle, Bellinian Andante, 'Se al nuovo dì pugnando', he entrusts his family to the care of Arrigo should he die in battle. The friends embrace and Arrigo leaves. Marcovaldo now enters: he has intercepted Lida's letter, and shows it to Rolando. In a furious cabaletta, 'Ahi scellerate alme d'inferno', Rolando swears vengeance on his wife and friend.

ACT 3 Scene iii *A room high in the tower* Arrigo, alone on the balcony as the curtain rises, decides to write a letter of farewell to his mother. Lida enters and the couple confess their love in a simple recitative. They are interrupted by Rolando, whose offstage voice causes Lida to hide on the balcony. Rolando appears and immediately discovers Lida, thus precipitating the Terzetto finale. The first movement,'Ah! d'un consorte, o perfidi', is all flux and change, while in the central Andante, 'Vendetta d'un momento', the two lovers desperately call for death. But Rolando has other plans. The set piece finished, Arrigo hears trumpets calling him to the Knights of Death and prepares to leave; but Rolando has decided that his punishment will be 'disgrace' and rushes out, locking the door behind him. Arrigo cannot stand the shame that will result if he fails to join the Knights, and with a final cry of 'Viva Italia!' throws himself from the balcony into the moat below.

ACT 4:   'To Die for the Homeland!'

The vestibule of a church, giving on to a piazza in Milan   As a choir
sings inside the church, Imelda tells Lida that Arrigo survived his
fall and reached the Knights of Death. They join the chorus in a
prayer. Distant sounds of rejoicing announce victory over the German
army. All unite in a celebratory hymn, but at its close a funeral march
is heard in the distance. Arrigo is brought in, mortally wounded. He
again protests Lida's innocence and begins the final trio of reconciliation, 'Per la salvata Italia'. The last, soaring phrase, sung by Arrigo,
Lida and then by the entire company, sums up the opera's message:
'Chi muore per la patria alma sì rea non ha!' ('He who dies for the
homeland cannot have such an evil soul!').

*

La battaglia di Legnano was from the start dogged by the special
circumstances of its creation: in the early years by problems with the
censor, and later perhaps by its too intense association with a particular historical period. But Verdi's plans to revise the work in the
1850s are surely significant, suggesting that he thought the opera
comparable to *Macbeth*, *Stiffelio* and *Luisa Miller*. *La battaglia* is
impressive above all in its inner workings, which show the concern
for orchestral and harmonic detail that never left Verdi after his decisive encounter with French operatic style. In today's climate, in which
almost all Verdi's early operas are occasionally revived, *La battaglia*
stands as one of Verdi's most unjustly neglected works.

Luisa Miller

Melodramma tragico in three acts set to a libretto by Salvadore Cammarano after Friedrich von Schiller's play *Kabale und Liebe*; first performed in Naples, at the Teatro San Carlo, on 8 December 1849.

The first cast included Marietta Gazzaniga (Luisa), Achille DeBassini (Miller), Antonio Selva (Walter) and Settimio Malvezzi (Rodolfo).

Count Walter	bass
Rodolfo *his son*	tenor
Federica *Duchess of Ostheim,Walter's niece*	contralto
Wurm *Walter's steward*	bass
Miller *a retired old soldier*	baritone
Luisa *his daughter*	soprano
Laura *a peasant girl*	mezzo-soprano
A Peasant	tenor

Federica's ladies-in-waiting,pages, retainers, archers, villagers

Setting The Tyrol, in the first half of the 17th century

Verdi's relationship with Naples, never entirely happy, continued inauspiciously during the late 1840s: in 1848, despite his efforts to withdraw, the Neapolitan authorities held him to a longstanding contract for a new opera at the San Carlo. The librettist was to be Salvadore Cammarano, resident poet at the theatre and a man of vast experience in both the practical and the artistic side of operatic production. Verdi's first idea was for a setting of Francesco Guerrazzi's recent historical novel, *L'assedio di Firenze*, a large-scale subject designed to suit the dimensions of the San Carlo and, one imagines, intended to follow the line of Verdi's current preoccupation, *La battaglia di Legnano*. However, by April 1849 this idea – hardly surprisingly given the counter-revolutionary political climate

– had been rejected by the Neapolitan censors. Cammarano then suggested using Schiller's *Kabale und Liebe*, a play Verdi himself had earlier considered. The composer accepted, although not without asking for a considerablenumber of structural alterations to the synopsis Cammarano sent him (not all of which the poet, who was no Piave in matters of acquiescence, agreed to).

Negotiations had thus far been undertaken with Verdi in Paris, where he had set up house with Giuseppina Strepponi while supervising the première of *Jérusalem*. In the late summer of 1849 he returned to Italy to work on *Luisa Miller* (as Schiller's play had been retitled); he arrived in Naples in late October to supervise the staging of the opera, first performed some five weeks later. The première was probably a success (press reports are lacking), but even though the opera received a respectable number of revivals it never attained the popularity of *Nabucco* or *Ernani* and faded from the repertory later in the century. *Luisa* was 'rediscovered' in the 1920s as part of the German Verdi 'renaissance' and has subsequently become – with *Nabucco*, *Ernani* and *Macbeth* – one of the few Verdi scores written before 1850 to enjoy a firm place in the international repertory.

*

The overture, in C minor, is unlike any other Verdi wrote in that it is monothematic and built primarily around a process of modulation rather than on a succession of contrasting melodies; the composer's clear intention was to emulate a Germanic, 'symphonic' movement rather than the usual, Italian potpourri type. The modulations and other symphonic devises, show that Verdi was perfectly able to understand and reproduce such symphonic devices when the mood took him.

ACT 1:   'Love'

ACT 1 Scene i   *A pleasant village*   A pastoral atmosphere is immediately created by the orchestra's 6/8 movement and prominent wind writing, and is confirmed by the chorus's simple, rocking melody 'Ti desta, Luisa', which bids Luisa awake on a beautiful April dawn. Miller and Luisa enter, Miller casting doubts on his daughter's relationship with 'Carlo', an unknown young man who has arrived with the new Count. Luisa expresses her naive love in the cavatina 'Lo vidi, e 'l primo palpito', which is simple and cabaletta-like, continuing elaborate woodwind effects in the accompaniment. Villagers present Luisa with flowers and 'Carlo' (Rodolfo in disguise) emerges from the crowd. The lovers join Miller in a closing terzetto, 'T'amo d'amor ch'esprimere', Miller avoiding the main melody to mutter his suspicions and discontent in a staccato counter-theme.

As the stage clears, Miller is detained by Wurm, who angrily demands Luisa's hand in marriage. In the spacious, conventionally organized Andante, 'Sacra la scelta è d'un consorte', Miller insists that his daughter will make her own choice of husband. But Wurm reveals the true identity of 'Carlo' and Miller bursts into a cabaletta of rage and grief, 'Ah! fu giusto il mio sospetto!'.

ACT 1 Scene ii   *A room in Walter's castle*   Walter and Wurm are in mid-conversation, Wurm having told the Count of Rodolfo's involvement with Luisa. When Wurm leaves, Walter releases his confused paternal feelings in the minor-major *romanza* 'Il mio sangue, la vita darei', another expanded form in which the major section takes an unexpected plunge back into minor reflections. Rodolfo appears and his father orders him to marry the recently widowed Duchess Federica. Before Rodolfo can explain his predicament Federica appears, heralded by a delicate chorus, 'Quale un sorriso d'amica sorte'. Federica and Rodolfo are left alone, and the Duchess admits her love in the first movement of a two-movement duet (the Andante 'Dall'aule raggianti'), which begins lyrically but diverts into fragmentary dialogue as Rodolfo admits he loves another. The ensuing cabaletta, 'Deh! la parola amara', confirms their divided position.

ACT 1 Scene iii   *A room in Miller's house*   An offstage chorus tells of a hunt in progress. Luisa is anxiously awaiting 'Carlo' but is instead confronted by her father, who reveals her lover's true identity and his forthcoming marriage. Rodolfo intervenes to swear his continuing love, telling Miller he knows a terrible secret that will protect them from the Count's wrath. Walter himself arrives to precipitate the first movement of the concertato finale, an Allegro dominated by a driving violin melody reminiscent of the overture theme. Walter summons soldiers and orders the arrest of Miller and his daughter, ignoring both the protests of Miller and Rodolfo and the entreaties of Luisa. The ensuing Andantino, the central lyrical movement 'Fra' mortali ancora oppressa', allows the principals to present their differing reactions with unusual definition. The act then quickly comes to a close: in an arioso of gathering intensity Rodolfo pleads with his father and, at the climax, threatens to reveal the dreadful secret. Walter immediately frees Luisa, the chorus thanks heaven, and the curtain falls with no concluding stretta.

ACT 2: 'The Intrigue'

ACT 2 Scene i   *A room in Miller's house*   (as in Act 1 Scene iii) Villagers rush on and in a formal narrative tell Luisa that her father has been taken to prison. As they disperse Wurm enters and tells Luisa that, to save her father, she must write a letter to Wurm's dictation, saying that she never loved Rodolfo and now wishes to elope with Wurm. Before signing the letter, Luisa offers a prayer, the famous 'Tu puniscimi, o Signore', an Andante agitato remarkable for its lack of formal repetition. Wurm continues his demands: that she will swear the letter is her own and that she loves Wurm. She closes the scene with a cabaletta, 'A brani, a brani, o perfido', that swings from minor to major as she moves from anticipation of death to the thought that her father will be at hand to minister to her final moments.

ACT 2 Scene ii   *Walter's room in the castle*   Walter, brooding, is joined by Wurm, who tells him of the progress of their plot against Luisa. They join in a narrative duet, 'L'alto retaggio non ho bramato', recalling their murder of the old Count and Rodolfo's discovery of the secret. The duet begins with an objectivity typical of operatic narrative, but becomes increasingly fragmented as the description of events unfolds, culminating in the cabaletta-like 'O meco incolume' in which Walter vows to protect Wurm or accompany him to the gallows.

Federica appears and Wurm is dismissed. Walter tells her that Rodolfo is now ready to marry, and produces Luisa who in a dialogue movement controlled by orchestral melody denies Rodolfo and declares her love for Wurm. This last statement precipitates the lyrical Andante 'Come celar le smanie', unusual in its complete lack of orchestral accompaniment.

ACT 2 Scene iii   *The castle gardens*   Rodolfo now has Luisa's infamous letter, and sorrowfully reminisces in the famous Andante 'Quando le sere al placido', an early example of Verdi's use of the French *couplet* form. Wurm appears and Rodolfo challenges him to an immediate duel, which Wurm evades by firing his pistol into the air and rushing off. Walter appears with some followers and, after Rodolfo has told him of Luisa's 'betrayal', Walter persuades his son to marry Federica as revenge. Rodolfo, in a confusion of distress, closes the act with the cabaletta 'L'ara, o l'avello apprestami'.

ACT 3:   'The poison'

A room in Miller's house (as in Act 1 Scene iii) An orchestral reminiscence of past themes introduces 'Come in un giorno solo', in which the villagers lament Luisa's sorrowful countenance. Luisa, who exchanges words with the chorus while writing a letter, is joined by Miller, who has learnt from Wurm the true nature of her sacrifice. Their ensuing duet is in the usual four movements, during the first of which Miller discovers that Luisa's letter proposes a suicide pact with Rodolfo. In the second movement, 'La tomba è un letto', Luisa returns to her naive, first-act musical style as she looks forward to an innocent grave while Miller counters with an impassioned plea in the parallel minor. The movement ends with Luisa tearing up the letter; there is a heartfelt reconciliation, and father and daughter join in a cabaletta, 'Andrem, raminghi e poveri', in which they look forward to leaving the village to live a simple, wandering existence.

As Miller departs, Luisa hears an organ from a nearby church; she kneels in prayer. Rodolfo enters and in a long, passionate recitative full of violent orchestral interjections forces her to admit to writing

PLATE 1

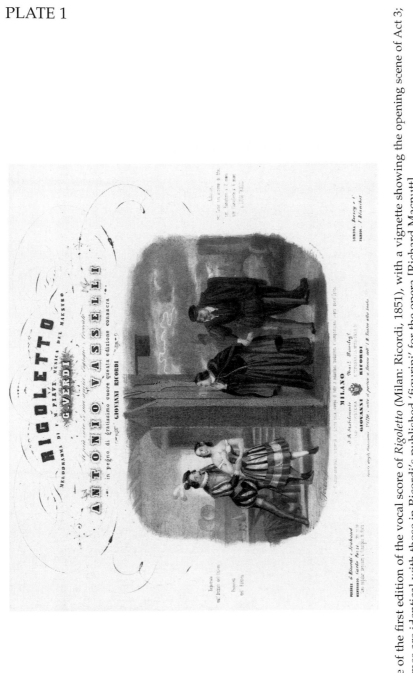

Title-page of the first edition of the vocal score of *Rigoletto* (Milan: Ricordi, 1851), with a vignette showing the opening scene of Act 3; the costumes are identical with those in Ricordi's published 'figurini' for the opera [Richard Macnutt]

PLATE 2

Rigoletto: design by Giuseppe and Pietro Bertoja for Act 1 scene ii (the most deserted corner of a blind alley) of the original production at La Fenice, Venice, 11 March 1851 [Museo Correr (photo Civici Musei Veneziani d'Arte e di Storia)]

PLATE 3

Scene from Colonello's production of *I Lombardi alla prima crociata* in the Verona Arena 1984 [Arena di Verona Press Office Archive (photo Franco Fainello)]

PLATE 4

Aida, Act 2 scene ii (one of the city gates of Thebes): engraving showing the first production at the Paris Opéra (Salle Garnier), 22 March 1880 [Civica Raccolta delle Stampe 'Achille Bertarelli', Castello Sforzesco]

PLATE 5

Giuseppe Verdi: photograph by Nadar, 1860s [Museo Teatrale alla Scala, Milan]

PLATE 6

Tito Gobbi in the title role of *Simon Boccanegra* [Stuart-Liff Collection]

PLATE 7

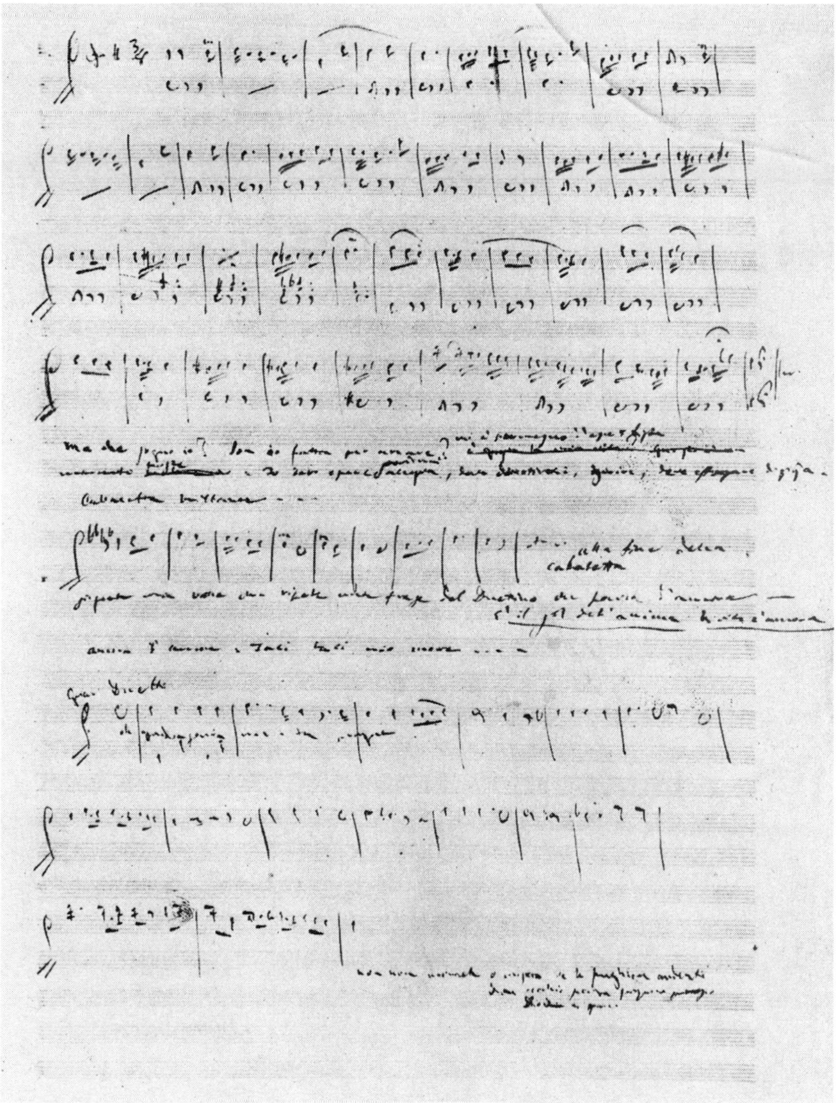

Verdi's preliminary sketches (possibly from late 1852) for Violetta's double aria at the end of Act 1 of *La traviata*: 'Ah fors'è lui' (top four systems) and 'Sempre libera degg'io' (central system); the passage marked 'Gran Duetto' was not used in the definitive version. The fact that there is no text underlay, and that the melodies are connected by a prose commentary, suggests that Verdi had not yet received the final version of the libretto [C. Gatti, *Verdi nelle immagini* (Milan, 1941)]

PLATE 8

Amelita Galli-Curci as Violetta in *La traviata* [Stuart-Liff Collection]

the letter; then he shares with her a drink which he has surreptitiously poisoned. The duet moves into regular musical periods at the Andante, 'Piangi, piangi, il tuo dolore', whose lyricism seems all the more intense for having so long been denied in the duet. Rodolfo admits that he has poisoned them both; Luisa at last feels free to confess her deception, and they join in the stretta, 'Maledetto il dì ch'io nacqui', Rodolfo cursing the day he was born, Luisa trying to comfort him. The arrival of Miller, who quickly discovers all, leads to a terzetto finale, 'Padre, ricevi l'estremo addio', at the close of which Rodolfo, seeing Luisa fall dead, kills Wurm before himself collapsing by the side of his beloved.

*

For that perceptive early critic of Verdi, Abramo Basevi, *Luisa Miller* marks the beginning of Verdi's 'second manner', one in which he drew more on Donizetti's example and less on Rossini's, and in which his musical dramaturgy took on a more subtle and varied form. Modern commentators have sometimes endorsed this judgment, signalling the opera as an important step towards *Rigoletto*. However, while the rustic ambience of the opera undoubtedly called forth from Verdi a new and compelling attention to local colour, it is difficult to see in the formal aspect of *Luisa* an essential stylistic turning-point, particularly when compared with *Macbeth*, which had appeared two years earlier. Nevertheless, few would argue about the opera's important position among pre- *Rigoletto* operas: not so much for its formal experiments as for its control of conventional musical forms, especially the grand duet. And in this respect, the middle-period work *Luisa* most resembles is not *Rigoletto* but *Il trovatore*, whose driving energy within conventional contexts is apparent through much of the earlier opera, in particular in its final act.

Stiffelio

Opera in three acts set to a libretto by Francesco Maria Piave after Emile Souvestre's and Eugène Bourgeois' play *Le pasteur, ou L'évangile et le foyer*; first performed in Trieste, at the Teatro Grande, on 16 November 1850.

The première cast included Gaetano Fraschini (Stiffelio), Marietta Gazzaniga Malaspina (Lina) and Filippo Colini (Stankar).

Stiffelio *an Ahasuerian preacher*	tenor
Lina *his wife*	soprano
Stankar *an old colonel, count of the Empire and Lina's father*	baritone
Raffaele von Leuthold *a nobleman* tenor Jorg *an old preacher*	bass
Federico di Frengel *Lina's cousin*	tenor
Dorotea *Lina's cousin*	mezzo-soprano

The Count's friends, Stiffelio's disciples, Ahasuerians

Setting Austria, in and around Stankar's castle by the river Salzbach, at the beginning of the 19th century

As was becoming the pattern, Verdi's April 1850 contract for the work that would become *Stiffelio* was signed not with a theatre but with a publisher, in this as in most other cases Ricordi. The librettist was again to be Piave, who himself suggested an adaptation of *Le pasteur*, a French play that had received its première only the previous year but was already available in Italian translation. It was a bold choice, a far cry from the melodramatic plots of Byron (*Il corsaro*, *I due Foscari*) and Hugo (*Ernani*): modern, 'realistic' subjects were unusual in Italian opera, and the religious subject matter seemed bound to cause problems with the censor.

Giovanni Ricordi decided to have the première staged at Trieste – the theatre that had recently given such a lukewarm reception to *Il corsaro* – and, true to expectation, the local censorship insisted on a number of important changes, in particular muting the action of the final scene so as (in the composer's view) to make it ridiculous. The work's reception was not much better than that accorded *Il corsaro*. *Stiffelio* had occasional revivals in subsequent years, but was continually dogged by censorship difficulties, and in the mid-1850s Verdi decided to 'rescue' his music by revising it to fit a different, less sensitive plot, Aroldo.

The original *Stiffelio* disappeared from the repertory and won its first modern revival only in the 1960s. Since then it has received a fair number of performances, and is ranked by many as Verdi's most unjustly neglected opera.

*

The overture is of the potpourri type: a sequence of contrasting melodies, some of which return in the subsequent action. Its predominantly martial atmosphere (even the main cantabile melody is scored for solo trumpet) seems, curiously, better suited to *Aroldo* than to the original subject.

ACT 1 Scene i   *A hall on the ground floor of Stankar's castle*   The opera immediately pronounces its unusual formal exterior by beginning without the customary introductory chorus. Instead, Jorg offers up an intense, chromatic prayer on behalf of Stiffelio, who has just returned from a mission. Stiffelio appears, surrounded by his family and friends, and in the ensuing narration, 'Di qua varcando sul primo albore', relates that a boatman reported to him how at first light he saw a young man and a woman at an upstairs window of the castle, clearly up to no good, and how the man threw himself from the window into the river, dropping some papers as he did so. Stifled outbursts from Lina and Raffaele suggest their guilty consciences, but Stiffelio puts their fears to rest by magnanimously casting the documents into the fire. All join in a septet, 'Colla cenere disperso', after which Stiffelio's friends sing a welcoming chorus, 'A te Stiffelio un canto', based on a theme heard in the overture.

The crowd disperses, leaving Stiffelio alone with his wife. The first part of his ensuing double aria is a complex, articulated structure, responding as it does to Lina's reactions. First comes 'Vidi

117

dovunque gemere', in which he describes the moral collapse he has seen everywhere on his journey; then he has a reassuring word for his wife in 'Ah no, il perdono è facile'; and finally come the loving words of 'Allor dunque sorridimi' as he takes her hand and asks for a smile such as she gave him on their wedding day. But his melody suddenly breaks off as he sees that her ring is missing. She can give no answer to his inquiries about it and his suspicions burst out in the cabaletta 'Ah! v'appare in fronte scritto'. The final bars are interrupted by Stankar, who asks Stiffelio to join his friends; with a reminder that he will soon return, the pastor hurries away.

Lina offers a prayer, 'A te ascenda, o Dio clemente', delicately scored and with those elaborate cadential harmonies so characteristic of the later Verdi. She decides to write her husband a letter of confession but is interrupted by Stankar, who reads the first line and is confirmed in his suspicions of her infidelity. Their ensuing duet follows the conventional four-movement pattern. The first movement is dominated by an accusing Stankar, while the second, 'Ed io pure in faccia agl'uomini', is of the 'dissimilar' type, Lina answering his impassioned declamation with obsessively repeated 'sobbing' figures. Stankar, fearful of dishonour for his family, forbids Lina to reveal the truth; she reluctantly agrees and they seal the bargain with the cabaletta 'Or meco venite', sung *sotto voce* almost throughout.

In a brief *scena*, Raffaele conceals a letter to Lina inside a book, Klopstock's *Messias*. Federico enters to take the book away and, observed by Jorg, he and Raffaele depart.

ACT 1 Scene ii   *A reception hall in the castle*   The jubilant opening chorus, 'Plaudiam! Di Stiffelio s'allegri', fashioned on a waltz-time variant of one of the overture's main themes, is interspersed with fragments of conversation as Jorg tells Stiffelio of the hidden letter and his (mistaken) suspicions about Federico. Stiffelio is called upon to describe his forthcoming sermon, and with bitter declamation says it will concern the evils of betrayal. As if to illustrate his point, he asks Federico for the *Messias*. But the book is locked, and Stiffelio's demand for Lina's key leads to the Adagio of the concertato finale, 'Oh qual m'invade ed agita', a magnificently imposing movement that builds to a climax of rare power. Stiffelio forces the lock; the letter falls out, but Stankar seizes it and, in spite of the preacher's protests, tears it up. Stiffelio's anger bursts on Stankar in the stretta 'Chi ti salva o sciagurato', Lina pleading for her father's protection while Stankar proposes a duel with Raffaele.

ACT 2   *An ancient graveyard*   The sombre orchestral prelude is one of Verdi's most evocative to date. Lina, drawn by an 'unknown force', finds the tomb of her mother and in the Largo 'Ah! dagli scanni eterei' – whose luminous scoring makes a striking contrast to the prelude – begs for divine support. Raffaele appears, refusing to renounce his love for Lina even when she directs at him the imploring cabaletta 'Perder dunque voi volete'. But they are interrupted by Stankar, who provokes Raffaele to a duel by insulting his lineage. They defy each other and begin to clash swords as Stiffelio appears, calling on them to stop in the name of God. The intervention is too much for Stankar, who blurts out that Raffaele is Lina's seducer. This precipitates a magnificent concertato quartet movement, 'Ah no, è impossibile!', one which prefigures the famous quartet in *Rigoletto* in its welding together of strongly contrasting musical material. It is dominated by Stiffelio, who develops an imposing musical presence through his powerful declamatory style. Stiffelio continues to control the next movement, in which he takes upon himself Stankar's challenge to Raffaele. At the height of the action a chorus within the church is heard singing of divine forgiveness. In spite of the others' pleading, Stiffelio cannot renounce his thirst for vengeance, and eventually falls down in a faint at the sight of a nearby cross.

ACT 3 Scene i   *An antechamber with doors leading to various rooms*   First comes a double aria for Stankar in which his sense of dishonour leads him to thoughts of suicide. After an unusually complex recitative, the Andante 'Lina, pensai che un angelo' shows Verdi already along the road to the baritone cantabile movements of his later works, while the cabaletta 'O gioia inesprimibile', performed almost entirely *sotto voce*, approaches the level of suppressed energy so pervasive in *Il trovatore*. As Stankar leaves, Stiffelio appears with Jorg, whom he immediately sends off to warn the congregation of his arrival. He meets Raffaele and, questioning him about Lina's future, leads him to a side room where, Stiffelio says, he will 'hear all'. Lina herself now appears before Stiffelio. This is the key confrontation in the opera: a duet difficult to understand in terms of the standard four-movement pattern, so closely are its various stages fashioned around the rapidly changing reactions of the main characters. First comes Stiffelio's 'Opposto è il calle', in which, to a deceptively simple melody charged with harmonic tension, he demands divorce. Lina's violent response is countered by a yet more restricted period from Stiffelio, but then Lina takes over and in 'Non allo sposo' begs him to listen as a priest if not as a husband. Her final plea, 'Egli un patto proponeva', accompanied by solo english horn, is the most touching of all: she declares that her love for Stiffelio has never wavered. Stiffelio, understanding that Raffaele is to blame, goes to the side room to confront him. But Stankar appears, bloody sword in hand, to announce that honour is now satisfied. The closing cabaletta, 'Ah sì, voliamo al tempio', is (as befits the moment) of the 'dissimilar' type, and concludes as Stiffelio is dragged by Jorg towards the church.

ACT 3 Scene ii *The interior of a Gothic church* This very brief final scene is remarkable in being based almost entirely on stage effect: there are hardly any sustained melodies, merely declamation and atmospheric choral interpolations. The congregation, Lina included, is at prayer as Stiffelio and Jorg appear. Stiffelio opens the Bible, determined to take inspiration from whatever passage he finds. He reads the episode of the woman taken in adultery and, as he reaches the phrase 'and she rose up, forgiven', the congregation repeats his words in a stirring choral close.

*

Much has been made of *Stiffelio* in recent times, some even claiming that it deserves an equal place beside the operas it immediately precedes, *Rigoletto*, *Il trovatore* and *La traviata*. Its 'modern' plot and subject matter are certainly in tune with contemporary sensibilities, and the tendency of its most powerful moments to avoid or radically manipulate traditional structures has been much praised. There are, though, a few drawbacks, not least the manner in which the progress of the action is occasionally unclear; nor is the reason for Lina's adultery established. And even the 'forward-looking' dramaturgical structures seem at times to lack necessary durational weight, almost as though the composer were working out new formal balances as he progressed. It is, for instance, significant that many of the alterations made for *Aroldo* are not governed by the new plot but are inserted because Verdi felt he could improve the dramatic articulation. However, *Stiffelio* undoubtedly deserves a better fate than its present neglect, and has in its protagonist one of Verdi's finest tenor roles.

Rigoletto

Melodramma in three acts set to a libretto by Francesco Maria Piave after Victor Hugo's play *Le roi s'amuse*; first performed in Venice, at the Teatro La Fenice, on 11 March 1851.

The first cast included Raffaele Mirate (Duke), Felice Varesi (Rigoletto) and Teresa Brambilla (Gilda).

The Duke of Mantua	tenor
Rigoletto *his court jester*	baritone
Gilda *Rigoletto's daughter*	soprano
Sparafucile *a hired assassin*	bass
Maddalena *his sister*	contralto
Giovanna *Gilda's duenna*	soprano
Count Monterone	bass
Marullo *a nobleman*	baritone
Borsa *a courtier*	tenor
Count Ceprano	bass
Countess Ceprano	mezzo-soprano
Court Usher	bass
Page	mezzo-soprano

Noblemen

Walk-on parts: Ladies, pages, halberdiers

Setting In and around Mantua during the 16th century

Verdi first mentioned the idea of setting a version of Victor Hugo's drama as early as September 1849, shortly after he had returned to Italy, with Salvadore Cammarano to be the librettist; but it was a contract with La Fenice, Venice, signed in April 1850, that eventually brought the opera into being. Perhaps encouraged by the presence in Venice of the accomplished baritone Felice Varesi (who had created the title role of *Macbeth* in 1847), Verdi suggested to Piave, the resident poet at La Fenice, that they adapt Hugo's *Le roi s'amuse*, 'one of the greatest creations of the modern theatre'. He had fears that there might be problems with the censor, but Piave – after seeking advice in Venice – managed to reassure him and the plan went ahead under the working title of *La maledizione*. By summer 1850, however, signs from Venice over the suitability of the subject were not encouraging. Verdi insisted on continuing, saying that he had now found the musical colour of the subject and so could not turn back.

By early October 1850 the cast for the première had been fixed and Piave had submitted a draft libretto. Verdi, still involved with *Stiffelio* at Trieste, had little time to begin composition in earnest and probably did not start drafting the score until late November. However, soon after that, the Venetian police censors intervened: calling attention to the 'disgusting immorality and obscene triviality' of the libretto, they imposed an absolute ban on its performance in Venice. Verdi was enraged, blamed Piave and, refusing to consider writing a fresh opera, offered La Fenice *Stiffelio* instead. Piave, whose doglike devotion to the composer never wavered, hastened to make an acceptable adaptation; entitled *Il duca di Vendome*, this accommodated the censor's objections and was officially approved on 9 December. But Verdi remained steadfast. In a long letter of 14 December, he went into great detail about the dramatic essentials of the subject, insisting (among many aspects that *Il duca di Vendome* had obscured or excised) that the principal tenor retain absolute power over his subjects, and that Triboletto (as the protagonist was then called) remain a hunchback. By the end of the month, a compromise had been reached with the authorities at La Fenice – one which in effect allowed Verdi to retain what he considered dramatically essential – and, soon after, the opera acquired a new title, *Rigoletto*.

Verdi spent the first six weeks of 1851 busy with his score, and arrived in Venice in mid-February to begin piano rehearsals with the principals and to complete the orchestration. The première was an enormous success, and the opera, in spite of continuing problems with local censors, almost immediately became part of the basic repertory, being performed more than 250 times in its first ten years.

Rigoletto has never lost this position and remains one of the most frequently performed operas in the international repertory.

*

The prelude, as was to become common in mature Verdi, is a kind of synopsis of the opera's dramatic essentials. The brass, led by solo trumpet and trombone, intone a restrained motif later to be associated with the curse placed on Rigoletto; this builds in intensity and eventually explodes into a passionate sobbing figure for full orchestra; the figure peters out, the brass motif returns, and simple cadences effect a solemn close.

ACT 1 Scene i   *A magnificent hall in the ducal palace*   The opening scene begins with a lengthy sequence of dance tunes played by an offstage band, over which the Duke and his courtiers converse casually. The Duke has seen a mysterious young woman in church and is determined to pursue her. To drive home his libertine character, he sings a lively two-verse ballad in praise of women, 'Questa o quella'. The Duke then turns his attention to Countess Ceprano, courting her to the accompaniment of a graceful minuet, before Rigoletto enters to mock her unfortunate husband, Count Ceprano. To a reprise of the opening dance sequence, two conversations take place: Marullo tells the courtiers that Rigoletto has been seen with a mistress; and Rigoletto advises the Duke to banish or even execute Ceprano. The ensuing ensemble (Ceprano and others muttering vengeance against Rigoletto, whose mockery they have often endured) is interrupted by Monterone, come to upbraid the Duke for dishonouring his daughter. Rigoletto's sarcastic reply brings down on him Monterone's terrifying anathema; the scene ends in a further ensemble, with Rigoletto visibly shaken by the old man's curse. This opening sequence is clearly based on the traditional *introduzione* format, but with the difference that it boasts an unprecedented level of musical variety: from the brash dances of the stage-band, to the Duke's light, comic-opera ballad, to the elegant minuet, to Rigoletto's grotesque musical parodies, to Monterone's high drama and the stunned reaction it provokes. But there are also connecting devices (for example the descending melodic motif that opens the dance sequence) and a superb sense of dramatic economy; these serve to bind the episode together, making it one of the richest and most complex opening scenes hitherto attempted in 19th-century Italian opera.

ACT 1 Scene ii   *The most deserted corner of a blind alley*   Rigoletto, returning home, meets the hired assassin Sparafucile, who offers his services. Rigoletto questions him but eventually sends him away. This brief duet, which is preceded by Rigoletto's intoned reminiscence of Monterone's curse, 'Quel vecchio maledivami!', bears no relation to the formal norms of Italian opera. It is in a single movement, and the primary continuity is supplied by an orchestral melody played on solo cello and bass. Over this, the voices converse with the greatest naturalness, indeed with a restraint that belies the violence of the subject matter. The effect is calm, sinister and seductive: a necessary pause after the preceding hectic activity, but one that adds an important new colour to the dramatic ambience.

Rigoletto reaches his house and offers the first of his long, freely structured soliloquies, 'Pari siamo', in which the contrasting aspects of his personality are tellingly explored within the flexibility of recitative but with the potential emotional charge of aria. The ensuing duet with Gilda returns us to the formal world of early 19th-century opera, with a conventional four-movement sequence. An opening movement dominated by a syncopated violin melody gives way to 'Deh non parlare al misero', in which Rigoletto's increasingly agonized reminiscences of Gilda's mother are answered by his daughter's broken semiquavers and sobbing appoggiatura ornament. The transition section, as will happen increasingly in later Verdi, also develops lyrical ideas, notably 'Culto, famiglia, patria', in which Rigoletto tells Gilda that she is everything to him. But Gilda wishes for freedom to leave the house. Rigoletto, horrified, calls Giovanna and, in the cabaletta 'Ah! veglia, o donna', enjoins her to watch carefully over her charge. This final movement has none of the driving energy of the early Verdian cabaletta, being far more reminiscent of the relaxed, Donizettian type. But there is room for a remarkable intrusion of stage action: having reached the reprise of the main melody, Rigoletto breaks off, hearing a noise outside; as he goes to investigate, the

Duke slips in unnoticed. The cabaletta then continues, but with a hidden presence that will lead the action forward.

Left alone with Giovanna, Gilda muses on the young man she has seen at church, hoping that he is poor and of common blood. The Duke emerges from his hiding place to declare his love and so initiate a further four-movement duet, though one much reduced in scope and duration in comparison with the preceding number. After a hectic dialogue movement in which Gilda begs him to leave, the Duke declares his love in a simple 3/8 Andante, 'È il sol dell'anima', at the end of which he is joined by Gilda in an elaborate double cadenza. In a brief connecting movement he declares himself to be 'Gualtier Maldè', a poor student; Ceprano and Borsa appear in the street outside and Giovanna, who has not taken her employer's injunction very seriously, warns the lovers to part. The cabaletta of farewell, 'Addio ... speranza ed anima', is extremely condensed, with the principals sharing the exposition of melodic material.

Gilda, again left alone, muses on her lover's name in the famous aria 'Caro nome'. The opening melodic phrases, as befits the character, are of extreme simplicity, but the aria develops in a highly unusual manner, as a contrasting series of strictly controlled ornamental variants, quite unlike the 'open'-structured ornamental arias of the previous generation. The aria is further held together by its delicately distinctive orchestration, in which solo woodwind play an important part. As the opening melody returns in a coda-like ending, Marullo, Ceprano, Borsa and other courtiers again appear outside and can be heard preparing Gilda's abduction.

Rigoletto returns to the scene, and briefly recalls Monterone's curse before Marullo tells him that they are planning to abduct Countess Ceprano, who lives nearby. While fitting Rigoletto with a mask, Marullo succeeds in blindfolding him. The courtiers sing a conspiratorial chorus, 'Zitti, zitti', mostly *pianissimo* but full of explosive accents. Rigoletto holds a ladder as the courtiers emerge with Gilda, her mouth stopped by a handkerchief. He does not hear her cries for help, but soon tires of holding the ladder and takes off the mask to find his house open and Gilda's scarf lying in the street. To an inexorable orchestral crescendo he drags Giovanna from the house but is unable to speak except once more to recall Monterone's curse, 'Ah! ah! ah! . . . la maledizione!'

ACT 2 *A hall in the Duke's Palace* First comes a Scena ed Aria for the Duke, in the conventional mode and a necessary close focus on a character who will see no more of the action during Act 2. 'Ella mi fu rapita!' ('She was stolen from me!'), he cries, and in a lyrical Adagio pours out his feelings at the presumed loss of Gilda. 'Parmi veder le lagrime' is formally structured along familiar lines, but is intricately worked, proving not for the first or the last time that formal conventionality in no sense blunted Verdi's musical or dramatic skills. The courtiers enter to announce in a jaunty narrative that they have duped Rigoletto and have his 'mistress' (actually of course Gilda) nearby; this change of perspective immediately allows the Duke, who is aware of her identity, to launch into a cabaletta of joy and expectation, 'Possente amor mi chiama'. This aria's rather back-ward-looking melodic and orchestral brashness causes it often to be cut in performance, although doing so unbalances both the scene and the characterization of the Duke, who needs the somewhat vulgar catharsis of this moment to be fully convincing in his Act 3 persona.

The Duke leaves to take advantage of Gilda and Rigoletto enters for a very different kind of Scena ed Aria. Affecting indifference before the courtiers, he mixes a nonchalant, public 'la ra, la ra' – though one in which the 'sobbing' notes are all too apparent – with stifled asides as he searches for his daughter. The innocent questions of a page eventually reveal to him that Gilda is with the Duke, and against the background of a string figure of gathering intensity he reveals that Gilda is his daughter and demands access to her. The courtiers block his way, and in frustration he unleashes a remarkable aria. 'Cortigiani, vil razza dannata', unclassifiable in conventional formal terms, is in three distinct parts, each marking a stage in Rigoletto's psychological progress. First, against an obsessively repeated string figure, he rails against the courtiers with fierce declamatory force. Then comes fragmentation, a breaking of the accompaniment rhythm, and of the voice: a frightening disintegra-tion. And finally, the third stage, Rigoletto gains a new dignity and continuity: aided by a solo cello and english horn he asks pity for a father's sorrow.

Gilda enters and throws herself into her father's arms, and so begins yet another four-movement duet. Rigoletto solemnly dismisses the courtiers and bids her tell her story. 'Tutte le feste al tempio', unlike the parallel lyrical duet movements of Act 1, is begun by Gilda: it is she who now achieves a new status from the circumstances that have befallen her. And as with Rigoletto's previous monologue, the duet moves through strongly contrasting sections, from her opening narration, a kind of duet with solo oboe, to Rigoletto's obsessively fixed response, and finally to another clarifying third stage, in which Rigoletto bids his daughter weep and in which she joins him with a completely new kind of vocal ornamentation, only superficially resembling that found in Act 1. Monterone passes by on his way to prison, and this time Rigoletto assures him that he will have vengeance. Staring at a portrait of the Duke, the jester joins with his daughter in a cabaletta, 'Sì, vendetta, tremenda vendetta', that brings the act to a close.

ACT 3 *A deserted bank of the River Mincio* An orchestral prelude, in Verdi's severe, 'academic' vein, leads to a brief exchange between Rigoletto and Gilda. Time has passed, but Gilda still loves the Duke. Rigoletto, promising to show her the true man, has her gaze into Sparafucile's house through a chink in the wall. The Duke appears, asks loudly for wine and the woman of the house (Maddalena), and breaks into a song in praise of women's fickleness. 'La donna è mobile' is certainly the best-known music in the score, perhaps unfortunately, as its brashness and simplicity make their full effect only in the surrounding gloomy context. The Duke's song dies away, to be followed by the famous quartet. Its first half, 'Un dì, se ben rammentomi', is dominated by a violin melody that carries reminiscences of earlier material (in particular Gilda's 'Caro nome'), over which the Duke and Maddalena converse lightheartedly. Then comes the main lyrical portion, 'Bella figlia dell'amore', in which Rigoletto and Gilda join them in a static portrayal of contrasting emotional states. The dramatic aptness of this section is made especially powerful by the manner in which the three principals involved all offer a kind of digest of their vocal characters elsewhere in the opera: the Duke (who carries the main melodic thread) ardent and lyrical, Gilda overcome with appoggiatura 'sobbing', Rigoletto declamatory and unmoving.

A storm is gathering as Sparafucile emerges, and over fragmentary bursts of orchestral colour he and Rigoletto agree on a price for the murder of the Duke. Rigoletto will return at midnight to throw the body in the river. The hunchback retires and the Duke is conducted to a room, there dreamily recalling 'La donna è mobile' before falling asleep. As the storm gathers force, Maddalena, attracted to the Duke, tries to persuade Sparafucile to spare him. Professional honour forbids that he kill Rigoletto instead, but he agrees that, if another should come along before the time allotted, a substitution can be made. Gilda overhears this and, in a trio characterized by its relentless rhythmic drive ('Se pria ch'abbia il mezzo'), decides to sacrifice herself. She enters the house, and a terrifying orchestral storm depicts the gruesome events that occur within.

The final scene shows great economy of means. The storm recedes as Rigoletto reappears to claim the body, which has been placed in a sack for easy disposal. He is about to dispatch it when he hears the voice of the Duke, again singing 'La donna è mobile'. Horrified, he opens the sack to find Gilda, on the point of death. Their final duet, 'V'ho ingannato!', is necessarily brief, leaving time only for Gilda to look towards her arrival in heaven – with the obligatory flute arpeggios – and for Rigoletto to declaim in ever more broken lines. He recalls the curse one last time, and the curtain falls.

*

Rigoletto is almost always placed as the true beginning of Verdi's maturity, the essential dividing line between 'early' works and the succession of repertory pieces that will follow; and this special placing is commonly seen as exemplified in the striking formal freedom of various scenes. But thus to concentrate on such matters risks a certain distortion: most of the opera's formal innovations have been prefigured in earlier works, and many of its most powerful sections exist unambiguously and comfortably within the formal conventions of the time. However, no earlier work is as impeccably paced as *Rigoletto*, nor does any show its overall consistency of style; and perhaps these matters are best seen as linked not so much to formal matters as to a new sense of musical characterization. With Rigoletto and Gilda in particular, Verdi managed to create musical portraits that function for the most part within the formal norms of Italian opera but that nevertheless manage to develop individually as the drama unfolds. This was as much a technical as an emotional advance; it entailed, that is, a kind of mature acceptance of conventional discourse, as well as an acutely developed perspective on precisely when it could be ignored and when exploited. Though this acceptance was to appear in various guises in the works of Verdi's maturity, it was something that rarely left the composer during the remainder of his long career.

Il trovatore
('The troubadour')

Dramma in four parts set to a libretto by Salvadore Cammarano (with additions by Leone Emanuele Bardare) after Antonio García Gutiérrez's play *El trovador*; first performed at Rome, at the Teatro Apollo, on 19 January 1853. The revised version, *Le trouvère*, was first performed at the Paris, Opéra on 12 January 1857.

The première cast included Giovanni Guicciardi (Luna), Rosina Penco (Leonora), Emilia Goggi (Azucena) and Carlo Baucardé (Manrico).

Count di Luna *a young nobleman of Aragon*	baritone
Leonora *a lady-in-waiting to the Princess of Aragon*	soprano
Azucena *a gypsy*	mezzo-soprano
Manrico *an officer in the army of Prince Urgel,* *and the supposed son of Azucena*	tenor
Ferrando *a captain in the Count's army*	bass
Ines *Leonora's confidante*	soprano
Ruiz *a soldier in Manrico's service*	tenor
An Old Gypsy	bass
A Messenger	tenor

Leonora's female attendants, nuns, servants and armed retainers of the Count, gypsies, followers of Manrico, etc.

Setting Biscay and Aragon, in 1409

Verdi was still in Venice enjoying the success of *Rigoletto* (in March 1851) when he wrote to Cammarano suggesting García Gutiérrez's play (first performed in 1836) as a subject for his next opera. It is clear from his early letters that he saw the drama as a sequel to *Rigoletto*, this time with an unconventional female character, the gypsy Azucena, at the centre of the action. Azucena, like Rigoletto, was to be fired by two opposing passions: filial love and a desire for vengeance. More than this, it is clear that Verdi wished to develop

131

further the formal freedoms he had experimented with in parts of *Rigoletto*. In an early letter to Cammarano, for example, he urged:

> As for the distribution of the pieces, let me tell you that when I'm presented with poetry to be set to music, any form, any distribution is good, and I'm all the happier if they are new and bizarre. If in operas there were no more cavatinas, duets, trios, choruses, finales, etc. etc., and if the entire opera were, let's say, a single piece, I would find it more reasonable and just.

But, as so often with Verdi, his revolutionary statements in his writings were considerably toned down when it came to practical matters. Cammarano's draft libretto turned out to be fashioned along conventional lines, and Verdi made little objection.

In part owing to personal difficulties, work on the new opera moved along rather slowly. Verdi, who had become the most famous and frequently performed Italian composer in Europe, and who could by now write for more or less whichever theatre he chose in Italy, considered a number of places for the première, being particularly concerned with the availability of a first-rate Azucena. Eventually, in the middle of 1852, the Teatro Apollo in Rome was decided upon. But then, in July 1852, Cammarano died, leaving a draft of *Il trovatore* with many details in need of attention. Leone Emanuele Bardare was brought in, and was particularly involved in the expansion of Leonora's role, which Verdi had originally wished to minimize but now fashioned as a dramatic equal to Azucena, thus forming a symmetry with the pair of opposed male roles, Manrico and the Count. The opera was a huge success. It very soon became the most popular of Verdi's works, both in Italy and around the world. In the mid-1850s Verdi created a revised version for a performance at the Paris Opéra, in part to ensure his French rights to the score. This revision, in a translation by Emilien Pacini, and entitled *Le trouvère*, included a ballet (placed after the opening chorus of Part 3), omitted Leonora's Part 4 cabaletta, 'Tu vedrai che amore in terra', and involved a substantial rewriting of the end of the opera (during which the 'Miserere' music returns in a lengthy coda).

*

Part 1:   'The Duel'

ACT 1 Scene i   *A hall in the Aliaferia palace*   There is no overture or formal prelude, merely a series of martial arpeggios and horn
calls to set the scene. Ferrando bids the sentries and servants keep
alert: the Count fears that the troubadour who has sometimes been
seen in the garden is his rival in love. At the chorus's bidding,
Ferrando narrates the story of Garzia, the Count's brother. One day,
when still a baby, Garzia was found with an old witch at his cradle.
She was driven off, but the boy sickened and was thought to have
been given the evil eye. The witch was sought out and burnt at the
stake, but her daughter exacted a terrible revenge: on the day of the
execution young Garzia disappeared, and the charred remains of a
baby were found in the embers of the witch's funeral pyre. All this
is told in a two-stanza narrative, each stanza divided into a relatively
free introductory passage ('Di due figli'), and then a more formal
'aria' ('Abbietta zingara') in which violins double the voice in
octaves (a typical trait of 'gypsy' style). The chorus rounds off each
stanza with horrified comments. In freer recitative, run through with
a good deal of winding chromaticism, Ferrando continues his narration. The old Count fell into a decline and died; nothing more was
heard of the gypsy's daughter, though the old witch herself is said
still to roam the skies at night. The chorus joins Ferrando in 'Sull'orlo
dei tetti', a rapid stretta that conjures up the ghostly forces around
them. At the climax, the chiming of the midnight bell causes universal
panic, and all hurriedly disperse.

ACT 1 Scene ii   *The palace gardens* Leonora, restlessly wandering,
tells her maid Ines how she fell in love with a mysterious knight at
a tournament and how he vanished when civil war broke out, between
the house of Aragon and Prince Urgel of Biscay's supporters. This
is for the most part delivered in the spare, functional recitative typical
of the opera, a style that makes the moments of arioso all the more
effective. Leonora continues her story in the formal mould of a two-
stanza Andante, 'Tacea la notte placida', a piece that moves from
minor to major, flowering into an angular rising line as she describes

how her lover has now returned as a troubadour to serenade her with melancholy songs. Ines suggests that Leonora should forget her lover, but in a highly ornamental cabaletta, 'Di tale amor', Leonora swears that she will die rather than lose him.

The ladies depart and the Count enters to declare his consuming passion for Leonora. He is about to climb up to her apartment when he hears a distant serenade: Manrico's 'Deserto sulla terra', a simple two-stanza canzone. Leonora hurries down to greet the troubadour, in the darkness mistakenly addresses the Count, and is then accused of treachery by Manrico. The three principals finish the act with a two-movement trio, first an Allegro agitato ('Qual voce!') dominated by a breathless, disjointed figure from the violins, and then – ignoring the usual lyrical slow section – straight to a furious stretta ('Di geloso amor sprezzato'). The final curtain sees the Count and Manrico striding off to fight a duel as Leonora falls senseless to the ground.

Part 2: 'The Gypsy'

ACT 2 Scene i *A ruined hovel on the lower slopes of a mountain in Biscay* The tonality, rhythms and melodic gestures of the orchestral introduction bring us back to the musical world of Part 1 scene i as the gypsies celebrate their return to work with the famous 'anvil' chorus, 'Chi del gitano i giorni abbella?' This is immediately juxtaposed with Azucena's canzone, 'Stride la vampa', an invocation of fire and destruction that hovers obsessively around the note *b'*. The gypsies retire (to a muted reprise of their chorus); Azucena tells Manrico of her mother's death at the stake, and of how she planned to take revenge by casting the old Count's son on to the embers of the fire. Her narrative, 'Condotta ell'era in ceppi', starts out formally controlled; but as the tale unfolds the music breaks from its tonal and rhythmic confines, coming to an intense declamatory climax as Azucena admits that she mistakenly threw her own baby on to the fire.

Manrico asks whether he is, then, Azucena's son, but the gypsy diverts him with assurances of love and encourages him, in turn, to tell a story. Manrico's 'Mal reggendo' recounts his duel with the

Count and how a strange voice commanded him not to deal the fatal blow; but with Azucena's answer it turns into the first lyrical movement of a 'dissimilar' duet (in which each singer has different musical material). They are interrupted by Ruiz, who bears a letter telling Manrico that Leonora, thinking him dead, is about to enter a convent. Manrico resolves to go to her immediately, and so begins the duet cabaletta, 'Perigliarti ancor languente', in which Azucena begs him in vain not to court danger yet again.

Act 2 Scene ii *The cloister of a convent near Castellor* The Count is resolved to steal Leonora away from the convent and apostrophizes her in 'Il balen del suo sorriso', an 'aristocratically' graced Largo that exposes the baritone's full expressive range. A bell from the convent urges action, and the Count and his followers disperse to hide, the male chorus's 'Ardir, andiam' serving as a frame for the Count's vigorous cabaletta of expectation, 'Per me ora fatale'. A chorale-like chant from offstage nuns, which mingles with a restrained reprise of the chorus's 'Ardir, andiam', introduces Leonora. Her affecting arioso is cut short by the Count and then, to general amazement, by Manrico, whose sudden appearance precipitates the main lyrical section of the concertato finale, 'E deggio e posso crederlo?' Led off by a breathless Leonora, continued by the patterned opposition of the two male principals, the movement comes to a magnificent climax with Leonora's rising line, 'Sei tu dal ciel disceso, o in ciel son io con te?'. Action once more boils up as Manrico's followers surround the Count's men. With a final reprise of 'Sei tu dal ciel' (whose lyrical power functions in place of the usual stretta movement), Leonora rushes off with Manrico.

Part 3: 'The Gypsy's Son'

Act 3 Scene i *A military encampment* The Count's men are eager to mount an attack on Castellor and when Ferrando tells them they will move at dawn the next day they celebrate with the famous chorus 'Squilli, echeggi la tromba guerriera'. The Count is still in agony over his loss of Leonora when Ferrando brings in Azucena, who has been

135

captured nearby. To divert attention under interrogation, Azucena lapses into her 'gypsy' mode, singing 'Giorni poveri vivea', a simple minor-mode song that unexpectedly flowers into the major as she mentions the love she has for her son. But Ferrando has guessed her true identity and in a concluding stretta, 'Deh! rallentate, o barbari', she begs for mercy, the Count exults and Ferrando and the chorus look forward to her death at the stake.

ACT 3 Scene ii *A room adjoining the chapel at Castellor, with a balcony at the back* We move to the rival camp, where Leonora and Manrico are about to be married. Manrico calms his bride's fear with the Adagio 'Ah sì, ben mio, coll'essere', in which the tenor approaches most closely the 'aristocratic' musical world of Leonora and the Count. The lovers indulge in a brief duet before Ruiz interrupts to inform Manrico of Azucena's capture. Manrico immediately summons his followers and prepares to mount a rescue operation, pausing only to sing the cabaletta 'Di quella pira'. This movement, which rudely casts Manrico back into the more direct musical world of the gypsies and is probably best known for its (unauthentic) high C's, hides within its blunt exterior a good number of those subtle harmonic and orchestral gestures that Verdi seemed so effortlessly to integrate with his most energetic music.

Part 4: 'The Execution'

ACT 4 Scene i *A wing of the Aliaferia palace* It is now too late in the drama for even brief narratives, and we must grasp by deduction that Manrico's attack has failed and that he is now a prisoner of the Count. Leonora arrives to try to save him, and from outside the prison sings of her love in the Adagio 'D'amor sull'ali rosee', which retains her 'aristocratic' ornamental style, but now colours it with dark instrumental sonorities and a predominantly falling line. The ensuing *tempo di mezzo*, perhaps the most famous in Italian opera, magnificently combines three contrasting musical ideas: a solemn 'Miserere' sounding from within; Leonora's fragmented response, underpinned by a quiet yet insistent 'death' rhythm from the full orchestra; and Manrico's farewell to his beloved, 'Ah che la morte ognora', a simple melody that recalls his Act 1 serenade. The number concludes with Leonora's reiteration of her love in the cabaletta 'Tu vedrai che amore in terra' (often omitted in performance for fear of overtaxing the soprano).

The Count appears, determined to execute both Manrico and Azucena. The arrival of Leonora initiates a conventionally structured though powerfully condensed four-movement duet. The first movement involves rapid dialogue over an orchestral melody; then the opponents move to a formally fixed statement of their positions (the Andante mosso 'Mira di acerbe lagrime'), Leonora begging for the life of Manrico, the Count obstinate in his desire for revenge. But then, in the third movement, Leonora strikes a Tosca-like bargain: herself in exchange for her lover's life. The Count jubilantly agrees, failing to see that Leonora has secretly taken poison. They join in the celebratory cabaletta 'Vivrà! . . . Contende il giubilo'.

ACT 4 Scene ii   *A grim prison*   The Finale ultimo finds Manrico and Azucena languishing in prison. Azucena has a frightening vision of the death that awaits her, the orchestra recalling her 'Stride la vampa' of Part 2. With reassurances from Manrico, sleep gradually overcomes her. They join in the narcotic duet 'Sì, la stanchezza', which begins in the minor but moves to the parallel major for Manrico's 'Riposa, o madre' and Azucena's picture of the simple gypsy life, 'Ai nostri monti'. Leonora appears, telling Manrico that he is free to go; but he quickly guesses the nature of her bargain with the Count. He accuses her in the concertato 'Parlar non vuoi?', which includes Leonora's frantic attempts to defend herself and, in the later part, Azucena's somnolent reprise of 'Ai nostri monti'. Leonora collapses at Manrico's feet as the ensemble finishes; the poison begins to take effect, and soon the truth is out. In a second formal ensemble, 'Prima che d'altri vivere', Manrico and Leonora bid a tender farewell, the Count entering to add his comments in the later stages. As Leonora dies, the Count assumes control: Manrico is led off to the scaffold, and Azucena is forced to watch his execution. As the fatal blow falls, she tells the Count that he has just killed his own brother, and brings down the curtain with a final, exultant cry: her mother has been avenged.

*

Il trovatore, though without doubt one of the two or three most popular Verdi operas, has until recently fared rather badly with critics and commentators, mostly because of its unabashedly formalistic exterior in comparison with the works on either side of it, *Rigoletto* and *La traviata*. This attitude at last shows signs of changing, perhaps as our criteria for judging Verdi's musical dramas alter with time. Indeed, many of the most important stages in the critical rehabilitation of this opera have concentrated attention on just those aspects that were earlier castigated. The libretto, for example, with its immovable character types and 'unrealistic' stage action, has recently been seen as one of the work's great strengths, its economy of dramatic means and immediacy of language forming the perfect basis on which to build Verdian musical drama. Similarly, the extreme formalism of the musical language has been seen as serving to concentrate and define the various stages of the drama, above all channelling them into those key confrontations that mark its inexorable progress.

But if one trait can be singled out that best accounts for the opera's success, it is probably the sheer musical energy apparent in all the numbers. Time and again we find a relentless rhythmic propulsion in the accompaniment, and a tendency for the melodic lines to be forced into a restrictive compass, freeing themselves rarely but with consequent explosive power. This internal energy often runs through entire numbers, making a sense of progress across the various formal stages – from arioso to cantabile to cabaletta – that is just as convincing as the more radical, 'external' experiments with form encountered in the surrounding operas.

La traviata
('The fallen woman')

Opera in three acts set to a libretto by Francesco Maria Piave after Alexandre Dumas *fils'* play *La dame aux camélias*; first performed in Venice, at the Teatro La Fenice, on 6 March 1853.

The première cast included Fanny Salvini-Donatelli as Violetta, Ludovico Graziani as Alfredo and Felice Varesi, as Giorgio Germont.

Violetta Valéry *a courtesan*	soprano
Flora Bervoix *her friend*	mezzo-soprano
Annina *Violetta's maid*	soprano
Alfredo Germont	tenor
Giorgio Germont *his father*	baritone
Gastone, Vicomte de Letorières *friend of Alfredo*	tenor
Baron Douphol *Violetta's protector*	baritone
Marchese D'Obigny *friend of Flora*	bass
Doctor Grenvil	bass
Giuseppe *Violetta's servant*	tenor
Flora's Servant	bass
Commissioner	bass

Ladies and gentlemen, friends of Violetta and Flora, matadors, picadors, gypsies, servants of Violetta and Flora, masks etc.

Setting In and around Paris, about 1700

By April 1852 Verdi had agreed to write a new opera for the Carnival 1853 season at the Teatro La Fenice in Venice, with Francesco Maria Piave as librettist. But even as late as October no subject had been decided upon: the unusually tight schedule was due in part to Verdi's continuing work on *Il trovatore*, whose première in Rome eventually took place less than two months before that of *La traviata*. By the beginning of November, however, Verdi and Piave had elected to base their opera on Dumas *fils'* play, which had first been performed in Paris earlier that year. The working title of the opera, later changed at the insistence of the Venetian censors, was *Amore e morte* ('Love and Death'). As Verdi wrote to his friend Cesare De Sanctis on 1 January 1853, it was 'a subject of the times. Others would not have done it because of the conventions, the epoch and for a thousand other stupid scruples'. The composer even proposed that, contrary to custom, the opera should be performed in modern costume; but again the Venetian authorities would not agree, and the period was put back to the beginning of the 18th century.

La traviata, it seems, was written in something like record time. Even though the above-quoted letter to De Sanctis dates from just over two months before the première, it is primarily concerned with compositional problems surrounding the still unfinished *Trovatore*; it is clear that *La traviata* was largely unwritten at the time. Its première was the most celebrated fiasco of Verdi's later career, a circumstance probably attributable more to the singers – Salvini-Donatelli was physically unsuited to Violetta and Varesi was too far past his prime to tackle such an exposed role – than to problems the audience may have had with the musical style. Verdi was reluctant to allow further performances until he could find a more suitable cast, but eventually allowed a second staging (on 6 May 1854) at the Teatro San Benedetto, Venice, making various alterations to the score, the most important of which were to the central Act 2 duet between Violetta and Germont. This time success was unequivocal, and the opera soon became one of the composer's most popular works. It has retained this position into modern times, in spite of the fact that the heroine's role is one of the most feared in the soprano repertory.

*

The prelude to *La traviata* is a curious narrative experiment: it paints a three-stage portrait of the heroine, but in reverse chronological order. First comes a musical rendering of her final decline in Act 3, with high, chromatic strings dissolving into 'sobbing' appoggiaturas; then a direct statement of love, the melody that will in Act 2 become 'Amami, Alfredo'; and finally this same melody repeated on the lower strings, surrounded by the delicate ornamentation associated with Violetta in Act 1.

Act 1   *A salon in Violetta's house*   It is August. In a festive atmosphere, the action underpinned by a sequence of lively orchestral
dances, Violetta and friends greet their guests, among whom is
Alfredo Germont, a young man who has loved Violetta from afar for
some time. Eventually all sit down to supper and Violetta calls for
a toast. Alfredo takes up the cup to sing the famous brindisi 'Libiamo
ne' lieti calici', a simple, bouncing melody repeated by Violetta and
finally (with judicious transposition) by the entire chorus. A band in
an adjoining room now starts up a succession of waltzes and the
guests prepare to dance; but Violetta feels unsteady (the symptoms
suggest she is consumptive) and begs the others to go on without
her. Alfredo remains behind and, with the dance music still sounding,
warns Violetta that her way of life will kill her if she persists. He
offers to protect her and admits his love in the first movement of the
duet: 'Un dì felice, eterea' begins hesitantly but builds to the
passionate outpouring of 'Di quell'amor ch'è palpito', a melody that
will reappear later as a kind of emblem of Alfredo's devoted love.
Violetta answers with an attempt to defuse the situation, telling him
he will soon forget her, and surrounding his passionately insistent
melody with showers of vocal ornamentation. The dance music
(which unobtrusively disappeared during the duet) now returns as
Violetta playfully gives Alfredo a flower, telling him to return when
it has faded. To round off the scene the returning guests, seeing dawn
approaching, prepare to leave in the concluding stretta, 'Si ridesta in
ciel l'aurora'.

Left alone, Violetta closes the act with a formal double aria. She
muses fondly of her new conquest in the Andantino 'Ah fors'è lui',
which – like Alfredo's declaration – begins hesitantly but then flowers
into 'Di quell'amor'. This sequence is then literally repeated (in the
style, that is, of a French *couplet* rather than an Italian cantabile)
before Violetta violently shrugs off her sentimental thoughts and
resolves that a life of pleasure is her only choice. She closes the act
with the cabaletta 'Sempre libera degg'io', full of daring, almost
desperate coloratura effects. But in the closing stages her melody is
mixed with 'Di quell'amor', sung by Alfredo from below the balcony.

ACT 2 Scene i *A country house near Paris* It is the following January; three months have passed since Violetta and Alfredo set up house together in the country. Alfredo sings of his youthful ardour in 'Dei miei bollenti spiriti', an unusually condensed Andante with no repetition of the initial melodic phrase. Annina then hurries in to inform Alfredo that Violetta has been selling her belongings to finance their country life together. Alfredo immediately decides to raise money himself and rushes off to Paris after expressing his remorse in the conventionally structured cabaletta 'Oh mio rimorso!' (often cut in modern performances).

Violetta appears and is joined by a visitor who turns out to be Giorgio Germont. Their ensuing grand duet is unusually long; typically for Verdi, the formal expansion is concentrated on the opening section of the conventional four-movement structure. After an initial passage of recitative this first movement involves three main sub-sections: a kind of lyrical dialogue between the principals. First comes an Allegro moderato ('Pura siccome un angelo') in which Germont describes the plight of his daughter, whose forthcoming marriage is threatened by Alfredo's scandalous relationship with Violetta. After a brief transition, Violetta reveals the seriousness of her illness and protests that Alfredo is all she has in the world (the breathless 'Non sapete quale affetto'). But Germont is adamant and in 'Bella voi siete, e giovane' assures Violetta that she will find others to love. Eventually Violetta capitulates: the second movement of the duet, 'Dite alla giovine', begins with her heartbroken agreement to leave Alfredo, and gives ample opportunity for the voices to interweave. The final two movements are relatively brief and conventional: Violetta agrees to break the news to Alfredo in her own way, begging Germont to remain to comfort his son; and then in the cabaletta 'Morrò! la mia memoria' she asks Germont to tell Alfredo the truth after her death.

As Germont retires, Violetta begins to write a letter to Alfredo, but cannot finish before her lover appears. He is disturbed by her agitation, but she answers his questions with a simple, passionate declaration of love, 'Amami, Alfredo' (the melody that served as the basis for the opera's prelude) before rushing out. The remainder of the scene might well, of course, focus on Alfredo, but operatic convention requires a formal double aria for the baritone (who has no other opportunity for an extended solo), so Alfredo's reactions are sandwiched into the transition passages. Soon after Violetta has left, a servant brings Alfredo her letter saying that she must leave him forever, and his anguished reaction is immediately countered by Germont's lyrical Andante, 'Di Provenza il mar, il suol', which conjures up a nostalgic picture of their family home. But Alfredo will not be consoled and at the end of Germont's cabaletta, 'No, non udrai rimproveri', his anger boils over: knowing that she has received an invitation to a party in Paris, he assumes that Violetta has deserted him to return to her old friends.

ACT 2 Scene ii   *A salon in Flora's town house*   A boisterous orchestral opening, over which Flora and her new lover discuss the separation of Violetta and Alfredo, is followed by a two-part *divertissement* as a chorus of gypsies (with more than an echo of the musical world of *Il trovatore*) and then of matadors, dance and sing. Alfredo enters and, to an obsessively repeated motif on the lower strings and wind, begins playing recklessly at cards, apparently uncaring when Violetta appears on the arm of Baron Douphol. As Alfredo and the Baron bet against each other with barely concealed hostility, Violetta repeatedly laments her position in an anguished rising line. Supper is served, and Violetta manages to see Alfredo privately. In answer to his accusations she desperately claims that she now loves the Baron, at which Alfredo calls the guests together and, in a declamatory passage of rising fury, denounces Violetta and throws his winnings in her face as 'payment' for their time together. This precipitates the concertato, which begins with a rapid passage of choral outrage before Germont, who has just arrived, leads off the main Largo. This large-scale movement depicts the contrasting moods of the main characters: Germont reproachful and lyrically contained; Alfredo distressed and remorseful with a fragmentary line; and Violetta, privately begging Alfredo to understand her distress with a line which eventually dominates through its simplicity and emotive power. Such is the charge of the movement that the act can end there, without the conventional concluding stretta.

ACT 3 *Violetta's bedroom* It is February. The orchestral prelude opens with the idea that began the entire opera, and then develops into an intense solo for the first violins, full of 'sobbing' appoggiaturas. In the spare recitative that follows we learn from a doctor that Violetta is near death. To a restrained orchestral reprise of 'Di quell'amor', Violetta reads a letter from Germont, telling her that Alfredo (who fled abroad after fighting a duel with the Baron) now knows the truth about her sacrifice and is hurrying back to her. But she knows that time is short, and in the aria 'Addio, del passato' bids farewell to the past and to life, the oboe solo adding poignancy to her painfully restricted vocal line. A chorus of revellers heard outside underlines the gloom of Violetta's isolation, but then, to a sustained orchestral crescendo, Alfredo is announced and arrives to throw himself into Violetta's arms. After the initial greeting Alfredo leads off the Andante movement of the duet, 'Parigi, o cara': a simple waltz-time melody reminiscent of Act 1, in which the lovers look forward to a life together away from Paris. It is significant, though, that Violetta's attempts at Act 1-style ornamentation are now severely restricted in range. Violetta decides that she and Alfredo should go to church to celebrate his return, but the strain even of getting to her feet is too much and she repeatedly falls back. This painful realization of her weakness precipitates the cabaletta 'Gran Dio! morir sì giovane', in which Violetta gives way to a despair that Alfredo can do little to assuage. Germont appears, and a brief but passionate exchange between him and Violetta leads to the final concertato, 'Prendi: quest'è l'immagine', in which Violetta gives Alfredo a locket with her portrait, telling him that, should he marry, he can give it to his bride. The movement begins with an insistent full-orchestra rhythmic figure, similar to that used in the 'Miserere' scene of *Il trovatore* and clearly associated with Violetta's imminent death; later, Violetta develops the simple, intense vocal style that has characterized her in this act. A last orchestral reprise of 'Di quell'amor' sounds as the final blow approaches. Violetta feels a sudden rush of life, sings a final 'Oh gioia!', but then collapses dead on to a sofa.

*

As we have seen, *La traviata* was written in great haste and its genesis was thoroughly entangled with the creation of Verdi's previous opera, *Il trovatore*. Perhaps not surprisingly, there are a series of startling musical resemblances between the two operas. But these similarities are on what one might call the musical surface; in dramatic structure and general atmosphere the two works are remarkably different, in some senses even antithetical. *La traviata* is above all a chamber opera: in spite of the 'public' scenes of the first and second acts, it succeeds best in an intimate setting, where there can be maximum concentration on those key moments in which the heroine's attitude to her surroundings are forced to change. Perhaps for this reason, the cabalettas, those 'public' moments which are so inevitable and essential to the mood of *Il trovatore*, tend to sit uneasily; we remember *La traviata* above all for its moments of lyrical introspection.

It is nevertheless easy to see why *La traviata* is among the best loved of Verdi's operas, perhaps even *the* best loved. In many senses it is the composer's most 'realistic' drama. The cultural ambience of the subject matter and the musical expression are very closely related: no suspension of disbelief is required to feel that the waltz tunes that saturate the score are naturally born out of the Parisian setting. And, perhaps most important, this sense of 'authenticity' extends to the heroine, a character whose psychological progress through the opera is mirrored by her changing vocal character: from the exuberant ornamentation of Act 1, to the passionate declamation of Act 2, to the final, well-nigh ethereal qualities she shows in Act 3. Violetta – Stiffelio, Rigoletto and Gilda notwithstanding – is Verdi's most complete musical personality to date.

Les vêpres siciliennes
[*I vespri siciliani*]
('The Sicilian Vespers')

Opéra in five acts set to a libretto by Eugène Scribe and Charles Duveyrier after their libretto *Le duc d'Albe*; first performed in Paris, at the Opéra, on 13 June 1855.

The first cast included Marc Bonnehée (Montfort), Louis Guéymard (Henri), Louis-Henri Obin (Jean Procida) and Sophie Cruvelli (Hélène).

Guy de Montfort (Montforte) *Governor of Sicily under*	
Charles d'Anjou, King of Naples	baritone
Le Sire de Béthune *French officers*	bass
Count de Vaudemont *French officers*	bass
Henri (Arrigo) *a young Sicilian*	tenor
Jean Procida *a Sicilian doctor*	bass
Duchess Hélène (Elena) *sister of Duke Frédéric of*	
Austria	soprano
Ninetta *her maid*	contralto
Daniéli *a Sicilian*	tenor
Thibault (Tebaldo) *French soldiers*	tenor
Robert (Roberto) *French soldiers*	baritone
Mainfroid (Manfredo) *a Sicilian*	tenor

Sicilian men and women, French soldiers, monks, *corps de ballet*

Setting In and around Palermo, 1282

After the performances of *Jérusalem* at the Opéra in 1847 Verdi had intended to produce an entirely new opera for the first theatre of Paris, but the revolutions of 1848 caused the plan to be shelved. He renewed negotiations with the Opéra, however, in 1852, and a contract was drawn up for a full-scale French grand opera in five acts, with a libretto by Eugène Scribe, the acknowledged poetic master of the genre. After various subjects had been proposed, poet and composer eventually agreed to use a revised version of an existing libretto, *Le duc d'Albe*, written by Scribe and Charles Duveyrier for Halévy (who did not use it) and partly set to music by Donizetti in 1839.

Verdi spent most of 1854 working at the score, making a reluctant Scribe undertake some important revisions and complaining about the sheer length demanded by audiences at the Opéra. The première was well received, even by such severe critics as Berlioz, but the work failed to enter the standard repertory of the Opéra. Its revolutionary subject caused difficulties with the Italian censors and it was first performed in Italian at Parma in a bowdlerized version translated by Eugenio Caimi and entitled *Giovanna de Guzman*. Later performances as *I vespri siciliani* retained most aspects of Caimi's translation and it is almost invariably in this Italian version that the opera is encountered today. For a revival at the Opéra in 1863, Verdi replaced 'O jour de peine' with the tenor *romance* 'O toi que j'ai chéri'.

*

The overture, the longest Verdi wrote and still sometimes revived in the concert hall, follows convention in being made up of themes drawn from the opera. It falls into two movements: a Largo, full of rhythmic 'death' figures, even in its more lyrical, major-mode section; and an Allegro agitato, whose main theme is taken from the Henri-Montfort duet in Act 3 and is repeated twice before a noisy Prestissimo brings the piece to a close.

ACT 1   *The main piazza in Palermo*   The opening chorus, 'Beau pays de France!' ('Al cielo natio'), musically juxtaposes the victorious French soldiers with the resentful Sicilian people and includes a brief episode in which a drunken soldier, Robert, looks forward to claiming his share of the vanquished Sicilian women.

Hélène enters dressed in mourning; Béthune explains to Vaudemont that she is a hostage of Montfort and has come to pray for her brother Duke Frédéric, executed by Montfort a year ago. Robert staggers up, asking her for a song; she complies with a freely structured aria made up of three brief episodes and a closing cabaletta, 'Courage! . . . du courage!' ('Coraggio, su, coraggio'), in which she rallies the Sicilians around her. As the cabaletta draws to a close, the Sicilians advance on the French; but they are interrupted by the appearance of Montfort, who precipitates a largely unaccompanied quartet 'Quelle horreur m'environne!' ('D'ira fremo all'aspetto'), in which Hélène and Montfort explore their conflicting positions. Henri now arrives and, unaware of who Montfort is, explains to Hélène that he has inexplicably been released from prison by the Governor of Sicily but would dearly love to meet the tyrant face to face. At this Montfort reveals his identity and dismisses the women, thus preparing the ground for the closing duet finale. Like Hélène's aria, the duet passes through a number of short contrasting sections (as Montfort learns of Henri's history, offers him a commission in the French army and advises him to avoid Hélène) before closing with a cabaletta, 'Téméraire! téméraire!' ('Temerario! qual ardire!'), in which the characters' mutual defiance is reflected in a clash of strongly contrasting individual themes.

ACT 2   *A delightful valley near Palermo*   An orchestral introduction suggesting the movement of a boat accompanies the disembarkment of the fanatical patriot Prociada. He greets his homeland in a brief recitative before beginning the famous Andante, 'Et toi, Palerme' ('O tu, Palermo'), fashioned in ternary form with a striking level of orchestral detail in the middle section. Procida's followers appear and together they sing the cabaletta 'Dans l'ombre et le silence' ('Nell'ombra e nel silenzio'), in which a stealthy, staccato choral passage precedes the main solo melody. Henri and Hélène arrive and are told by Procida that Spanish forces have agreed to aid the Sicilian cause, but that the Spaniards will not act unless there is a local uprising. Procida departs, to allow Henri and Hélène a two-movement duet – the first half of the traditional four-movement Italian model. In the first movement, the Allegro 'Comment, dans ma reconnaissance' ('Quale, o prode'), rapid dialogue precedes Henri's declaration of love; in 'Près du tombeau peut-être' ('Presso alla tomba'), the couple sing together (though with highly differentiated lines), Hélène agreeing to accept Henri if he will avenge her brother's death.

Béthune appears, summoning Henri to a ball at Montfort's house that evening; when Henri refuses he is surrounded and dragged away. Hélène explains to Procida what has happened, but he is nevertheless determined to continue his plan of attack. To the strains of a festive tarantella, the stage fills with young Sicilian men and women, among them 12 brides and their prospective husbands. Some French soldiers arrive and Procida encourages them to take advantage of the local women – to such good effect that at the end of the dance the soldiers abduct the young brides at swordpoint. The chorus of outrage that follows, 'Interdits, accablés' ('Il rossor mi coprì!'), again obsessively repeating rhythmic 'death' figures, is interrupted by offstage voices singing a barcarolle: a boat is seen in the distance carrying French officers and Sicilian women. In a brief interlude, Procida decides that Montfort will be assassinated that very night; and the two very different choruses join in cleverly worked counterpoint to bring the act to a close.

Act 3 Scene i *A study in Montfort's palace* A brief orchestral prelude introduces Montfort, alone and brooding on his past: the woman he abducted many years ago has died, but she brought up their son Henri (who does not know his father's identity) to hate Montfort. The governor summons Henri to his presence before singing the famous 'Au sein de la puissance' ('In braccio alle dovizie'), a freely structured aria full of surprising harmonic excursions, in which he muses on his outward power and inward emptiness. Henri, entering, begins a lengthy duet, 'Quand ma bonté toujours nouvelle' ('Quando al mio sen'), which departs notably from standard Italian formal practice. There is a rapid alternation of tempos and moods in which Montfort presents Henri with proof of their relationship and, to a statement of the main theme of the overture (a melody that also dominates the final section of the duet), rejoices in his revelation. Henri is shocked, fears he must now lose Hélène and, in spite of Montfort's continued pleading, rejects the embrace of his father.

Act 3 Scene ii *A magnificent hall laid out for a grand ball* The long ballet that begins this scene is entitled 'Les quatre saisons' ('Le quattro stagioni') and, at least at the first production, entailed an elaborate mixture of mime and dance, with gods, zephyrs, naiads, fauns and a final dance to Bacchus. Verdi's succession of brief contrasting movements shows the requisite instrumental invention and rhythmic vitality, though it is perhaps too one-dimensional to be of much interest outside its immediate context.

The Act 3 finale is a large choral tableau, typical of French grand opera in its setting of private emotions within a public frame. The festive opening chorus, 'O fête brillante' ('O splendide feste!'), is interrupted by various dance tunes as Procida and Hélène approach Henri to tell him of the plot to murder Montfort. Henri warns Montfort of the danger but still refuses to side with his father. However, when Hélène tries to stab Montfort, Henri defends him and the conspirators are immediately arrested. The ensuing Adagio concertato, 'Coup terrible' ('Colpo orrendo'), which closes the act, is made up of two contrasting musical segments: first, a section of stunned surprise in which a tiny rhythmic motif is isolated and repeated; and then, its antithesis, a long lyrical melody in which all participants join to effect a stirring close.

ACT 4 *The courtyard of a fortress* A robust orchestral introduction presents Henri, who shows a pass allowing him to visit the prisoners. He laments his position in 'O jour de peine' ('Giorno di pianto'), a strophic aria whose angular melodic arch and harmonic underpinning are quite unlike the Verdian norm and which ends with a fast coda. Hélène then arrives to precipitate the first movement of the grand duet, 'De courroux et d'effroi' ('O sdegni miei'), in which fragmentary responses coalesce into a patterned melody as Henri begs for understanding, the melody momentarily breaking into recitative when Henri admits the identity of his father. The second movement, 'Ami! . . . le coeur d'Hélène' ('Arrigo! ah parli a un core'), is a miniature minor-major *romanza* for Hélène, in which she reconciles herself to Henri, though with no hope of their union; and the duet closes with a curtailed cabaletta, 'Pour moi rayonne' ('È dolce raggio').

Procida enters; he has been informed that Spanish forces are ready to aid the revolutionaries; he is quickly followed by Montfort, who orders the prisoners' immediate execution. Procida then leads off the quartet, 'Adieu, mon pays' ('Addio, mia patria'), in which the principals explore their differing emotions. Montfort offers clemency if only Henri will call him 'father'. A *de profundis* is heard offstage, the place of execution is revealed and eventually, to a slow, high violin melody, Henri submits. The prisoners are released and all join in a final stretta.

ACT 5 *Luxurious gardens in Montfort's palace in Palermo* The final act begins with three 'atmospheric' numbers in which the plot is barely advanced but local colour is richly explored. First comes the chorus 'Célébrons ensemble' ('Si celebri alfine'), quickly followed by Hélène's *sicilienne*, 'Merci, jeunes amies' ('Mercè, dilette amiche'), a *couplet* form entailing considerable virtuosity. Finally, there is Henri's lightly scored *mélodie* 'La brise souffle au loin' ('La brezza aleggia'), a song in praise of the evening breezes. Procida, his fanatical hatred undimmed, enters to announce the imminent uprising, which will begin at the sound of the wedding bells. He upbraids Hélène when he sees her love for Henri; she is horrified at the coming massacre. Henri leads off the first movement of the terzetto finale, 'Sort fatal!' ('Sorte fatal!'). Hélène tries to stop the progress of events by refusing to go through with the wedding, but in spite of her pleading Henri refuses to leave the scene and in the closing stretta of the trio, 'Trahison! imposture!' ('M'ingannasti, o traditrice'), the principals' conflicting positions are again explored. Montfort enters and signals for the wedding bells to sound. The Sicilians rush in with daggers drawn and fall on Montfort and the French.

*

Les vêpres siciliennes, in common with almost all French grand operas, has fallen from the repertory, its sheer length and the complexity of its vocal and scenic demands placing severe pressure on modern opera-house economics. There may also be purely musical reasons for the opera's comparative neglect: with a very few exceptions, its main lyrical numbers lack the melodic immediacy of the trio of Italian operas (*Rigoletto*, *Il trovatore* and *La traviata*) that

151

immediately preceded it. However, for those wishing to understand Verdi's musical development during the 1850s, *Les vêpres siciliennes* is of enormous importance. In both strictly formal terms and in larger matters of operatic structure, it marks a decisive turn away from the language of the middle-period Italian operas and the emergence of many stylistic features we associate with the later Verdi. There is no subsequent Verdi opera in which the experience of *Les vêpres* will not be recalled and refined.

Simon Boccanegra

Opera in a prologue and three acts set to a libretto by Francesco Maria Piave (with additions by Giuseppe Montanelli) after Antonio García gutiérrez's play *Simón Bocanegra*; first performed in Venice, at the Teatro La Fenice, on 12 March 1857. The revised version, with additions and alterations by Arrigo Boito, was first performed in Milan, at the Teatro alla Scala, on 24 March 1881.

The cast at the première included Leone Giraldoni (Boccanegra), Giuseppe Echeverria (Fiesco), Luigia Bendazzi (Amelia) and Carlo Negrini (Gabriele). For the revised version the cast included Victor Maurel (Boccanegra), Edouard de Reszke (Fiesco), Anna D'Angeri (Amelia) and Francesco Tamagno (Gabriele).

PROLOGUE

Simon Boccanegra *a corsair in the service of the Genoese Republic*	baritone
Jacopo Fiesco *a Genoese nobleman*	bass
Paolo Albiania *Genoese goldsmith*	bass
Pietro *a Genoese popular leader*	baritone

Sailors, populace, Fiesco's servants etc.

DRAMMA

Simon Boccanegra *the first Doge of Genoa*	baritone
Maria Boccanegra *his daughter, under the name Amelia Grimaldi*	soprano
JacopoFiesco *under the name Andrea*	bass
Gabriele Adorno *a Genoese gentleman*	tenor
Paolo Albiani *the Doge's favourite courtier*	bass
Pietro *another courtier*	baritone
A Captain of the Crossbowmen	tenor
Amelia's Maidservant	mezzo-soprano

Soldiers, sailors, populace, senators, the Doge's court, African prisoners of both sexes

Setting In and around Genoa, about the middle of the 14th century; between the Prologue and Act 1, 25 years pass

Verdi was approached to write a new opera for the Teatro La Fenice in Venice (his last première there had been of *La traviata* in 1853) at the instigation of the librettist Francesco Maria Piave in the spring of 1856. By May of that year a contract had been agreed with the theatre, the subject to be Gutiérrez's *Simón Bocanegra*, and Piave set to work according to precise instructions from the composer. In fact, Verdi himself supplied a complete prose sketch of the action, one so detailed that he insisted that his sketch rather than a draft of the libretto be submitted to the censors for approval. From August 1856 Verdi was in Paris, and in part because communication was difficult with the Italian-based Piave, he took on a local collaborator, the exiled revolutionary Giuseppe Montanelli, who drafted several scenes. Verdi began composing in the autumn of 1856 and, as the date of the première approached, showed his usual close concern with the staging and choice of performers. The première was only a moderate success; the libretto in particular received some harsh criticism. Subsequent revivals in the late 1850s were occasionally successful, although the 1859 La Scala première was a complete fiasco.

Doubtless in reaction to this lack of public acclaim, Verdi considered revising the score during the 1860s; but it was not until 1879 that he finally decided to make substantial alterations, in part to test the possibility of working with Arrigo Boito as librettist on the larger project of *Otello*. Looking over the score, Verdi pronounced it 'too sad' and decided that, although the prologue and final two acts could remain more or less unchanged, the first act needed a thorough overhaul, in particular by the injection of contrast and variety. This idea eventually gave rise to the famous Council Chamber scene; but in the end Verdi (somewhat reluctantly) found it necessary to make large adjustments to several other portions of the score (details are given below). The revised version had a resoundingly successful première at La Scala, directed by Franco Faccio.

*

PROLOGUE *A square in Genoa* The 1857 version begins with a prelude in which various themes from the opera are briefly juxtaposed; the opening scene is the barest of declamatory recitatives. In 1881 Verdi underpinned the opening conversation between Paolo and Pietro with an undulating string theme, rich in harmonic inflections and clearly meant to introduce the maritime flavour of the score. The two men discuss who is to be the next Doge, Pietro persuading Paolo to support the corsair Boccanegra. As Pietro departs to rally the plebeian vote, Boccanegra himself appears. He is at first indifferent to assuming high office, but is persuaded to seek it by Paolo's reminder that his position will help win him his beloved Maria – she is imprisoned in her father Fiesco's home as a result of her love affair and Fiesco's strong disapproval of the plebeian Boccanegra. From here to the end of the prologue the two versions largely correspond, although Verdi made numerous small revisions for 1881. First comes a chorus during which Paolo and Pietro convince the workers that they should vote for Boccanegra. The scene, remarkable for its restraint, centres on 'L'atra magion vedete?', in which Paolo describes the Fieschi's gloomy palace, which holds Maria prisoner.

As the crowd disperses, Fiesco emerges from his home, stricken with grief: his daughter has just died. After a stern recitative he sings the famous 'Il lacerato spirito', a minor-major *romanza* notable for its extreme melodic simplicity but powerful emotional effect. Fiesco is then joined by Boccanegra for the first grand duet of the opera. The first movement shows the usual violent alternation of moods: Fiesco accuses, Boccanegra tries to placate him, the old man agrees to pardon Boccanegra if he will give up the daughter Maria has borne him. But in a second movement, 'Del mar sul lido', again dominated by maritime figures in the orchestra, Boccanegra narrates how his daughter has mysteriously disappeared from the remote hiding place where she was lodged during her absence at sea. Fiesco, who contributes little to this movement, turns his back on Boccanegra, pretending to leave, but hides nearby. In a third movement, full of

155

passionately anxious string figures, Boccanegra enters the palace in search of Maria. His cries of anguish at discovering her body are immediately countered by offstage cheers. To a jarring festive theme – a kind of cabaletta substitute – the people enter to hail Boccanegra as their new leader.

ACT 1 Scene i   *The gardens of the Grimaldi palace outside Genoa* 25 years have passed. An evocative orchestral prelude depicting the rising dawn introduces Amelia, whose French-style ternary aria, 'Come in quest'ora bruna', is notable for its delicately varied accompaniment and its injection of narrative mystery in the middle section. Gabriele's offstage voice is now heard in two stanzas of a *Trovatore*-like serenade, 'Cielo di stelle orbato'. In the 1857 version this leads to a cabaletta for Amelia, 'Il palpito deh frena', which in 1881 was replaced by a few bars of recitative. In the first movement of the lovers' ensuing duet, Gabriele tries to calm Amelia's fears for the future; in the second, the gentle Andantino 'Vieni a mirar la cerula', they pause to admire the sea around Genoa, although thinking too of enemies within the city walls. At the close of the Andantino the pair are joined by Pietro, who asks permission for the Doge to visit later that day. Amelia, sure that he is planning for her to marry Paolo, sends Gabriele away to prepare for their own wedding. In a final cabaletta, 'Sì, sì, dell'ara il giubilo', much reduced in 1881, they swear to defy the whole world.

Amelia hurries into the palace, but Gabriele is detained by Fiesco (who is posing under the name Andrea, and has long been watching over Amelia; he is very fond of her, although unaware of her real identity). Fiesco, informed of Amelia's and Gabriele's marriage plans, warns Gabriele that his intended bride is not of noble birth but an orphan who replaced the real Amelia Grimaldi, long since dead. In 1857 the episode was rounded off by a duet cursing Boccanegra, thought responsible for the death; in 1881 there is a *religioso* duet in which Fiesco gives a father's blessing to Gabriele.

Offstage trumpets herald Boccanegra. In a brief scene the Doge gives Amelia a paper showing that he has pardoned her presumed brothers (the Grimaldi, who have plotted against him). In the first movement of the ensuing duet, 'Dinne, perchè in quest'eremo', which is underpinned by a sinuous orchestral melody, Amelia admits her love for Gabriele and, feeling gratitude to Boccanegra, decides to tell him of her lowly birth. This she does in a second movement, the narration 'Orfanella il tetto umile', in the last section of which Boccanegra joins her with a gathering sense of her true identity. The third movement, in which Boccanegra confirms that she is his long-lost daughter, quickly gives way to a cabaletta of mutual joy, 'Figlia! a tal nome io palpito', subtly varied in the 1881 version to increase the sense that both individuals have distinct musical personalities. Amelia leaves, and Boccanegra roughly tells Paolo to abandon hope of marrying her. When Boccanegra himself departs, Paolo tells Pietro of his plan to abduct Amelia.

ACT 1 Scene ii *The Council Chamber of the Doge's Palace* This scene was almost entirely recomposed for the 1881 version. The 1857 finale is set in a large square in Genoa, and is a conventional four-movement concertato finale, a grand ceremonial scene in which the Doge appears amid festivities and is interrupted by Fiesco and Gabriele who accuse him of abducting Amelia. As the scene reaches its climax Amelia herself appears, protesting the Doge's innocence and thus precipitating the central Andantino. Amelia then narrates her abduction and escape, but she refuses to reveal publicly who was responsible, and all join in a stretta calling for the guilty one to be brought to justice.

In 1881 Verdi altered this traditional plan, vastly expanding the first movement, eliminating the last, and fashioning new music almost throughout. The scene begins with a stormy orchestral introduction, after which the Doge urges the Council to preserve peace between Genoa and Venice. A riot is heard outside as the plebeians demand death for the patricians and the Doge. Boccanegra orders the crowd to be brought in, and a mass of people appears with Fiesco and Gabriele as captives, accused of killing Lorenzino, a leader of the plebeians. Gabriele in turn accuses the Doge of having Amelia abducted and is about to stab him when Amelia enters and interposes herself between them. She narrates her abduction and escape in

157

'Nell'ora soave', but refuses to reveal publicly who was responsible. A new argument develops between the opposing factions, this time violently quelled by the Doge, who launches the central Andante mosso, 'Plebe! Patrizi!', a magnificent ensemble movement in which the Doge's and Amelia's pleas for peace calm the crowd. The Andante over, the Doge pronounces a solemn curse on Amelia's abductor, forcing Paolo to repeat the words. As the chorus reiterate the curse, Paolo falls down in horror.

ACT 2 *The Doge's room in the Ducal Palace at Genoa* In 1881 Verdi expanded Paolo's brief 1857 scena into a powerful recitative during which he meditates on the curse that has fallen on him and then puts poison in Boccanegra's drink. Fiesco and Gabriele are led in and, in spite of his hatred for Boccanegra, Fiesco refuses to be involved in Paolo's plot against the Doge. Fiesco leaves and Paolo informs Gabriele that the Doge wishes Amelia for himself. Left alone, Gabriele breaks into a fit of jealous anger that culminates in the two-movement aria 'Sento avvampar nell'anima', the first movement driven by a furious orchestral figure, the second a lyrical Largo enhanced by delicate chromatic details in the vocal line.

There follows a highly condensed four-movement duet for Amelia and Gabriele. During the opening movement Gabriele accuses Amelia of betrayal; she denies this but will elaborate no further. In the second-movement Andante, 'Parla, in tuo cor virgineo', Gabriele begs her to explain herself while she continues to protest her inno-cence. A tiny connecting movement starts as Amelia hears the Doge approaching. Gabriele refuses to leave, but in a short cabaletta she succeeds in making him hide on the balcony. The Doge enters and in a stormy recitative learns that she loves Gabriele, whom he now knows to be conspiring against him. Left alone, he drinks from the poisoned cup and lapses into sleep. Gabriele reappears and after some deliberation decides to murder the Doge; but he is stopped by the sudden appearance of Amelia. Boccanegra awakes and eventually reveals that Amelia is his daughter, the three principals cementing their newfound connection in the lyrical Andante 'Perdon, perdon, Amelia'. But a warlike chorus is heard in the distance: the people are rebelling against the Doge. Gabriele offers to sue for peace, and vows to fight at Boccanegra's side.

ACT 3 *Inside the Doge's Palace* An orchestral introduction and choral cries in praise of the Doge precede the appearance of Fiesco and Paolo. In an impassioned recitative, Paolo reveals that it was he who abducted Amelia and poisoned the Doge. He is led off to execution. A Captain orders that all the lights in the city be extinguished in honour of the dead. The Doge himself appears, a sluggish, chromatic string theme depicting the moving of the poison through his body. In a shimmering arioso, he delights in his beloved Genoese sea, 'Oh refrigerio! ... la marina brezza!', before being joined by Fiesco. In the first movement of their duet, 'Delle faci festanti al barlume', which contains the usual series of sharply contrasting episodes, Fiesco challenges the Doge and then admits his true identity. As the lights are gradually extinguished, Boccanegra reveals that 'Amelia' is really Fiesco's granddaughter. At this Fiesco breaks into tears, and the lyrical second movement, the Largo 'Piango, perchè mi parla', sees bass and baritone gradually reconciled. But ominous rhythmic figures in the orchestra warn us that Boccanegra is nearing death, and Fiesco tells him he has been poisoned. Amelia and Gabriele appear and Boccanegra blesses them in a final concertato, 'Gran Dio, li benedici'. With his dying breath he nominates Gabriele as his successor.

*

Simon Boccanegra is the mature Verdian opera most thoroughly revised by the composer, and the fact that these revisions were effected more than 20 years after the original version leaves the opera with some startling stylistic disjunctions. The 1857 drama was remarkably forward-looking for its time, particularly from the point of view of conventional operatic characterization: there are no secondary female characters, but a preponderance of low male voices; and though a baritone protagonist was no longer exceptional, Boccanegra has very few opportunities to show vocal brilliance and is assigned no conventional arias. However, this excitingly unusual vocal constellation is connected with, and in part causes, an important problem, one of which Verdi himself was well aware: the opera was, he felt, too consistently dark in colour, too gloomy.

The 1881 revisions do much to improve this aspect of the work. Though the distribution of voices remains the same, in retouching various scenes the mature Verdi invariably added new levels of harmonic and instrumental colour to the opera. And, perhaps most importantly, by adding the new Act 1 finale (the famous Council Chamber scene), he injected into the heart of the work an episode of enormous vividness and power, enriching the character of Boccanegra in such a way that his subsequent death scene gains considerably in impressiveness.

It has been argued, however, that the revisions – especially the addition of the new Act 1 finale – create a further general problem, one of what we might call dramatic balance. The sheer weight of Boccanegra's new presence tends to overpower the other principals, Gabriele in particular, making their concerns seem unimportant or at least under-articulated. But perhaps critics tend to exaggerate the extent to which these essentially 'narrative' matters are crucial to the success of an opera. In recent years, audiences have been in no doubt that *Simon Boccanegra* contains some of the mature Verdi's greatest dramatic music, and there seems little doubt that the opera will retain its new status as one of the composer's most compelling creations.

Aroldo

Opera in four acts by set to a libretto by Francesco Maria Piave after their earlier opera Stiffelio; first performed in Rimini, at the Teatro Nuovo, on 16 August 1857.

The original cast included Emilio Pancani (Aroldo), Marcellina Lotti (Mina) and Gaetano Ferri (Egberto).

Aroldo *a Saxon knight*	tenor
Mina *his wife*	soprano
Egberto *her father, an old knight, vassal of Kent*	baritone
Briano *a pious hermit*	bass
Godvino *an adventurer knight, guest of Egberto*	tenor
Enrico *Mina's cousin*	tenor
Elena *also her cousin*	soprano
Jorg *Aroldo's servant*	spoken

Crusader knights, ladies and gentlemen of Kent, squires, pages, heralds, huntsmen, Saxons, Scottish peasants

Setting In Egberto's castle in Kent, and on the shores of Loch Lomond in Scotland, in about 1200

The first performance of *Stiffelio*, at Trieste in November 1850, had encountered severe problems with local religious censorship, particular objection being made to the final scene, which had to be changed radically and – Verdi thought – damagingly. The few subsequent revivals also tended to run into trouble, and in 1854 Verdi decided to collaborate with Piave on rescuing the opera by setting it to a different, less sensitive plot. In 1856 they started work, changing the tale of a 19th-century Protestant pastor into that of a 13th-century Saxon knight returned from the Crusades, Verdi taking the opportunity to make a number of further modifications. The brilliant young conductor Angelo Mariani directed the première at Rimini. The revised opera was a huge success, but revivals fared less well and

Aroldo soon disappeared from the general repertory, receiving only the occasional performance. In the discussion below, musical detail will be mentioned only if a passage differs substantially from *Stiffelio* or is new to *Aroldo*.

*

ACT 1 Scene i   *A drawing room in Egberto's home*   The overture is substantially that of *Stiffelio*, but the opening of the act is new to *Aroldo*. A festive unaccompanied chorus, 'Tocchiamo! a gaudio insolito', welcomes Aroldo home from the Crusades. After an intense orchestral introduction, Mina enters to give voice to her remorse and offer a brief prayer, 'Salvami tu, gran Dio', an opening that immediately makes her a more forceful presence than was Lina in *Stiffelio*. Aroldo now arrives and introduces the hermit Briano, who saved his life in battle. His ensuing double aria carries frequent anguished interpolations from Mina. The Andante, 'Sotto il sol di Siria', which describes how his thoughts on the battlefield were always for his wife, takes its theme from the overture; but (as in *Stiffelio*) the absence of Mina's ring arouses suspicions which he voices in the cabaletta 'Non sai che la sue perdita'.

Mina, left alone, decides to write to her husband. She is interrupted by Egberto; the words and music of the ensuing duet are, apart from a few details, identical with those in *Stiffelio*.

ACT 1 Scene ii   *A suite of rooms illuminated for a grand celebration*   To a further theme borrowed from the overture, ladies and knights appear downstage as Godvino slips a letter to Mina into a book, observed – though only from behind – by Briano. In the interval between bursts of choral celebration, Enrico comes on, dressed like Godvino, and takes up the book. Briano is now convinced that Enrico placed the letter there, and warns Aroldo. Egberto enters, and asks for a returning warrior to narrate the adventures of King Richard in Palestine. Aroldo obliges with 'Vi fu in Palestina', a largely declamatory episode that tells of a dishonourable man who betrayed his guests by writing a secret love letter to the lady of the house. He takes up the book to further illustrate the point, finds it locked and tells a terrified Mina to open it. The ensuing concertato, 'Oh qual m'invade ed agita', is taken directly from *Stiffelio*, though with various expansions and musical changes, in particular to the main melodic line of the stretta.

ACT 2 *An old graveyard in the castle in Kent* The opening part of the scene, together with Mina's prayer 'Ah! dagli scanni eterei', is taken from *Stiffelio*, but at the appearance of Godvino new music takes over in preparation for a new cabaletta, 'Ah dal sen di quella tomba', which – in line with the changes made to Mina's role in Act 1 – requires an impressive musical and emotional range from the soprano. The remainder of the act follows *Stiffelio*: Egberto's duel with Godvino is interrupted by Aroldo; Egberto reveals to Aroldo that Godvino is Mina's seducer; and Briano narrowly prevents Aroldo from fighting a duel with Godvino.

ACT 3 *An antechamber in Egberto's home* The act is identical with Act 3 scene i of *Stiffelio*, although with occasional alterations to and expansions of Mina's role. Egberto contemplates suicide in his double aria; Aroldo and Godvino have a brief scene; and finally there is the long duet of confrontation between Aroldo and Mina, during which Egberto murders Godvino.

ACT 4 *A deep valley in Scotland* An opening chorus, 'Cade il giorno', offers generic local colour to mark the new geographical location. Aroldo and Briano, dressed as hermits, join the chorus in a prayer, 'Angiol di Dio', that makes prominent use of contrapuntal effects. A storm has been brewing and now breaks out to an orchestral accompaniment as elaborate in its instrumental virtuosity as anything Verdi had written to date. To the relief of the chorus, a boat seen approaching on the lake survives the storm, and as the bad weather subsides the boat moors and from it disembark Mina and Egberto. They go to the hermit's cottage to seek shelter. The ensuing Quartetto finale breaks into two large sections. First comes an Allegro, 'Ah da me fuggi', in which sharply differing emotional reactions are juxtaposed: Aroldo's violent rejection of his wife, then Egberto's narration of his and Mina's painful exile after Godvino's death, and finally Mina's disjointed pleas for forgiveness. But Mina takes control and leads off the final Largo, 'Allora che gl'anni', in which she begs Aroldo at least to forgive her when she is old and near death. At last the conflicting voices join, and a sententious phrase about forgiveness from Briano eventually persuades Aroldo to pronounce the words 'Sei perdonata!' ('You are forgiven!').

*

As will be clear from the above, *Aroldo* differs from *Stiffelio* primarily in its first and last acts. However, there is surprisingly little stylistic disparity in the later opera, a fact that in part demonstrates the forward looking nature of so much of *Stiffelio*. The relative merits of the operas are not such as to recommend one firmly over the other. *Aroldo* has a more forceful soprano presence, and its final act makes a weightier close than the brief though effective choral finale of *Stiffelio*. On the other hand, Lina's reticence in the earlier opera is one of its most effective dramatic ploys, and *Stiffelio's* compelling sense of religious claustrophobia is somewhat diffused by the *Aroldo* story, which wavers uncertainly between the warlike and the religious. It is tempting to conclude that both operas deserve more performances than they at present receive.

Un ballo in maschera
('A Masked Ball')

Melodramma in three acts by set to a libretto by Antonio Somma after Eugène Scribe's libretto *Gustave III, ou Le bal masqué*; first performed in Rome, at the Teatro Apollo, 17 February 1859.

The cast at the première included GaetanoFraschini (Riccardo), Leone Giraldoni (Renato), Eugenia Julienne-Dejean (Amelia)and Zelina Sbriscia (Ulrica).

Riccardo *Count of Warwick, Governor of Boston*	tenor
Renato *a Creole, his secretary, and husband of Amelia*	baritone
Amelia	soprano
Ulrica *a negro fortune-teller*	contralto
Oscar *a page*	soprano
Silvano *a sailor*	bass
Samuel ⎫ *enemies of the Count*	bass
Tom ⎭	bass
A Judge	tenor
Amelia's Servant	tenor

Deputies, officers, sailors, guards, men, women, children, gentlemen, associates of Tom and Samuel, sercants, masks, dancing couples

Setting In and around Boston, at the end of the 17th century

By February 1857 Verdi had agreed to write a new opera for the Teatro San Carlo in Naples, to be performed in the carnival season 1857–8. His first idea was to use *King Lear*, a setting of which he had planned with the playwright Antonio Somma, but (not for the first time) the San Carlo singers were not to his liking and the project was postponed. By September 1857 the composer was becoming anxious about his approaching deadline, and eventually proposed to Somma and the San Carlo – albeit with some reservations about the libretto's convention- ality – that he set a remodelled and translated version of an old Scribe libretto entitled *Gustave III, ou Le bal masqué*, written for Auber in

1833. Somma and the theatre agreed, and Verdi set to work advising his librettist, who had no experience of writing for the musical theatre, on the necessary poetic proportions of the subject.

As soon as a synopsis reached the Neapolitan censors, it became clear that the opera, which dealt with the assassination of the Swedish king Gustavus III, would have to be changed considerably if it was to be performed in Naples. Verdi agreed to change the king into a duke and to set the action back in time, and a new version of the story was patched together. However, soon after the composer arrived in Naples the censor rejected this version, making a series of new, more stringent demands, notably that Amelia become a sister rather than a wife, that there be no drawing of lots by the conspirators, and that the murder take place offstage. The authorities of the San Carlo attempted to answer these objections by cobbling together a new version entitled *Adelia degli Adimari*, but this Verdi angrily rejected. Eventually negotiations broke down, the planned performances fell through, and Verdi undertook to satisfy his contract at a later date.

When it became clear that Naples would not stage the opera, Verdi decided to have it given at the Teatro Apollo, in Rome, even though it soon became clear that Roman censorship, though far less exigent than that at Naples, would require at least a change of locale and the demoting of the king to some lesser noble. Eventually, however, Somma and Verdi established Riccardo, Conte di Warwick and a setting in the colonies of North America, although as a protest Somma did not allow his name to appear on the printed libretto. The première was a great success, and *Un ballo inmaschera* became one of Verdi's most popular operas. Though not attaining the dissemination of *Rigoletto*, *Il trovatore* or *Latraviata*, it has never lost its place in the international repertory.

Many modern performances restore the opera to its original, 18th-century Swedish setting, even though such restoration seems not to have had Verdi's explicit approval. In the Swedish setting the names are as follows:

Riccardo	Gustavus III *King of Sweden*
Renato	Captain Anckarstroem *Gustavus's secretary*
Amelia	Amelia
Ulrica	Mam'zelle Arvidson
Oscar	Oscar
Silvano	Christian
Samuel	Count Ribbing
Tom	Count Horn
A Judge	Armfelt *Minister of Justice*

*

The brief prelude presents three of the main musical ideas of the opening scene, first a chorale-like opening chorus, then a fugato associated with the conspirators and finally Riccardo's first aria; the whole argument is punctuated by a tiny rhythmic figure first heard in the second bar.

Act 1 Scene i   *A hall in the Governor's house*   The opening chorus, 'Posa in pace, a' bei sogni ristora', continues the prelude's musical juxtaposition of Riccardo's loyal followers with the conspirators who are planning to overthrow him, led by Samuel and Tom. Riccardo appears and, in a style reminiscent of *opera buffa*, reviews with Oscar the guest list for the coming masked ball. At seeing the name of Amelia, however, he is visibly moved, and advances to the footlights to sing a brief aria privately expressing his guilty love for her, 'La rivedrà nell' estasi'. Its opening phrase, will return later as a musical symbol of the love around which the story of the opera revolves. As the chorus disperses, the secretary Renato enters to warn Riccardo of plots against his life. His aria, 'Alla vita che t'arride', though formally more extended than Riccardo's, displays the same tendency towards condensation of traditional elements. Next to appear is a judge, requesting that Riccardo exile Ulrica, a fortune-teller suspected of supernatural practices. Oscar chooses to defend Ulrica in the ballata 'Volta la terrea', a French two-stanza form studded with that light coloratura which will typify the page throughout. Riccardo decides that he and his followers will disguise themselves and pay a personal call on Ulrica. He leads off the final stretta, 'Ogni cura si doni al diletto', a number that continues the Gallic atmosphere in its celebration of the pleasures of life, despite the continued mutterings of the conspirators in the musical background.

ACT 1 Scene ii *The fortune-teller's dwelling* After an atmospheric orchestral introduction, full of low woodwind sonorities and sinister tritones, Ulrica sings the invocation 'Re dell'abisso', an aria that begins in the minor, is interrupted by Riccardo's entrance in disguise, and continues with a cabaletta substitute in the major. The atmosphere of foreboding is rudely interrupted by Silvano, a sailor who has seen no preferment and who – in the brief, sprightly solo 'Su, fatemi largo' – asks Ulrica to divine his future. Ulrica predicts wealth and a commission, something that Riccardo promptly brings to pass by secreting gold and the appropriate papers into Silvano's pocket. Silvano discovers his new-found wealth and all join in praise of Ulrica. They are interrupted by Amelia's servant, who requests for her mistress an interview with Ulrica. Ulrica dismisses the crowd; but Riccardo, who has recognized the servant, remains in his hiding place as Amelia comes in.

In an impassioned arioso, Amelia asks Ulrica to rid her of the love that torments her. Ulrica's reply is the sinuous, chromatic 'Della città all'occaso', which tells of a healing plant that grows in the gallows-field nearby. In the brief terzetto that ensues, 'Consentimi, o Signore', Amelia prays that she may be healed, while Ulrica tries to comfort her and Riccardo, still hidden, vows to follow her on her quest. As Amelia departs, the stage is filled with Riccardo's entourage. Riccardo poses as a fisherman and sings the characteristic two-stanza canzone 'Di' tu se fedele', replete with the conventions of maritime musical language. He presents his hand to Ulrica who, in an imposing arioso, predicts that he will soon die by the hand of a friend. Riccardo attempts to disperse the tension by leading off the famous quintet 'È scherzo od è follia', in which his breathless, 'laughing' line is accompanied by sinister chattering from Samuel and Tom, and by a sustained, high-lying melody for Oscar. Riccardo asks the identity of his murderer: Ulrica says it will be the first person who shakes his hand, a prophecy seemingly made absurd by Renato, who hurries on soon after and immediately clasps his master's hand. The act closes with a martial hymn, 'O figlio d'Inghilterra', in which the principals emerge from the vocal mass to restate their differing positions.

ACT 2   *A lonely field on the outskirts of Boston*   Amelia's grand scene is preceded by a lengthy, impassioned orchestral prelude which features her melody from the Act 1 terzetto. Heavily veiled, she is terrified by her surroundings and in the aria 'Ma dall'arido stelo divulsa' prays for assistance in her ordeal. The aria, with the mournful english horn obbligato that is a traditional pointer of the isolated heroine, is interrupted by a terrifying vision as midnight sounds, but her final prayer re-establishes a kind of resigned calm. Riccardo appears, and so begins one of Verdi's greatest soprano-tenor duets, a number that, as was becoming common in middle-period Verdi, has a succession of contrasting 'dialogue' movements before its more conventional close with the cabaletta together. In the opening Allegro agitato the pace of exchange is rapid as Riccardo declares his love and Amelia begs him to leave; the musical continuity comes for the most part from a driving string melody. In a second movement, 'Non sai tu che se l'anima mia', their individual attitudes are explored at greater length, with a particularly impressive modulation as the discourse turns from Riccardo to Amelia; but eventually Riccardo's pleas win the day and, to a passionate, soaring melody sustained by a pedal A major chord, Amelia admits her love for him. A brief linking section leads to the cabaletta, 'Oh qual soave brivido', whose two stanzas and lively arpeggiated melody are separated by yet another impassioned declaration of mutual love.

The couple separate at the sound of footsteps: Riccardo recognizes Renato; Amelia, terrified, lowers her veil. In the first movement of the ensuing trio, 'Per salvarti da lor', Renato warns of the approaching conspirators, and lends his cloak to Riccardo in order to effect the latter's escape. Riccardo will leave only after muffled pleas from Amelia, and he solemnly charges Renato to escort her, still veiled, to the gates of the city. Before Riccardo rushes off, the three principals pause for a furiously paced second trio movement, 'Odi tu come fremono cupi', in which the driving rhythm encloses a strictly patterned alternation of solo statements. Riccardo is safely away when the conspirators appear, singing the contrapuntal music first heard in the prelude to the opera. They are challenged by Renato and, finding their prey has disappeared, decide to amuse themselves by seeing the face of the mysterious woman. When it becomes clear that Renato, in his loyalty to the count, will fight rather than permit this, Amelia herself raises her veil. Renato is astounded: the conspirators cannot contain their mirth at the notion of Renato's nocturnal assignation with his own wife, and break into the nonchalant 'laughing' chorus, 'Ve' se di notte qui colla sposa'. In between statements of the main idea, Renato accuses Amelia while she begs for mercy. As a parting gesture, Renato arranges a meeting with Samuel and Tom later that morning; the conspirators stroll off together, still vastly amused, their laughter echoing as the curtain comes down.

ACT 3 Scene i *A study in Renato's house* A stormy orchestral introduction ushers in Renato and Amelia. In an impassioned arioso, Renato insists that his wife must die. Although she admits her love for Riccardo, she insists that she has not betrayed her husband. Renato, however, is inflexible, and in the sorrowful aria 'Morrò ma prima in grazia', Amelia begs to see her child before dying, a cello obbligato adding to the pathos of the scene. Renato agrees to her request and once she has departed hurls furious insults at the portrait of Riccardo, which has a prominent place in his study. His anger coalesces into the famous aria 'Eri tu', a minor-major *romanza* which in the second part turns from angry accusations to the pain of his lost love.

Yet again the contrapuntal theme introduces Samuel and Tom. Renato shows them that he knows of their conspiracy, but now offers to join in its execution, offering his son's life as proof of his good word. Samuel and Tom accept his word, and all three swear blood brotherhood in the martial hymn 'Dunque l'onta di tutti sol una'. They elect to draw lots to decide who will strike the fatal blow, and Renato takes advantage of Amelia's return to force her to draw the name from an urn. To dotted rhythms and tremolando strings, Amelia draws Renato's name, and the conspirators again join in the martial hymn, this time with a terrified descant from Amelia.

170

In one of those abrupt changes of mood so characteristic of the opera, Oscar now appears, bringing with him once again the musical atmosphere of French comic opera. He has an invitation to tonight's masked ball, which Renato, Samuel and Tom all accept. To close the scene, they join in a stretta led off by Oscar, 'Di che fulgor', in which the terror and exultation of the principals are subsumed under Oscar's delicate musical idiom.

ACT 3 Scene ii *The Count's sumptuous study* In an opening recitative, Riccardo decides to sign a paper sending Renato and Amelia back to England. He then muses on the loss of his love in the *romanza* 'Ma se m'è forza perderti', which moves from minor to major, but via an unusual intermediate section in which he feels a strange presentiment of death. Dance music is heard offstage, and Oscar brings an anonymous message warning Riccardo that he risks assassination at the ball. But Riccardo, as ever heedless of the danger concludes the scene with a passionate recollection of his Act 1 aria of love for Amelia.

ACT 3 Scene iii *A vast, richly decorated ballroom* The opening chorus, 'Fervono amori e danze', repeats the music heard offstage in scene ii. As Renato, Samuel, Tom and their followers appear, a new, minor-mode theme emerges over which the conspirators exchange passwords and search for the Count. A third theme is heard as Oscar recognizes Renato. However, in spite of Renato's anxious questions, Oscar refuses to reveal the Count's costume, singing instead a lively French *couplet* form, 'Saper vorreste'. The opening chorus is heard again, and Renato renews his questions, pleading important business. Oscar finally reveals that the Count is wearing a black cloak with red ribbon, after which he mingles with the crowd to yet more of the opening chorus. A new dance melody, this time a delicate mazurka, underpins a stifled conversation between Amelia and Riccardo: Amelia begs the Count to escape; he reiterates his love but tells her that she is to return to England with her husband. They are bidding a last, tender farewell when Renato flings himself between them and stabs Riccardo. In the subsequent confusion, Oscar rips off Renato's

171

mask and the chorus expresses its fury in a wild Prestissimo. But then the gentle mazurka briefly returns (the offstage dance orchestra as yet unaware of the events) as Riccardo bids his people release Renato. Leading off the final concertato, 'Ella è pura', Riccardo assures Renato that Amelia's honour is intact. He bids his subjects farewell, and a brief stretta of universal horror brings down the curtain.

*

Un ballo in maschera, as many have remarked, is a masterpiece of variety, of the blending of stylistic elements. Verdi's experiment with a 'pure' version of French grand opera in the mid-1850s, *Les vêpres siciliennes*, was not entirely happy; here we see him instead gesturing to the lighter side of French opera, primarily with the character of Oscar, but also in aspects of Riccardo's musical personality. The juxtaposition of this style with the intense, interior version of Italian serious opera that Verdi had preferred in the early 1850s is extremely bold, particularly in sections such as Act 1 scene ii (where Riccardo confronts Ulrica) or in the finale to Act 2 (the so-called laughing chorus), in both of which the two styles meet head on with little mediation. One of the reasons why the blend is so successful is that Verdi's treatment of the traditional forms at the backbone of his 'Italian' manner was itself changing, adapting towards the more elliptical manner of French models. *Ballo* is notable for the shortness and intensity of its principal arias, for the absence of grand design.

Another reason for the opera's success undoubtedly lies in its delicate balance of musical personalities. At the outer limits of the style, as it were, lie two musical extremes; Oscar, whose role throughout is cast in an unambiguously Gallic mould of light comedy; and Ulrica, whose musical personality is unrelievedly dark and austere. Within these two extremes lie Renato and Amelia, characters cast in the Italian style, fixed in their emotional range, but from time to time infected by the influence of their 'French' surroundings. And at the centre comes Riccardo, who freely partakes of both worlds, and who mediates between them so movingly and persuasively.

La forza del destino
('The Power of Fate' [The Force of Destiny])

Opera in four acts set to a libretto by Francesco Maria Piave after Angel de Saavedra, Duke of Rivas's play *Don Alvaro, o La fuerza del sino*, with a scene from friedrich von Schiller's play *Wallensteins Lager*, translated by Andrea Maffei. *La forza del destino* was first performed in St Petersburg, at the Imperial Theatre, on 29 October/10 November 1862. The revised version, with additional text by Antonio Ghislanzoni, was first performed in Milan, at the Teatro alla Scala, on 27 February 1869.

The première starred Caroline Barbot (Leonora), Francesco Graziani (Carlo), Enrico Tamberlik (Alvaro) and Constance Nantier-Didiée (Preziosilla). The cast for the revised version included Teresa Stolz (Leonora), Luigi Colonnese (Carlo), Mario Tiberini (Alvaro) and Ida Benza (Preziosilla).

The Marquis of Calatrava	bass
Donna Leonora *his daughter*	soprano
Don Carlo di Vargas *his son*	baritone
Don Alvaro	tenor
Preziosilla *a young gypsy*	mezzo-soprano
The Padre Guardiano	bass
Fra Melitone *a Franciscan*	baritone
Curra *Leonora's maid*	mezzo-soprano
An Alcalde	bass
Mastro Trabuco *a muleteer, then pedlar*	tenor
A Surgeon (*in the Spanish army*)	bass

Muleteers, Spanish and Italian peasants, Spanish and Italian soldiers of various rank, their orderlies, Italian recruits, Franciscan friars, poor mendicants, vivandières

Dancers: Peasants, Spanish and Italian vivandières, Spanish and Italian soldiers

Walk-on parts: Innkeeper, innkeeper's wife, servants at the inn, muleteers, Spanish and Italian soldiers, drummers, buglers, peasants and children of both nations, a tumbler, pedlars

Setting Spain and Italy, around the middle of the 18th century

After *Un ballo in maschera* (finished in early 1858), Verdi experienced his most serious compositional hiatus to date, repeatedly telling friends that he had ceased to be a composer and that his farmlands at San Agata now took up all his time. The breakthrough to fresh creativity came in late 1860 when the famous tenor Enrico Tamberlik wrote to Verdi offering him a commission from the Imperial Theatre at St Petersburg. Verdi first suggested Victor Hugo's *Ruy Blas*, which initially met with censorship problems and then apparently failed to hold the composer's interest. By the middle of 1861 he had decided on Rivas's *Don Alvaro*, a Spanish romantic melodrama, written under the influence of Hugo. The librettist was again to be Piave, although Verdi approached his friend and former collaborator Andrea Maffei about using material from Schiller's *Wallensteins Lager* – a move that immediately indicated his intention of writing an opera of wide-ranging dramatic ambience. Serious work began on the opera in August 1861 and by November it was more or less complete (except, as usual, for the orchestration, which Verdi still preferred to complete nearer the time of performance, when he had experienced the singers and the theatrical acoustics at first hand). Verdi left for Russia in late 1861, but the première was postponed owing to the illness of the prima donna. He undertook several lengthy European trips during the first half of 1862 and returned to supervise rehearsals at St Petersburg in September of that year. The first performance was praised in some journals, but was at best only a moderate success.

It is clear that Verdi was not entirely happy with this or subsequent performances, and by 1863 he was talking of making alterations to the score, notably to the endings of Acts 3 and 4. Various large-scale structural alterations were discussed during the next few years with a view to a Parisian première in the mid-1860s, but pressure of other work caused plans to be shelved. Then in 1868 – after the première of *Don Carlos* at the Opéra – Verdi agreed to a new production of *La forza* at La Scala the following year. The librettist Antonio Ghislanzoni was drafted to help with modifications (the devoted Piave had in 1867 succumbed to a stroke which incapacitated him for the rest of his life); Verdi eventually elected to replace the *preludio* with a full-scale overture, to revise portions of Act 3, to make various minor alterations to other passages and, perhaps most important, to replace the bitter catastrophe of the final scene (in which all three principals die) with a scene of religious consolation. The performance, ably conducted by Angelo Mariani, was a considerable success and *La forza* remained a popular element of the repertory during the later years of the 19th century. There is some evidence that Verdi was actively involved in a cut-down French version of the score, first heard in Antwerp in 1882; but this version seems to have survived only in vocal score and was never sanctioned by Verdi's publisher Ricordi.

*

The overture (which, as mentioned above, belongs to the 1869 version, though deriving from the shorter *preludio* of 1862) is a potpourri of the score's most memorable tunes. It begins with a solemn three-note unison (usually called the 'fate' motif) and then a driving string theme that proves to be the dominant idea. Subsequent melodies are taken, in order of appearance, from the final-act duet between Alvaro and Carlo, from Leonora's Act 2 aria, 'Madre, pietosa Vergine', and from Leonora's Act 2 duet with Padre Guardiano (two themes, one associated with Leonora, one with the priest). The overture makes few concessions to classical ideas of balance, though it is given at least a surface impression of greater coherence by continual 'motivic' references to the main theme.

ACT 1 *The Marquis of Calatrava's house in Seville* After twice sounding the three-note unison that began the overture, the scene begins with a restrained string theme, though one whose syncopations and minor inflections hint at troubled undercurrents. The Marquis of Calatrava bids goodnight to his daughter, concerned by her sadness. Leonora can offer only anguished asides. As the Marquis

175

retires, Curra begins preparations for Leonora's elopement. Leonora's indecision is intense, but Curra outlines the bloody consequences for her lover Alvaro whi is thought racially inferior if he is now deserted. In the aria 'Me pellegrina ed orfana', which is in two contrasting sections and – as befits its dramatic position – involves no large-scale internal repetitions, Leonora bids a tender farewell to her homeland. The sound of approaching horses heralds Alvaro, who climbs in through a window. He immediately launches a duet, in four movements, conventionally patterned though economical. The first movement, 'Ah, per sempre', is dominated by Alvaro's impetuosity, but when Leonora shows signs of reluctance he settles into a more lyrical second movement ('Pronti destrieri'), which begins as a typical 3/8 wooing piece for romantic tenor but develops unusual vocal power as Alvaro recalls the gods of his native land (he is South American). The third movement (somewhat revised for 1869) as usual injects new action: Leonora begs that the elopement be postponed another day, protesting her love amid weeping that makes Alvaro suspicious; he accuses her of not loving him; she passionately affirms her feelings – and so to the cabaletta, 'Seguirti fino agl'ultimi', in which the lovers prepare to depart, and which is skilfully structured so that the final, curtailed reprise is preceded and precipitated by the sound of approaching footsteps. A brief recitative, in which Alvaro draws his pistol, is followed by the 'scena-finale', an action movement dominated by the pulsating main theme of the overture, modulating rapidly and purposefully to match events on stage. The Marquis of Calatrava enters. He insults Alvaro, goading him to a duel; Alvaro refuses and throws down his pistol. But the weapon accidentally discharges, fatally wounding the old man, who with his dying breath curses his daughter. Alvaro and Leonora make their escape, thus closing one of the most tightly constructed, economical acts in all Verdi.

ACT 2 Scene i *The village of Hornachuelos and its surroundings*
This scene is as expansive and repetitious as the previous one was tight and economical. 18 months have passed. The sprightly opening chorus, 'Holà! Ben giungi, o mulattier', gives way to a peasant dance,

both pieces richly imbued with Spanish local colour (the first more than a little reminiscent of passages in *Il trovatore*). Supper is announced and a 'student' (in fact Don Carlo, in search of his sister and 'her seducer') says grace. The dance music continues. Leonora enters dressed as a young man, recognizes her brother and immediately retreats. The stage is now taken by Preziosilla, who encourages the young men to join battle against the Germans and sings a rousing canzone, 'Al suon del tamburo', a French-influenced strophic song with refrain which recalls Oscar's music in *Un ballo in maschera*. During the final stages of the song Preziosilla consents to read Carlo's fortune and predicts a miserable future.

A chorus of pilgrims is heard in the distance; their chant forms the basis of a large-scale concertato movement, 'Padre Eterno Signor', which is punctuated by Leonora's desperate cries for divine mercy. As the pilgrims depart, Carlo takes centre stage and treats the company to a narrative ballata, 'Son Pereda, son ricco d'onore': his name is Pereda and he has been helping a friend track down the friend's sister and her lover. The predictable form and simple rhythm retain something of the comic opera atmosphere, although contrasting internal episodes give hints of tragic undercurrents. But Preziosilla and the others are happy enough, and the scene ends with some elaborate exchanges of 'goodnight' and a lively reprise of the opening chorus and dance tune.

ACT 2 Scene ii *A small clearing on the slopes of a steep mountain* Leonora struggles towards the door of a monastery, and in a turbulent recitative recalls her horror at hearing her brother's story at the inn, especially his news that Alvaro, from whom she was separated in flight, has returned to his homeland in South America. She falls on her knees to beg divine forgiveness in the famous 'Madre, pietosa Vergine', which is cast as a minor-major *romanza*, the first part underpinned by an obsessive string motif, the second based on the aspiring melody that had served as climax to the overture.

Leonora rings the monastery bell and, as Melitone (a comic character) departs to find the Padre Guardiano (Father Superior), she sings a further arioso in which the overture's main theme is once again juxtaposed with the aspiring melody. The Padre appears and dismisses Melitone, so beginning one of the opera's grand duets. After a brief scena, the number falls into the conventional four movements, although with the basic difference that Leonora and the Padre have comparatively little interaction: both remain enclosed within their very different views of the world. The first movement, 'Infelice, delusa', is as usual a series of sharply contrasted episodes, as Leonora tells her story and begs for a refuge from life. The second movement, 'Chi può legger nel futuro', offers a brief respite as the two voices come together, but in the third contrast returns. Eventually the Padre agrees to help her, and they join in a final cabaletta, 'Sull'alba il piede all'eremo'.

The great door of the church opens and a long procession of monks files down the sides of the choir. In a solemn ritual, the Padre tells the monks that a hermit is to live in the holy cave, and that no one must invade his seclusion. All join in a curse on any violator, 'Il Cielo fulmini, incenerisca'. The act closes with a quiet, simple hymn, 'La Vergine degli Angeli', before Leonora sets off to her hermitage.

ACT 3 Scene i *In Italy, near Velletri: a wood, at dead of night* Both Alvaro and Carlo have become involved in the war that is raging. A robust orchestral introduction and offstage chorus are hushed as Alvaro comes forward to the strains of a long clarinet solo, which elaborates a theme first heard in the Act 1 love duet. In an arioso punctuated by wisps of clarinet sound, Alvaro explains his noble birth and unhappy childhood. Then, in 'Oh, tu che in seno agli angeli', he asks Leonora (whom he believes dead) to look down on him from heaven. The aria begins in conventionally patterned phrases but soon takes on that 'progressive' form so typical of Verdi's later style.

Offstage noises disrupt Alvaro's pensive mood and he departs to investigate. Moments later he returns with Carlo, having saved him from assassins. The two hurriedly exchange false names and then swear eternal allegiance in a brief, sparsely accompanied duet. Further offstage cries alert them to a renewed enemy attack, and they rush off together.

ACT 3 Scene ii   *Morning: the quarters of a senior officer of the Spanish army*   As the scene changes, the orchestra depicts a battle and a surgeon describes its progress. Although victory is announced, Alvaro is carried on severely wounded. Carlo tries to rally him, promising the Order of Calatrava; but Alvaro reacts violently to the name. The wounded man requests a private interview with Carlo, and in the famous duet 'Solenne in quest'ora' entrusts his new friend with the key to a case wherein lies a packet to be burnt if Alvaro dies. The 'duet', dominated by Alvaro, is reminiscent of a traditional minor-major *romanza*: the opening minor section as the tenor issues his solemn commands, the major emerging as he rejoices that he can now die in peace.

Left alone, Carlo recalls Alvaro's reaction at the name of Calatrava and begins to suspect that he may be Leonora's seducer. He is tempted to break open the packet, but in 'Urna fatale', a cantabile within whose early 19th-century conventionality is buried powerful progressive elements, he tells how his honour forbids him from finding the truth. He looks elsewhere in the case and soon finds a portrait of Leonora. Just then the surgeon announces that Alvaro will live and Carlo, knowing he will now be able to wreak his vengeance, breaks into a cabaletta of savage joy, 'Egli è salvo!'

ACT 3 Scene iii   *A military encampment near Velletri*   In the 1862 version the scene progresses from a long choral episode to the quarrel between Alvaro and Carlo, an offstage duel, and then a double aria for Alvaro; the 1869 version – which defers the choral episode to the end of the act, has the duel onstage and omits Alvaro's aria – has much to commend it, not least that it clarifies the action and shortens one of Verdi's most demanding tenor roles.

The scene opens with a a comic-opera style chorus, 'Compagni, sostiamo' (new for 1869), in which a patrol makes a tour of inspection. Alvaro enters, accompanied by the minor-mode version of the clarinet theme that introduced him earlier in the act. Carlo joins him and, after innocently inquiring whether his wounds are healed (we must assume that several days have passed), calls Alvaro by his true name, so precipitating a grand duet. The first movement is the

traditional series of contrasting sections: Carlo reveals his own identity, Alvaro protests his innocence and finally Carlo informs Alvaro
that Leonora is still alive. The second movement, 'No, d'un imene
il vincolo', is a powerfully 'dissimilar' Andantino, in which Alvaro
celebrates the news of his beloved's survival only to be confounded
by Carlo's insistence on revenge. This leads swiftly to a closing
cabaletta, 'Morte! Ov'io non cada', in which the two swear mutual
defiance and begin to fight. But they are separated by a passing patrol;
Carlo is dragged off, and Alvaro casts aside his sword, swearing that
he will seek refuge in the cloister.

Rolls on the side drum introduce the sequence of choruses and
brief solos that will close the act. First comes 'Lorchè pifferi e
tamburi', a brief, lively chorus that leads directly into Preziosilla's
two-strophe French-influenced song 'Venite all'indovina', in which
she offers to tell the soldiers' fortunes. A further brief round of choral
celebrations precedes Trabuco's 'A buon mercato', a Jewish pedlar
song in which the chorus again joins. The mood darkens with the
next episode, in which a group of beggars, their lands destroyed by
the war, are followed by a group of miserable conscripts. But some
vivandières and Preziosilla soon brighten the atmosphere, leading the
conscripts in a tarantella. Melitone enters as the dance is at full tilt
and treats the company to an elaborate comic sermon (the passage
is taken almost word for word from Maffei's translation of Schiller's
Wallensteins Lager). The soldiers eventually tire of Melitone and
chase him away, leaving Preziosilla to round off the act with the
famous 'Rataplan' chorus.

ACT 4 Scene i *Inside the monastery of Our Lady of the Angels,
near Hornachuelos* Five years have passed. A crowd of beggars
appears, quickly followed by Melitone carrying a cauldron of soup.
In a comic-opera *parlante*, Melitone chides the beggars for asking
too much, continuing even when the Padre Guardiano advises kind-
ness to the suffering poor. Eventually Melitone's patience runs out:
he kicks the pot over and orders the beggars away in the comic
cabaletta 'Il resto, a voi pren detevi'. In the subsequent recitative,
Melitone mentions to the Padre the strange behaviour of 'Father

Raffaele' (who, we soon guess, is none other than Alvaro). The Padre counsels patience in a brief closing duet, 'Del mondo i disinganni', which contrasts his solemn ecclesiastical style with Melitone's frankly comic idiom.

The monastery bell rings loudly; Melitone answers to find Carlo, who dispatches him to seek 'Father Raffaele'. In the ensuing recitative Carlo reiterates his desire to avenge the family honour. Alvaro enters, thus starting a grand duet in which the traditional four movements are still present though radically altered in the light of the dramatic situation. The first movement, 'Col sangue sol cancellasi', offers the usual stark contrasts: Carlo's calls for a duel are underpinned by a martial theme in the orchestra, while Alvaro's offers of peace are more lyrical and subdued. The central Andante, 'Le minaccie, i fieri accenti', based on the second theme of the overture, is of the 'dissimilar' type – each having different musical material – with Alvaro's opening melody repeated by Carlo with agitated orchestral accompaniment. The movement breaks down as Carlo taunts Alvaro as a half-breed: this is too much, and Alvaro takes up the challenge. Before rushing off to fight, the two offer mutual defiance in a very brief, coda-like cabaletta, 'Ah, segnasti la tua sorte!'

ACT 4 Scene ii *A valley amid inaccessible rocks* Strains of the overture's main theme introduce Leonora, pale, worn and in great agitation. Her famous aria, 'Pace, pace, mio Dio!', in which she restates her love for Alvaro and begs God for peace, is like a distant homage to Bellini, whose 'long, long, long melodies' Verdi had so admired. Length indeed is here, as is the simple arpeggiated accompaniment typical of Bellini, but Verdi's line is injected with declamatory asides and harmonic shifts, a perfect expression of the new aesthetic that had overtaken Italian opera. As the aria comes to a close, she takes up food left by Padre Guardiano, but retreats hurriedly as others approach.

In the 1862 version, the opera's final scene reached a bloody conclusion. Alvaro and Carlo enter duelling; Carlo falls mortally wounded; Alvaro summons Leonora. On recognizing each other they sing a brief duet before Carlo calls Leonora to him as he dies, and, vengeful to the last, stabs her fatally. The heroine has a final, intense arioso, 'Vedi destino! io muoio!', before dying in Alvaro's arms. Sounds are heard below, and the monks appear. Padre Guardiano calls Alvaro, but he retreats to the highest point of the mountain and hurls himself into the abyss. For 1869 Verdi decided on a radical change. The opening arioso, which includes the offstage duel up to Alvaro and Leonora's meeting, is largely the same, but there is no duettino for the lovers, merely a continuation of the declamation until Leonora departs to help her brother. Alvaro has time for a brief soliloquy before an offstage scream interrupts him. Leonora, mortally wounded, is led on by Padre Guardiano: furious, dissonant 'death figures' in the orchestra cause a breakdown in the musical flow. But from this arises the final, lyrical trio, 'Non imprecare, umiliati', led off in the minor by Padre Guardiano. At first the two lovers can offer only fragmentary comments, but then the music turns to major, and a new, transfiguring melody arises from the orchestra, over which Alvaro declaims that he is 'redeemed'. Leonora leads off the final section, which concludes the opera with a sense of resolution and lyrical space.

*

La forza del destino reached something of a low point in the early years of this century, its sprawling action and mixture of comic, tragic and picturesque finding no resonance in a climate dominated by the Wagnerian model. But times have changed, and since the 1930s the opera has become one of the most popular of Verdi's works after the three middle-period masterpieces. This swing of fortune suggests an important shift in our expectations of what constitutes satisfying musical drama, because *La forza* is undoubtedly Verdi's most daring attempt at creating a 'patchwork' drama – or, as he once called it, an 'opera of ideas'. We look in vain for the kind of unifying colours found in *Rigoletto* or *Il trovatore*, and it is surely no accident that Verdi's 1869 revision could so radically change certain sequences in the action, even – as in Act 3 – transferring passages from one part of a scene to another. The opera is, in other words, only loosely linear: a significant precursor of 'native' Russian operas such as *Prince Igor* and *Boris Godunov*.

The presence of certain recurring themes, in particular the main theme of the overture (frequently dubbed a 'destiny' or 'fate' motif) has often been mentioned by commentators and is sometimes advanced as exemplifying the score's 'musical unity'. Perhaps that is so, but one could equally well see these recurring elements as an attempt to give some semblance of musical connectedness to a score that conspicuously lacks the cohesion Verdi so effortlessly achieved in his middle-period works. Nor, of course, are the themes used in anything like a consistent manner. An opera such as this, whose time gaps and scope make necessary a steady sequence of narratives (all the major characters are obliged to explain their past actions to each other), might easily have used a system of recurring motifs on a large scale. Nothing like that is attempted; indeed, in one sense the recurring motifs by their very literalness alert us to the extravagant gaps that are constantly and excitingly thrown up by this most challenging of works.

Don Carlos

Opéra in five acts set to a libretto by Joseph Méry and Camille Du Locle after Friedrich von Schiller's dramatic poem *Don Carlos, Infant von Spanien*; first performed in Paris, at the Opéra, on 11 March 1867. The revised *Don Carlos*, in four acts (the French text was revised by Du Locle, and the Italian translation was by Achille de Lauzières and Angelo Zanardini), was first performed in Milan, at the Teatro alla Scala, 10 January 1884.

The cast at the première included Louis-Henri Obin (Philip), Paul Morère (Don Carlos), Jean-Baptiste Faure (Posa), Marie Sasse (Elisabeth) and Pauline Guéymard-Lauters (Eboli). The cast for the revised version included Alessandro Silvestri (Filippo), Francesco Tamagno (Don Carlo), Paul Lhérie (Rodrigo), Abigaille Bruschi-Chiatti (Elisabetta) and Giuseppina Pasqua (Eboli).

Philip II *King of Spain*	bass
Don Carlos *Infante of Spain*	tenor
Rodrigue *Marquis of Posa*	baritone
The Grand Inquisitor	bass
Elisabeth de Valois *Philip's queen*	soprano
Princess Eboli	mezzo-soprano
Thibault *Elisabeth de Valois' page*	soprano
The Countess of Aremberg	silent
The Count of Lerma	tenor
An Old Monk	bass
A Voice from Heaven	soprano
A Royal Herald	tenor
Flemish Deputies	basses
Inquisitors	basses

Lords and ladies of the French and Spanish court, woodcutters, populace, pages, guards of Henry II and Philip II, monks, officers of the Inquisition, soldiers

Setting France and Spain, about 1560

Schiller's *Don Carlos* had been suggested to Verdi – and rejected by him – as a possible subject for the Paris Opéra in the early 1850s, when negotiations were beginning for the work that would become *Les vêpres siciliennes*. In 1865, with another full-scale Verdi grand opera being planned for Paris's foremost theatre, the composer clearly saw new potential in the subject. Emile Perrin, the new director of the Opéra, had discussed various topics with Verdi, for the most part via the composer's French publisher and friend Léon Escudier. Verdi pronounced *King Lear*, ever near to his heart at this period, too lacking in spectacle for the Opéra; *Cleopatra* was better, but the lovers would not arouse sufficient sympathy. *Don Carlos*, however, was now 'a magnificent drama', even though Verdi immediately saw the need to add two new scenes to the scenario offered him: one between the Inquisitor and Philip, the other between Philip and Posa. As the libretto took shape, the composer took his usual active part in advising on everything from large structural matters to minute details of phrasing and vocabulary.

Verdi worked steadily on the opera during the first half of 1866 and arrived in Paris in July of that year with most of the score completed. Then came the notoriously long, arduous rehearsal period at the Opéra, during which Verdi made several important changes, including the addition of a scene for Elisabeth at the start of Act 5. As the rehearsals neared completion in February 1867 it became clear that the opera was far too long, and Verdi made substantial cuts, among which were the lengthy and impressive Prelude and Introduction to Act 1, part of the Philip-Posa duet in Act 2, and both the Elisabeth-Eboli and the Carlos-Philip duets in Act 4. The première was not a great success, and *Don Carlos* disappeared from the Opéra repertory after 1869.

Early Italian revivals, in a translation by Achille de Lauzières, were sometimes successful; but the opera's length continued to present problems, and it was frequently given in severely cut versions. In 1872 Verdi himself made further revisions, restoring and rewriting passages of the Philip-Posa duet and cutting a portion of the final duet between Carlos and Elisabeth. Then, in 1882–3, he made a thoroughgoing revision, in part to reduce the opera to more manageable proportions, in part to replace pieces he now found unsatisfactory. The most important cuts were the whole of Act 1 (though Carlos's aria was inserted into the following act), the ballet and its preceding scene in Act 3 and the Act 5 Chorus of the Inquisitors. Many other passages were revised, recomposed or reordered. The La Scala première of this new, four-act version, given in Italian translation. Some two years later a further version which restored the original Act 1 began to be performed and was published (we must assume with Verdi's approval).

It is important to bear in mind that, although the 1884 version was first given in Italian, the revisions Verdi made were to a French text: in other words, there is no 'Italian version' of *Don Carlos*, merely an 'Italian translation'. The following discussion will move through the opera by act, marking in italic the version to which various passages belong: *1867* means the version eventually performed at the Parisian première, *1884* the substantially revised four-act version. Where appropriate, French incipits are followed by their Italian equivalents.

*

ACT 1 (*1867*) *The forest at Fontainebleau* An impressive introductory chorus was cut during rehearsals, leaving the opera to start with a brief Allegro brillante; offstage fanfares and huntsmen's calls introduce the princess Elisabeth, who (observed by Carlos) gives alms to the woodcutters and then departs.

Carlos, who has come incognito from Spain, has now seen for the first time his betrothed, Elisabeth, and in the brief, italianate aria 'Je l'ai vue' ('Io la vidi') he announces love at first sight. He is about to follow Elisabeth when a horn call tells him that night is falling. Thibault and Elisabeth, lost in the wood, appear, and Carlos offers help, introducing himself simply as 'a Spaniard'. Thibault goes off for assistance, so making way for the duet that will dominate this brief act. The opening movement, 'Que faites-vous donc?' ('Che mai fate voi?'), is formed from a series of contrasting episodes, the tension rising as Elisabeth eagerly questions this stranger about the Infante Carlos whom she is to marry. Carlos presents her with a portrait of her betrothed, which she immediately recognizes as the man before

186

her. This precipitates the second movement, 'De quels transports' ('Di qual amor'), a cabaletta-like celebration of their good fortune, based on a melody that recurs through the opera as a symbol of their first love.

The joy is short-lived. Thibault returns to announce that Henry II has decided to give Elisabeth to the widowed Philip instead of to his son, so decisively putting an end to the war between Spain and France. The couple express their horror in the restrained, minor-mode 'L'heure fatale est sonnée!' ('L'ora fatale è suonata!'), which is immediately juxtaposed with the major-mode offstage chorus of celebration, 'O chants de fête' ('Inni di festa'). The Count of Lerma arrives to request Elisabeth's formal approval of the match, a female chorus adding their pleas for peace. Elisabeth reluctantly accepts, and the stage clears to a triumphant reprise of 'O chants de fête'. Carlos is left alone to bemoan his fate.

ACT 2 (*1867*)/1 (*1884*) Scene i *The cloister of the St Yuste monastery*

Both versions A solemn introduction for four horns precedes the offstage chorus 'Charles-Quint, l'auguste Empereur' ('Carlo, il sommo Imperatore'), a funeral dirge for Charles V. A solitary old Monk adds his prayer to theirs, but admits that Charles was guilty of folly and pride.

1867 Carlos enters: he has come to the monastery to forget the past. In a solemnly intoned, sequential passage, 'Mon fils, les douleurs de la terre', the Monk tells him that the sorrows of the world also invade this holy place. The Monk's voice reminds a terrified Carlos of the late emperor himself.

1884 Carlos's extended scena explores his anguish at losing Elisabeth and culminates in a revised version of 'Je l'ai vue' ('Io la vidi') from the original Act 1 (the act entirely omitted from this version). There follows a curtailed conversation with the Monk.

1867 Rodrigue, Marquis of Posa, appears and is greeted by Carlos. Posa launches into a description of the battles in Flanders (a first portion of this part of the duet, beginning 'J'étais en Flandre', was cut from the 1867 version during rehearsals), and Carlos responds with a lyrical declaration of friendship, 'Mon compagnon, mon ami'. Carlos then admits his secret love for Elisabeth, now the wife of his father Philip. Posa reiterates his friendship in a reprise of 'Mon compagnon', advising Carlos to forget his sorrows in the battle for Flanders.

1884 The above-described portion of the duet was further condensed and enriched, with a skilful link from the scene with the Monk, and with 'Mon compagnon' becoming 'Mon sauveur, mon ami' ('Mio salvator, mio fratel').

Both versions The final section of the duet, the cabaletta 'Dieu tu semas dans nos âmes' ('Dio, che nell'alma infondere'), is a 'shoulder-to-shoulder' number reminiscent of Verdi's earliest manner, the tenor and baritone vowing eternal friendship in parallel 3rds. In an impressively scored coda, Philip, Elisabeth and a procession of monks cross the stage and enter the monastery. Carlos and Posa join the chanting monks before a thrilling reprise of their cabaletta brings the scene to a close.

ACT 2/1 Scene ii *A pleasant spot outside the St Yuste monastery gates* Eboli and the other ladies-in-waiting are not allowed in the monastery, so they amuse themselves outside. The female chorus sets the scene with 'Sous ces bois au feuillage immense' ('Sotto ai folti, immensi abeti'), and then Eboli sings her famous 'Chanson du voile' (Veil Song), 'Au palais des fées' ('Nel giardin del bello'): the two-stanza song with refrain, packed with both harmonic and instrumental local colour, tells the story of Achmet, a Moorish king who one evening mistakenly wooed his own wife in the garden. A disconsolate Elisabeth appears, soon followed by Posa, who hands the Queen a letter from her mother in which is hidden a note from Carlos. As Elisabeth reads, Posa makes courtly conversation with Eboli; but in the background of their dalliance we hear from Elisabeth that Carlos's letter asks her to trust Posa. At a word from Elisabeth, Posa begins his two-stanza cantabile *romance*, 'L'Infant Carlos, notre espérance' ('Carlo, ch'è sol il nostro amore'), in which he tells how Carlos, rejected by his father, requests an interview with his new 'mother'.

In between stanzas, Eboli wonders whether Carlos's dejection has been caused by love for her, while Elisabeth trembles with confusion. With the completion of the second stanza, however, Elisabeth agrees to the interview; Posa and Eboli walk off together, and the ladies-in-waiting leave.

The ensuing duet between Carlos and Elisabeth, 'Je viens solliciter' ('Io vengo a domandar'), is one of Verdi's boldest attempts to match musical progress to the rapid alternations of spoken dialogue: there is little sense of a conventional four-movement form (except perhaps for a cabaletta-style ending), the duet instead passing through a rapid series of contrasting episodes, some sense of strictly musical connection coming from shared motifs. In a controlled opening, Carlos asks Elisabeth to intercede on his behalf with Philip, who will not allow him to leave for the Spanish possession of Flanders; there is trouble there stemming from religious persecution, and Carlos, who is in sympathy with the disidents feels strongly that he can calm the situation. Elisabeth agrees, but Carlos can restrain himself no further and pours out his love. Elisabeth at first attempts to deflect him, but eventually admits her feelings; Carlos falls into a swoon, and Elisabeth fears he is dying. As he awakens he begins a final, passionate declaration, 'Que sous mes pieds' ('Sotto al mio pie''), but when he attempts to embrace his beloved, she recovers herself and angrily rejects him, telling him sarcastically that to claim her he must kill his father. Carlos rushes off in despair, just as Philip himself appears, angry that Elisabeth has been left alone. He orders her lady-in-waiting, the Countess of Aremberg, back to France; Elisabeth bids the Countess a tender farewell in the two-stanza, minor-major *romance*, 'O ma chère compagne' ('Non pianger, mia compagna'). Philip, left alone, gestures for Posa to remain with him.

1867 After a brief recitative, Posa begins the first movement of a duet by describing his soldierly life ('Pour mon pays') and narrating his journeys in war-torn Flanders ('O Roi! j'arrive de Flandre'). Philip stresses the need for political control, and sternly curbs Posa's idealism. The impasse produces a lyrical second movement, 'Un souffle ardent', in which the two men are placed in patterned opposition before joining voice in a final section. Posa throws himself at

Philip's feet: Philip forgives his rashness, but bids him beware the Inquisitor. The king then confides in Posa, beginning the closing cabaletta, 'Enfant! à mon coeur éperdu', with an admission of his troubled personal feelings.

1884 In this radical revision, virtually all trace of the conventional four-movement form disappears from the duet, being replaced by the kind of fluid dialogue we find in *Otello*. Posa's 'O Roi! j'arrive de Flandre' ('O signor, di Fiandra arrivo') is retained, but most of the remaining music is new. Particularly impressive is Philip's advice to beware the Inquisitor, in which solemn chords serve momentarily to halt the musical flow. Philip is more explicit about his fears, going so far as to mention Carlos and Elisabeth; but he closes the duet with yet another sinister reference to the power of the Inquisitor.

ACT 3 (*1867*)/2 (*1884*) Scene i   *The Queen's gardens*

1867 Festivities are in progress; Philip is to be crowned the next day. In a further essay in local colour, the offstage chorus sings 'Que de fleurs et que d'étoiles' to the accompaniment of castanets. Elisabeth appears with Eboli: the queen is already weary of the celebrations and changes masks with Eboli so that she can retire to seek religious consolation. When Elisabeth leaves, Eboli has a brief solo, 'Me voilà reine pour une nuit', which recalls the central section of the Veil Song. She writes a letter of assignation to Carlos, hoping to entice him.

The ensuing ballet, entitled 'La Pérégrina', tells of a fisherman who happens on a magic cave containing the most marvellous pearls in the ocean. He dances with the White Pearl; gradually the other pearls join in. Philip's page enters to the strains of a Spanish hymn played by the brass; he has come to find for his master the most beautiful pearl in the world. At the climax of the ballet, Eboli (posing as Elisabeth) appears as La Pérégrina: the page's search is at an end. Verdi's music for the ballet, some 15 minutes long, is the traditional mixture of orchestral sophistication and extreme musical simplicity.

1884 A short, understated prelude is based on the first phrase of Carlos's 'Je l'ai vue' ('Io la vidi'); it clearly belongs to Verdi's late manner, particularly in the overt use of thematic transformation and the ease with which it moves between distantly related keys.

190

Both Carlos enters, reading the letter of assignation; this briefly sets the scene for the ensuing ensemble, which follows the common Italian four-movement pattern, led off by a condensed series of contrasting lyrical episodes, each punctuated by some dramatic revelation. As Eboli appears, Carlos breaks into a passionate declaration of love, thinking she is Elisabeth. Eboli responds with matching phrases, but the lyrical development abruptly breaks down as she removes her mask. Eboli at first misconstrues Carlos's confusion, and attempts to reassure him: but she soon guesses the truth, and accuses him of loving the Queen. At this point Posa arrives, and a brief transitional passage leads to the second main movement, 'Redoubtez tout de ma furie!' ('Al mio furor sfuggite invano'), in which the baritone's and mezzo's agitated rhythms are set against the tenor's long, impassioned melody. A brief transition movement during which Carlos restrains Posa from killing Eboli leads to the final stretta, 'Malheur sur toi, fils adultère' ('Trema per te, falso figliuolo'), in which Eboli brings down furious curses on the man who has rejected her and threatens to denounce him. She rushes off, leaving Carlos and Posa; they act out a brief coda in which Carlos – after some hesitation – entrusts his friend with some secret papers. The scene concludes with a brash orchestral reprise of their earlier cabaletta, 'Dieu tu semas dans nos âmes' ('Dio, che nell'alma infondere').

ACT 3/2 Scene ii   *A large square in front of Valladolid Cathedral*
This central finale, the grand sonic and scenic climax of *Don Carlos*, is formally laid out along traditional Italian lines but, in response to the added resources of the Opéra, is on a scale Verdi had never before attempted. The opening chorus, 'Ce jour heureux' ('Spuntato ecco il dì'), is a kind of rondo: the main theme alternates with a funereal theme to which monks escort heretics to the stake, and with a more lyrical idea in which the monks promise salvation to those who repent. A solemn procession fills the stage, after which a herald announces Philip, who appears on the steps of the cathedral. He is confronted by six Flemish deputies, escorted by Carlos. They kneel before him and, with a solemn prayer for their country, 'Sire, la dernière heure' ('Sire, no, l'ora estrema'), lead off a grand concertato movement in

which all the principals join, Elisabeth, Carlos and Posa adding their pleas, while Philip and the monks stubbornly resist. A transitional movement begins as Carlos steps forward, asking to be sent to Flanders (to undergo some training for kingship as much as to remove himself from the presence of Elisabeth. When Philip refuses, wary of Carlos's sympathy for the protestant Flemish, Carlos threateningly draws his sword. No one dares intervene until Posa steps forward and demands Carlos's surrender. To a soft, veiled reprise of their friendship cabaletta, Carlos relinquishes his weapon, upon which Philip pronounces Posa promoted to a dukedom. The scene closes with a grand reprise of the opening choral sequence. As the heretics go to their death, a voice from heaven assures them of future bliss.

ACT 4 (*1867*)/3 (1884) Scene i *The king's study* The king, alone with his official papers, sings the famous 'Elle ne m'aime pas!' ('Ella giammai m'amò!'). As a complex psychological portrait, the aria has few rivals in Verdi. The king's mood swings from self-pity at his emotional isolation (an arioso accompanied by obsessive string figures and culminating in the passionate outburst of 'Elle ne m'aime pas!'), to a sombre meditation on his mortality (mock-medieval horns accompany his picture of the stone vault in which he will lie), to a recognition of his power (a triplet bass melody hinting at the musical grandeur of the preceding concertato finale). But the aria closes with a reprise of its opening outburst: Philip's tragedy, at this point in the drama, is primarily a personal one.

The subsequent duet with the old and blind Grand Inquisitor, 'Suis-je devant le Roi?' ('Sono io dinanzi al Re?'), continues the aria's relative formal freedom, its sense that the music reacts immediately and flexibly to the shifting emotions of the dialogue. The opening orchestral idea, with its concentration on low strings, ostinato rhythms and restricted pitches, sets the scene for this power struggle between two basses. Philip seems in command as he asks the Inquisitor how to deal with Carlos and his support for the religious reforms in Flanders; but, as the controlled opening gives way to freer declamation, the Inquisitor takes over, stating that Posa, with his liberal idealism, is the more serious threat and demanding that he be turned over to the Inquisition. Philip resists, but in an imposing declamatory climax the Inquisitor warns him that even kings can be brought before the tribunal. As the opening orchestral idea returns, Philip attempts to restore peace; but the Inquisitor is indifferent and leaves Philip in no doubt as to how the struggle will be resolved.

The *scène* and quartet that follows (much revised for the 1884 version) is more conventionally structured. To the kind of lyrically enriched recitative that was now the Verdian norm, Elisabeth rushes in to announce the theft of her jewel case. Philip produces it – Eboli had purloined it – and invites her to reveal its contents; when she refuses he breaks the lock and finds inside a picture of Carlos. In spite of her protestations, he accuses her of adultery; the Queen faints, and Philip summons Posa and Eboli, who arrive to precipitate the formal quartet, 'Maudit soit le soupçon infâme' ('Ah! sii maledetto, sospetto fatale'). The ensemble is at first dominated by Philip, whose opening statements – fragmentary expressions of remorse – gradually form into a lyrical melody that interweaves with Posa's decision to take action and Eboli's cries of remorse. But towards the end Elisabeth's sorrowful lament takes on increasing urgency and focus.

Philip and Posa leave. Originally the scene continued with a duet for Elisabeth and Eboli, but this was cut during rehearsals for the 1867 première, when the cut extended some way into Eboli's confession; however, Verdi recomposed and expanded this for the 1884 version, in which Eboli first admits her love for Carlos and then, to a bare, almost motif-less rhythmic idea in the strings, reveals that she has been the king's mistress. Elisabeth orders Eboli to quit the court, and then departs. Eboli's ensuing aria, 'O don fatal' ('O don fatale'), in which she laments her fatal beauty, is cast in a conventional minor-major form, with the major section (in which she bids farewell to the Queen) strongly reminiscent in its chromaticism and wide-spaced orchestral sonority of Verdi's last style. In a cabaletta-like coda, Eboli resolves to spend her final hours at court in an attempt to save Carlos.

ACT 4/3 Scene ii   *Carlos's prison*   A string introduction of unusual depth and density introduces Posa to the waiting Carlos. Posa bids farewell to his friend in a rather old-fashioned *romance*, 'C'est mon jour suprême' ('Per me giunto è il dì supremo'), and then explains that Carlos's secret papers have been discovered on him. A shot rings out; Posa falls mortally wounded. After telling Carlos that Elisabeth awaits him at the monastery of St Yuste, he delivers a second *romance*, 'Ah! je meurs' ('Io morrò'), happy that he can die for the sake of his dear friend. A duet for Philip and Carlos that followed this episode (cut before the 1867 première, though Verdi drew on its material for the 'Lacrymosa' of the Requiem) was replaced with a riot scene (subsequently pruned for the 1884 version) in which Eboli appears at the head of a group intent on liberating Carlos. Philip also appears, but the crowd is silenced by the entry of the Inquisitor, who orders all to their knees before the king.

ACT 5/4   *The monastery at St Yuste*   An impressive and extended orchestral prelude introduces Elisabeth at the tomb of Charles V. Her aria, 'Toi qui sus le néant' ('Tu, che le vanità'), is in French ternary form: the outer sections are a powerful invocation of the dead emperor, and their firm, periodic structure stabilizes the number, allowing for remarkable variety and musical contrast during the long central section in which the Queen's thoughts stray to memories of the past. Carlos appears for their final duet (from here to the end of the opera, Verdi made a number of important revisions in 1884). The set piece begins with the conventional series of contrasting sections, in the most prominent of which, 'J'avais fait un beau rêve' ('Sogno dorato io feci!'), Carlos announces that he has done with dreaming and will now try to save Flanders. The final movement, 'Au revoir dans un monde' ('Ma lassù ci vedremo'), a kind of ethereal cabaletta in which the couple bid each other a tender farewell, is similar to the closing duet of *Aida* in its restraint and delicate orchestral fabric. As they say 'Adieu! et pour toujours' for the last time, Philip bursts in accompanied by the Inquisitor and various officials. The king tries to deliver his son to the priests, but Carlos retreats towards the tomb of Charles V. The tomb opens and the old Monk appears, wearing the emperor's crown and mantle. He gathers Carlos to him and, with a few sententious words, draws him into the cloister.

*

Soon after the first Paris performances of *Don Carlos*, Verdi voiced his doubts about the Parisian tradition of grand opera. While he was always ready to praise the care with which productions were mounted – particularly in comparison with much of Italy, where he often judged standards to be unbearably low – he was also aware that the sheer size of the undertaking, the number of different demands that had to be catered for, could take their toll on a work's balance and coherence of effect. He might well have had *Don Carlos* in mind. As we have seen, the opera in rehearsal proved impracticably long; the subsequent cuts were made for practical rather than dramatic reasons, leaving the 1867 version with many inconsistencies and imbalances. Clearly some of the outstanding problems were put straight by the composer's revisions of the 1870s and 1880s; but even the final versions of the opera pose uncomfortable dramatic questions.

Possibly the most serious difficulty comes in the comparative weight assumed by various characters. Philip and Eboli are the most successful and well-rounded portraits, though arguably Elisabeth achieves her proper sense of importance by means of her magnificent fifth-act aria and duet. Posa's musical physiognomy is strangely old-fashioned: his music almost all dates from the earliest layers of the score, and even then recalls the Verdi of the early 1850s (or even 1840s). On the other hand, it can be argued that this sense of anachronism is in keeping with Posa's dramatic position – as a nostalgic look at youthful days of action within the context of sterner political realities. With Carlos, however, few would deny an unsolved problem: his musical portrait never seems to find a centre, a true nexus of expression such as each of the other principals eventually achieves.

It is perhaps an indication of our changing views and tastes that, in spite of these difficulties, *Don Carlos* has of late become one of the best-loved and most respected of Verdi's operas. The simple fact is, of course, that Verdi dedicated to the work some of his greatest dramatic music. One need think only of the magnificent series of confrontational duets that form such a great part of the drama. As has been noted briefly above, several of these break decisively with traditional models, forging for themselves a vital new relationship between musical and dramatic progress. It is for such moments that *Don Carlos* will be remembered and treasured, and they will surely continue to prove more powerful than any large-scale dramatic obstacles the work might present.

Aida

Opera in four acts set to a libretto by Antonio Ghislanzoni after a scenario by Auguste Mariette; first performed in Cairo, at the Opera House, on 24 December 1871.

The first cast included Eleonora Grossi (Amneris), Antonietta Anastasi-Pozzoni (Aida), Pietro Mongini (Radames) and Francesco Steller (Amonasro).

The King of Egypt	bass
Amneris *his daughter*	mezzo-soprano
Aida *an Ethiopian slave*	soprano
Radames *Captain of the Guards*	tenor
Ramfis *Chief Priest*	bass
Amonasro *King of Ethiopia, Aida's father*	baritone
The High Priestess	soprano
A Messenger	tenor

Priests, priestesses, ministers, captains, soldiers, functionaries, Ethiopian slaves and prisoners, Egyptian populace, etc.

Setting Memphis and Thebes, during the reign of the Pharaohs

During the late 1860s the search for suitable librettos began to cause Verdi increasing problems. One of his most active helpers was the French librettist and impresario, with whom Verdi had collaborated in the making of *Don Carlos*. Du Locle sent Verdi a stream of possible subjects covering a wide variety of genres: from comic plots that might have continued the manner of *Un ballo in maschera* to large-scale topics suitable for conversion into grand opera. But Verdi became more and more difficult to please, finding the comic subjects structurally or temperamentally unsuitable, while often complaining of the 'patchwork' quality of grand opera, its inherent lack of coherence. The breakthrough came in the early months of 1870, when Du Locle sent Verdi a scenario by the archaeologist and Egyptologist

Auguste Mariette, based on an invented story set in Egyptian antiquity. Verdi had the previous year refused to supply an inaugural hymn as part of the celebrations to open the Suez Canal; but he accepted this new Egyptian idea – which was to open the new Cairo Opera House – almost immediately, appointing as librettist Antonio Ghislanzoni, his collaborator in the revised *La forza del destino*. Work on the opera, whose scenario was adapted and enlarged by both Du Locle and Verdi, proceeded through 1870, Verdi as usual taking a considerable hand in the libretto's formation, even in minor details of line length and wording; the staging of the production was carried out in Paris under the eye of Mariette.

As the composer decided not to attend the Cairo première, he proceeded to complete the orchestration of his score in Italy; but by that stage it was clear that production of the opera would be delayed by the Franco-Prussian war, the siege of Paris having trapped the sets and costumes there. There was in addition a series of intense struggles over the première cast, in which as usual Verdi took a close interest. Eventually *Aida* was first performed in Cairo – with predictable success – in late 1871, directed by the famous double bass player Giovanni Bottesini. Verdi also devoted great attention to the Italian première at La Scala, making various slight changes to the score and minutely rehearsing a carefully chosen group of principals. This second performance, conduced by Franco Faccio, took place on 8 February 1872, and included Maria Waldmann (Amneris), Teresa Stolz (Aida), Giuseppe Fancelli (Radames) and Francesco Pandolfini (Amonasro). It was again hugely successful with the public, although some critics voiced reservations about passages they found conventional or old-fashioned. Verdi was reluctant to allow further performances in Italy without assurances of a sensitive staging, but by the mid-1870s the opera had entered the general repertory, where it has remained to the present day. Some time before the Milanese première, Verdi wrote a full-scale overture; but after hearing it rehearsed he decided to withdraw it and reinstate the prelude.

*

The prelude juxtaposes and combines two themes: the first, chromatic and presented on high strings, will be associated with Aida throughout the opera; the second, scalar idea, contrapuntally developed, will be associated with the priests.

ACT 1 Scene i *A hall in the King's palace in Memphis* To the accompaniment of a restrained development of motifs from the prelude, Ramfis and Radames are in conversation: Ramfis advises that the Ethiopian enemy is again on the attack, and that Isis has named the commander of the Egyptian troops. As Ramfis departs, Radames eagerly anticipates becoming that leader, and then muses on his beloved Aida in the *romanza* 'Celeste Aida', a ternary-form piece shot through with atmospheric instrumental effects. Radames is then joined by Amneris, who loves the young warrior, but whose sinuous string melody underlines her suspicions about the direction of his affections. Their agitated duet, 'Quale inchiesta!', is interrupted by the appearance of Aida (and her characteristic theme), and Radames's longing glances confirm Amneris's jealousy. The duet turns into a trio as Amneris relentlessly questions the confused lovers.

A series of fanfares heralds the King of Egypt, Ramfis and a large group of followers. A messenger announces that Amonasro, King of the Ethiopians, is leading an army against them; the King of Egypt reveals that Isis has named Radames as their commander. All join in the martial hymn, 'Su! del Nilo', Aida's syncopated line underlining her distress at the forthcoming battle. After a final unison cry of 'Ritorna vincitor!' ('Return victor!'), the crowd disperses, leaving Aida alone. Her long, multi-sectioned arioso, which begins with an anguished verbal echo of the chorus's 'Ritorna vincitor!', explores in depth her predicament: Amonasro is her father, but the victory of her family would see the defeat of her beloved Radames. The soliloquy ends with a delicate but intense prayer, 'Numi, pietà', in which she begs the gods to have pity on her suffering.

ACT 1 Scene ii *Inside the temple of Vulcan in Memphis* The scene is an old-fashioned tableau, so beloved of French grand opera. An opening chorus, 'Possente Fthà', has many gestures to local colour, notably in its use of the melodic diminished 3rd. There follows a priestesses' dance during which Radames is conducted to the altar.

In solemn tones, Ramfis bids Radames protect the homeland, and then leads off the concertato 'Nume, custode e vindice', which gradually gains in power, mingles with the opening strains of the scene, and culminates in a triumphant cry of 'Immenso Fthà!'

ACT 2 Scene i *A room in Amneris's apartments* A chorus of female slaves, singing of Radames's recent victories, is followed by a dance of Moorish slaves, Amneris punctuating the choral song with a languorous appeal for her warrior to return. Aida is seen approaching and Amneris dismisses her slaves, to begin one of the great confrontational duets of Verdi's later operas, a number that has echoes of the traditional four-movement form though with equally significant divergences. First comes a succession of contrasting episodes, 'Fu la sorte dell'armi', in which Amneris, with her characteristic sinuous chromaticism, attempts to trap Aida into admitting her love for Radames. Aida's confusion crystallizes into an anguished statement of her identifying theme, but Amneris continues the interrogation by announcing Radames's death, and then by contradicting the news. The intensity of Aida's reactions leaves no doubt of her feelings and, in an *adagio* second movement, 'Pietà ti prenda del mio dolore', she begs in vain for Amneris to show mercy. They are interrupted by fanfares, and an offstage chorus singing the Act 1 'Su! del Nilo' (Verdi revised this final section after the first performance in Cairo). Over the choral musical background, Amneris and Aida sing a cabaletta substitute, 'Alla pompa che s'appresta', Amneris's line matching the martial atmosphere of the chorus, Aida's minor-mode answer – with syncopated accompaniment – in sharp contrast. Amneris storms out, to leave Aida alone for a last, desperate reprise of 'Numi, pietà'.

ACT 2 Scene ii *One of the city gates of Thebes* In celebration of victory, the grand concertato finale – one of Verdi's most spacious – begins with a chorus, 'Gloria all' Egitto', which features interludes for a female group and for the priests, who have a version of their characteristic contrapuntal theme. The stage gradually fills to strains of the famous march for 'Egyptian' trumpets; then comes a ballet sequence, full of harmonic and instrumental local colour; then a reprise of 'Gloria all'Egitto' during which the victorious Radames finally appears. Amneris places a laurel wreath on Radames's head, and the King grants him any wish he may desire. Radames asks that the prisoners be brought forth and Aida sees among them Amonasro. She inadvertently reveals to all that he is her father, but Amonasro quickly stops her from disclosing his identity. The Ethiopian king now takes centre stage to lead off the central Andante, which begins with his account of the battle and then shades into the main lyrical passage, a prayer for clemency, 'Ma tu, Re, tu signore possente'. The prayer is taken up by Aida and the prisoners, is sharply rejected by the priests (who demand death for the defeated), and develops into a broad and lengthy tutti. The set piece over, Radames asks the Egyptian king for clemency to be shown to the prisoners; Ramfis objects, but Radames carries the day. In a final gesture the king gives him a last reward: Amneris's hand in marriage. The scene concludes with a reprise of 'Gloria all'Egitto', varied and expanded to allow the principals to express their reactions to the new situation.

ACT 3   *The banks of the Nile*   A single note, G, is sustained by a complex blend of orchestral sonorities to invoke moonlight on the banks of the Nile. An offstage chorus adds to the effect by chanting a hymn to Isis, 'O tu che sei d'Osiride'. Amneris and Ramfis disembark from a boat and enter the temple to pray on the eve of Amneris's marriage. Aida's theme emerges as she cautiously enters for a clandestine meeting with Radames. In a *romanza* that Verdi added to the opera only at the last minute, 'Oh, patria mia', she invokes her long-lost homeland, the restless accompaniment and harmonies combining with a formal layout of remarkable freedom, even for the later Verdi.

Amonasro now appears; the ensuing duet is best seen as the first half of a conventional four-movement structure. After a brief scena in which Amonasro shows that he knows of her love for Radames, the first movement, 'Rivedrai le foreste imbalsamate', is the usual juxtaposition of contrasting lyrical sections: Amonasro invokes their beautiful homeland and reminds Aida of the cruelty of their enemies, but when she refuses to ask Radames about the route his troops will take, and so help the Ethiopians ambush the Egyptians, he angrily reproaches her in 'Su, dunque, sorgete'. Aida is by now broken down, and in the *andante* second movement, 'Padre! ... a costoro', painfully accepts her duty to the homeland: her fragmented line is 'healed' by Amonasro, and finally flowers into a lyrical acceptance of her fate. As Amonasro hides, Radames appears and a second, more conventional four-movement duet ensues. In a hectic first movement, Radames assures Aida of his love but warns that he must again lead his troops in battle. The *andantino* second movement, 'Fuggiam gli ardori inospiti', sees Aida recall the musical idiom of 'Oh, patria mia' in an effort to persuade Radames to run away with her. A brief transition movement, in which Aida accuses the still-reluctant Radames of not loving her, leads to the duet cabaletta, 'Si: fuggiam da queste mura', in which Radames emphatically agrees to join her in flight. The cabaletta ceases abruptly before its final cadences as Aida asks Radames of the route his army will take. As soon as Radames discloses the information, Amonasro emerges from the shadows, triumphantly announcing that his troops will be there to meet the Egyptians. In a closing terzetto, 'Tu! ... Amonasro!', Radames rails at his lost honour. Aida and Amonasro try to comfort him, but they delay too long: Amneris and Ramfis discover them; Amonasro tries to kill Amneris but is prevented by Radames; and, as father and daughter rush off, Radames gives himself up to justice at the hands of the priests.

ACT 4 Scene i *A hall in the King's palace* After an orchestral prelude based on the main theme of the terzetto in Act 1 scene i, Amneris sings an extended arioso in which she determines to save Radames. He is led on by the guards, and yet another multi-section duet ensues. In the first movement, 'Già i sacerdoti adunansi'. Amneris begs Radames to defend himself and Radames refuses, having lost all interest in life. The central lyrical movement, 'Ah! tu dei vivere', allows Amneris to declare her love, but Radames still wishes only for death. The main melody of the opening movement returns in the third as Amneris reveals that Aida, whom Radames believed dead along with Amonasro, is still alive. This revelation eventually precipitates a brief cabaletta, 'Chi ti salva', in which Amneris explodes with renewed jealousy and Radames rejoices that he can now die to protect his beloved.

Radames is led back to the dungeon, and a restrained version of the priests' theme, punctuated by anguished cries from Amneris, sounds as the priests and Ramfis follow him in. They chant a solemn prayer, 'Spirto del Nume', before beginning Radames's trial. Radames is accused by Ramfis three times: each time he refuses to answer, the priests brand him traitor ('Traditor!') and Amneris begs the gods for mercy. The priests then pronounce the horrible sentence: he will be entombed alive below the altar of the god he has outraged. In an unrestrained arioso, Amneris begs for mercy; but the priests are inflexible. As they depart, she is left to hurl after them a bitter curse, 'Empia razza! Anatema su voi!'

ACT 4 Scene ii   *The scene is on two levels: the upper represents the interior of the temple of Vulcan, gleaming with gold and light; the lower is a vault*   Priests close the stone over Radames's head as he sings his opening recitative, full of thoughts of Aida. But he hears a groan and quickly finds his beloved: she has stolen into the vault to die in his arms. Their duet has none of the usual contrasting movements, but is rather a sustained piece of delicate lyricism with three main ideas. First comes Radames's 'Morir! sì pura e bella!', in which he laments her death; Aida counters with 'Vedi? . . . di morte l'angelo', whose scoring and vocal style suggest that the heroine is already speeding to a celestial haven. And finally, with the background addition of chanting from above, comes the most substantial lyrical idea, 'O terra addio', whose extreme simplicity of formal outline is matched, perhaps permitted, by the unusually angular melodic arch. In the final moments, with the lovers singing 'O terra addio' in unison, Amneris kneels above the vault and implores peace for the soul that lies beneath.

*

Although *Aida* is still one of Verdi's most popular operas, its reputation has perhaps declined slightly of late, overtaken for the first time by works such as *Don Carlos* and *Simon Boccanegra*. The reasons for this reverse are doubtless complex, but the comparative conservatism of *Aida* must surely have played a part. If any rough division of Verdi's mature output were made according to 'experimental' versus 'conservative' works (with, say, *Rigoletto, La traviata* and *La forza del destino* in the first category, and *Il trovatore* and *Un ballo in maschera* in the second), then *Aida* would undoubtedly figure with the latter group. In formal terms it concentrates on the conventional set pieces of grand opera: the grand ceremonial scene and – most of all – the large-scale multi-sectional duet, of which there are several. True, there is a considerable array of variants within the recurring duet scheme, but both contemporary critics and more recent commentators have nevertheless seen certain elements of these formal structures as uncomfortable throwbacks to an earlier aesthetic. The level of musical characterization is also indicative of this conservative stance. In common with the characters of *Trovatore* and *Ballo*, the principal roles in *Aida* – with the partial exception of Amneris – hardly develop during the opera, tending to remain within their conventional vocal personalities as the plot moves their emotions hither and thither.

But to regard the restricted focus of *Aida* purely in these terms is to take a one-sided view of Verdi's capacities as a musical dramatist, and to emphasize unduly the radical aspect of his personality. Indeed, *Aida* 's greatest artistic successes are born of this 'conservatism': in magnificently controlled ceremonial scenes such as Act 2 scene ii – in which a kind of flexible variation technique allows episodes such as the opening chorus to reappear as the culmination of the scene; or in the telling effects gained when various multi-movement duets dovetail into each other, as in the sequence that closes Act 3.

There is, moreover, one important aspect in which *Aida* remains the most radical and 'modern' of Verdi's scores: its use of local colour. *Aida*, constantly alluding to its ambience in harmony and instrumentation, is the one Verdi opera that could not conceivably be transported to another geographical location. In this respect it was an important indication of the influence local colour would come to have over *fin-de-siècle* opera, and an object lesson on the delicacy and control with which this colour could be applied to the standard forms and expressive conventions of Italian opera.

Otello
('Othello')

Dramma lirico in four acts set to a libretto by Arrigo Boito after William Shakespeare's play *Othello, or The Moor of Venice*; first performed in Milan, at the Teatro alla Scala, on 5 February 1887.

The première, conducted by Franco Faccio, featured Francesco Tamagno (Otello), Victor Maurel (Iago) and Romilda Pantaleoni (Desdemona).

Otello *a Moor, general of the Venetian army*	tenor
Iago *an ensign*	baritone
Cassio *a platoon leader*	tenor
Roderigo *a Venetian gentleman*	tenor
Lodovico *an ambassador of the Venetian Republic*	bass
Montano *Otello's predecessor as Governor of Cyprus*	bass
A Herald	bass
Desdemona *Otello's wife*	soprano
Emilia *Iago's wife*	mezzo-soprano

Soldiers and sailors of the Venetian Republic, Venetian ladies and gentlemen, Cypriot populace of both sexes, Greek, Dalmatian and Albanian men-at-arms, island children, an innkeeper, four servants at the inn, common sailors

Setting A maritime city on the island of Cyprus, at the end of the 15th century

As the 1870s progressed, Verdi seemed increasingly isolated from current trends in Italian music, in particular by the tendency of both public and composers to look outside Italy (to France and, later, even more to Germany) for new ideas and aesthetic attitudes. It is against this background that we should examine his reluctance to write new works after the Requiem of 1874: Verdi was a composer who, after being at the forefront of Italian musical taste for two decades, suddenly found himself accused of being distinctly old-fashioned, out of touch with the times; and indeed he probably felt so too. Those who sought to lure him out of self-imposed retirement, among whom the prime mover was the young director of the Ricordi publishing house, Giulio Ricordi, had to tread carefully. Ricordi eventually teamed up with Arrigo Boito, the librettist and composer, who in the 1860s had been one of the most visible of the Italian avant garde, but whose respect for the old maestro was growing with the years. In June 1879 Ricordi and Boito mentioned to Verdi the possibility of his composing a version of Shakespeare's *Othello*; surely a canny choice given Verdi's lifelong veneration for the English playwright and his attempts after *Macbeth* to tackle further Shakespearean topics (notably *King Lear*). Verdi showed cautious enthusiasm for the new project, and by the end of the year Boito had produced a draft libretto, one full of ingenious new rhythmic devices but with an extremely firm dramatic thread.

Although Verdi eventually agreed – with a characteristic show of reluctance – to collaborate with Boito on *Otello*, the project was long in the making. First came two other tasks, the revisions to *Simon Boccanegra* (1881, effected with Boito's help) and to *Don Carlos* (1884), both of which can be seen in retrospect as trial runs for the new type of opera Verdi felt he must create in the changed Italian artistic climate. Verdi also bombarded Boito with alterations to the libretto draft of *Otello*, especially to the Act 3 finale, which he felt must furnish occasion for a grand concertato finale in the traditional manner. The opera was then composed in a series of intensive bursts, the comparative speed suggesting that Verdi had previously sketched the music rather thoroughly. The cast was carefully selected and intensively coached by Verdi himself, and the première was a predictable, indeed a well-nigh inevitable success, although some critics of course lamented the sophistication and lack of immediacy they found in Verdi's new manner. The opera was soon given in the major European capitals and became an important element of the operatic repertory. Though it has never reached the level of popularity of the middle-period masterpieces – something hardly surprising considering the severe vocal and orchestral demands made by the score – *Otello* remains one of the most universally respected of Verdi's operas, often admired even by those who find almost all his earlier works unappealing.

For the Paris première at the Théâtre de l'Opéra in 1894 Verdi added a ballet score to the third act and also made some significant revisions to the same act's concertato finale, reducing the musical detail in an effort to bring out the embedded conversations. These revisions were not incorporated into the Italian version and are rarely heard today.

*

ACT 1 *Outside the castle* A sudden burst of orchestral dissonance begins the opera with an immediacy Verdi had never before attempted: a clear sign that this work will engage a more realistic notion of musical drama. A violent storm is raging, and the onlookers from the shore, among them Iago, Cassio and Montano, comment on the fortunes of their leader Otello's ship. The crowd's reaction momentarily coalesces into 'Dio, fulgor della bufera', a desperate prayer to save the ship, but then all is again confusion until, to cries of 'È salvo!', Otello safely arrives. He greets his followers with a ringing salute, 'Esultate!', proudly announcing that the Turks have been beaten. The chorus then closes this opening 'storm' scene with a triumphant victory chorus, 'Vittoria! Sterminio!'

As the crowd goes about its work, Iago and Roderigo, in the inn, come to the fore. In a texture alternating simple recitative with arioso, the venomous Iago assures his friend that Desdemona will soon tire of her new husband, Otello, and thus become available to the besotted Roderigo. Iago then reveals his hatred for Cassio, whom he thinks has unjustly overtaken him in rank. Their conversation is followed by the fireside chorus 'Fuoco di gioia!', a series of contrasting sections tied together by brilliant orchestral effects imitating the crackling flames. As the fire dies down, Iago encourages Cassio to drink, eventually breaking into the brindisi 'Inaffia l'ugola', a three-stanza song with choral refrain, by the end of which Cassio is far the worse for wine. Roderigo provokes him to a fight, which is interrupted by Montano, who himself becomes embroiled with Cassio. Iago skilfully stage-manages the confusion by ordering Roderigo to call the alarm; soon there is general panic. At the height of the disturbance, Otello enters, sword in hand, and with an imperious gesture, 'Abbasso le spade!' ('Lower your swords!'), restores calm. His inquiry finds Cassio guilty and he dismisses him from service (to a stifled cry of triumph from Iago). Desdemona has by now appeared, and Otello dismisses the crowd, to be left alone with his new bride.

The ensuing love duet, although it bears a certain distant relationship to earlier 19th-century practices, is really *sui generis*, the form's tendency towards a series of short, contrasting sections all but obliterating vestiges of any larger, multi-movement structure. After a brief orchestral transition as the stage clears, a choir of solo cellos heralds the opening exchange, 'Già nella notte densa'; Otello evokes the nocturnal ambience before Desdemona turns to the past, and in the largest lyrical section, 'Quando narravi l'esule tua vita', recalls with Otello the manner in which his narrations of past exploits first won her over. At the close of this episode the lovers sing a patterned alternation, 'E tu m'amavi per le mie sventure', a paraphrase of Shakespeare's 'She lov'd me for the dangers I had passed, And I lov'd her that she did pity them'. In a Poco più mosso, Otello wishes for death at this moment of ecstasy, but soon their mutual feelings spread forth into a final gesture of intimacy: a thrice-repeated kiss ('Un bacio . . . ancora un bacio') whose intensity is reflected in the highly decorated violin melody that underpins the stage action. With a final gesture towards the night, 'Vien . . . Venere splende', Otello leads Desdemona back into the castle. The solo cellos return to effect a tender close.

ACT 2   *A room on the ground floor of the castle*   After an orchestral introduction suggesting Iago's busy energy, the villain is revealed, assuring Cassio that with help from Desdemona he will regain his place in Otello's estimation. Iago sends Cassio off to attend her and comes forward to deliver his famous soliloquy, 'Credo in un Dio crudel', a kind of evil Credo in which he plays to the hilt his demonic character. As befits Iago's slippery energy, this dynamic Credo hovers between arioso and aria, its devious harmonic and formal twists continuing to the last. Iago now notices Desdemona and Emilia in the garden and offers a *sotto voce* commentary as

Cassio approaches them with his suit. Then, seeing Otello approach, he positions himself for the crucial confrontation.

The Otello-Iago duet continues to the end of the act, although interrupted by a series of set pieces and dialogues that become increasingly caught up in the central action. The first phase of the duet, and its most fragmentary, involves the initial testing of Otello: Iago's teasing questions and repetitions, Otello's angry confusion, and then Iago's first mention of 'jealousy', to a sliding chromatic figure of great harmonic audacity. And the first set-piece interruption is a jarring one: Desdemona is seen again in the garden, and distant voices serenade her in a simple chorus, 'Dove guardi splendono raggi', a piece whose musical atmosphere recalls the choral evocations of Act 1 in both style and tonality. As the chorus ends, Desdemona approaches Otello to intercede on Cassio's behalf. But Otello's response is disturbed: so much so that Desdemona gently asks for pardon in a second set piece, the quartet 'Dammi la dolce e lieta parola', in which Otello bemoans his supposed loss while Iago extracts from Emilia a handkerchief of Desdemona's that has been cast aside in the preceding dialogue. As the quartet comes to a close, Otello dismisses Desdemona and Emilia, and is again left alone with Iago. This time the emotional temperature is near boiling point, and a few comments from Iago are enough to precipitate the aria 'Ora e per sempre addio', in which Otello bids farewell to his past life in a closed form that, appropriately given the dramatic situation, has strong hints of the younger Verdi's lyrical style. The aria disintegrates into furious orchestral figures as Otello demands proof of his wife's infidelity, eventually grabbing Iago by the throat and hurling him to the ground. Iago now takes over and gradually leads the atmosphere into those calmer waters where he can begin his story, 'Era la notte', in which – to a musical structure as complex and surprising as Otello's was simple and direct – he offers as 'proof' words he has overheard Cassio mumble in his sleep. From there to the end of the act, all is gathering dramatic energy. Iago produces Desdemona's handkerchief – which he claims to have seen in Cassio's hands – as a final, visible proof, and Otello unleashes the cabaletta, 'Sì, pel ciel', in which he and then Iago swear to exact a terrible vengeance.

ACT 3 *The great hall of the castle* An orchestral introduction derived from Iago's Act 2 description of jealousy shows that his machinations are still working. A herald announces the imminent arrival of Venetian ambassadors and Iago directs Otello to conceal himself and await the arrival of Cassio and further 'proof'. As Iago retires, Desdemona appears for the second of her extended duets with Otello; like the first, it is loosely structured around contrasting sections, with a prominent thematic reminiscence to aid the sense of closure. First comes 'Dio ti giocondi, o sposo', in which the semblance of lyrical normality (a patterned alternation of the voices, and periodic phrasing) soon gives way to agitated, fragmentary music as Desdemona mentions the plight of Cassio. Otello describes with repressed intensity the magical nature of the handkerchief Desdemona has mislaid, his anger rising further as she again attempts to deflect him into talk of Cassio. Finally he hurls out a brutal accusation of infidelity. Desdemona is crushed and at first can only murmur confusedly; but then, with 'io prego il cielo per te', her melody flows into the lyrical centre of the duet as she prays for Otello and bids him look at the first tears she has shed through grief. Otello at first seems calmed by this outburst, but soon his accusations return with added fury. As a cruel parting gesture, he recalls the calmer opening music of the duet, only to break it off with a gross insult and push Desdemona from the room.

Otello returns to centre stage for his most extended solo of the opera, the self-pitying soliloquy 'Dio! mi potevi scagliar', which begins in barely coherent fragments, rises gradually to a controlled lyricism, and again collapses, this time into furious invective. Iago appears and quickly takes charge, leading Otello aside where he can observe and listen to Cassio talking of Desdemona, and then involving Cassio in discussion of his dalliance with the courtesan Bianca. The terzetto 'Essa t'avvince coi vaghi rai', set in the form of a scherzo and trio, skilfully counterposes Iago's and Cassio's comic exchange with Otello's anguished commentary. Cassio even produces Desdemona's handkerchief (hidden in his lodgings by Iago), and Iago's elaborate description of this item forms a hectic stretta to the terzetto.

Offstage trumpets announce the arrival of the Venetian ambassadors. As the ceremonial sounds approach, Otello hurriedly discusses with Iago the method of Desdemona's death, which they agree should be strangulation in her bed. As Iago slips off to fetch Desdemona the dignitaries appear, welcomed by a choral salute. Lodovico gives Otello a letter from the Doge, but is disturbed by Otello's violent interruptions to his ensuing conversation with Desdemona, especially to her wish that Cassio be reinstated. Otello reports that the letter calls him back to Venice, with Cassio left in his place. During this speech, Otello directs a series of angry asides to Desdemona and at its close seizes his wife with such violence that she falls to the ground. The general amazement precipitates the Largo concertato, 'A terra! ... sì ... nel livido fango', led off by an unusually long and thematically developed solo from Desdemona, much of it later repeated by the ensemble. As the Largo unfolds, Iago works furiously in the musical background, assuring Otello that he will deal with Cassio and delegating Roderigo for the task. As the movement comes to a close, Otello wildly dismisses everyone, unleashing on Desdemona a final, terrible curse. Left alone with Iago, he can only mutter incoherently before fainting. Iago gestures triumphantly at the body and, with offstage voices still hailing Otello as the 'Lion of Venice', brings down the curtain with a derisive shout of 'Ecco il Leone!' ('Here is the Lion!').

ACT 4 *Desdemona's bedroom* A mournful english horn solo with fragmentary phrases sets the tone of this final act. Desdemona discusses with Emilia the present state of her husband and then, with presentiments of death upon her, sings the famous Willow Song, 'Piangea cantando', whose three stanzas with refrain poignantly tell of a young girl abandoned by her lover. After a final, heartfelt farewell to Emilia, Desdemona kneels to offer an 'Ave Maria', softly intoned over a gentle string accompaniment before flowering into 'Prega per chi adorando', Desdemona's personal entreaty for divine assistance. Accompanied by high strings of the utmost delicacy, Desdemona settles in her bed.

A mysterious, double bass solo introduces Otello to the bedchamber. Miming to an instrumental recitative punctuated by motivic fragments, he lays down his sword, puts out the torch that illuminates the room, approaches the bed and, to a repetition of the 'bacio' music from the end of Act 1, kisses the sleeping Desdemona. On the third kiss she awakens, so beginning the final and in many ways the freest of the Otello-Desdemona duets, a confrontation that even dispenses with the clear sectional form of earlier examples, reflecting through the proliferation and intensification of motivic repetitions an inexorable progress towards Desdemona's death. At the brutal climax of the scene, deaf to Desdemona's protestations of innocence and to her final pleas, Otello suffocates his wife with a terrible cry of 'È tardi!' ('It is too late!'). Only then does the orchestral surge finally flow back and attain some stasis. To a succession of weighty chords, Otello admits Emilia, who tells him that Cassio has killed Roderigo and has himself survived. She discovers the dying Desdemona, who with her final gasps desperately attempts to protect Otello. But Emilia guesses the truth and raises the alarm. Soon the room is filled with Lodovico, Cassio, Iago and armed men. Again the free, arioso musical texture takes over as Iago's plot is unravelled, first by Emilia's admission that Iago had obtained the handkerchief from her, then by the appearance of Lodovico, who reports that the dying Roderigo revealed his part in the conspiracy. Otello, finally understanding his tragic error, grabs his sword and, to slow, solemn chords, begins his final oration, 'Niun mi tema'. He reflects on his past glory, apostrophizes Desdemona in an unaccompanied passage that briefly flowers into lyricism and then, to general horror, stabs himself. His dying words as he drags himself towards Desdemona's body call forth yet another repetition of the 'bacio' music from Act 1.

*

The chronological position of *Otello* in Verdi's long list of tragic operas – the last work, separated from all the others by a considerable time gap – has inevitably made it seem a special case; indeed, for many earlier in the century, perhaps even for some today, it is his only serious opera to merit sustained critical attention. Recent critics have sometimes reacted against this by stressing the many traditional aspects of the score: its reliance, especially in Act 1, on 'characteristic' numbers such as the storm scene, victory chorus and brindisi; the clear remnants of traditional forms in the 'cabaletta substitutes' such as 'Sì, pel ciel'; and of course its most unequivocal gesture to traditional form, the great concertato finale that closes Act 3. Some have gone even further, and suggested for example that passages such as the Act 1 love duet should be regarded as further manipulations of the standard four-movement duet, and that there is in effect an unbroken tradition with Verdi's earlier works.

This last position may swing too far towards the claims of tradition. It is more profitable to regard *Otello* as an opera that attempts a break with the past in an effort to produce a new, more modern conception of musical drama. There may well be gestures towards the traditional, normative structures of earlier in the century – it would be difficult to imagine how any opera could completely avoid them. But for the most part the opera strives for a different, more fluid type of musical drama: one that is closer to prose drama in its willingness to admit a swift succession of emotional attitudes during a series of dramatic confrontations. Of course, no value judgments should be attached to this greater fluidity: musical drama is endlessly protean in the manner and the forms in which it may be expressed, and there is nothing intrinsically superior in a type of opera that approaches the rhythms of the spoken theatre. We should, however, preserve a sense of distance between *Otello* and Verdi's earlier operas, a fact that renders even more remarkable Verdi's creative energy and capacity for self-renewal during the last years of his life.

Falstaff

Commedia lirica in three acts set to a libretto by Arrigo Boito after William Shakespeare's plays *The Merry Wives of Windsor* and *King Henry IV*; first performed in Milan, at the Teatro alla Scala, on 9 February 1893.

At the première, conducted by Edoardo Mascheroni, the cast included Victor Maurel (Falstaff), Antonio Pini-Corsi (Ford), Edoardo Garbin (Fenton), Adelina Stehle (Nannetta) and Giuseppina Pasqua (Mistress Quickly).

Sir John Falstaff	baritone
Fenton	tenor
Dr Caius	tenor
Bardolfo [Bardolph] *follower of Falstaff*	tenor
Pistola [Pistol] *follower of Falstaff*	bass
Mrs Alice Ford	soprano
Ford *Alice's husband*	baritone
Nannetta *their daughter*	soprano
Mistress Quickly	mezzo-soprano
Mrs Meg Page	mezzo-soprano
Mine Host at the Garter	silent
Robin *Falstaff's page*	silent
Ford's Page	silent

Bourgeoisie and populace, Ford's servants, masquerade of imps, fairies, witches etc.

Setting Windsor, during the reign of Henry IV of England

Verdi, who by the time he wrote his last operas had become a national monument, talked intermittently of writing a comic opera during the latter part of his career, but never found a libretto to his taste until, some two years after the success of *Otello* in 1887, his librettist for that opera, Arrigo Boito, suggested a work largely based on Shakespeare's *The Merry Wives of Windsor*. Verdi was immediately enthusiastic about the draft scenario Boito concocted, made relatively few large structural suggestions, and by August 1889 even announced that he was writing a fugue (quite possibly the comic fugue that ends the opera). Composer and librettist worked closely together during the winter of 1889–90, and by the spring of 1890 the libretto was complete.

The composing of the opera took a considerable time, or rather was carried out in short bursts of activity interspersed with long fallow periods. Act 1 was completed – at least in short score – shortly after the libretto was finished, but then Verdi fell into a depression, the deaths of various close friends making him fear he would not live to finish the project. However, the remaining two acts were gradually completed and the remaining two acts were only gradually completed. It seems that, unusually for Verdi, certain scenes were finished out of chronological order (perhaps an indication of the relative independence of individual scenes). By September 1891 the opera was largely complete in short score, and a year later Verdi had finished the orchestration. The première at La Scala, which took place almost to the day six years after that of *Otello*. It was, perhaps inevitably at this stage of Verdi's career, a huge triumph, and was soon seen in the major international opera houses. Verdi made various minor changes to the score (notably recomposing and shortening the final minutes of Act 3 scene i) during these early revivals. *Falstaff* has always retained its place in the international repertory, though it is far less frequently heard than many of the middle-period works.

*

ACT 1 Scene i *Inside the Garter Inn* An offbeat C major chord and descending arpeggio set in immediate motion a scene (indeed an opera) that is remarkable above all for its sense of rapid change and relentless forward movement. Falstaff, who is busy sealing two letters as the curtain rises, is upbraided by Dr Caius, who accuses him of causing drunken confusion in Caius's house. Falstaff calmly accepts the charge, at which Caius accuses Pistol and Bardolph of getting him drunk and stealing his money. Pistol challenges the doctor to a mock duel and exchanges a furious round of insults with him. But Caius has had enough, and storms out after making a solemn promise never to get drunk with such scoundrels again. This hectic first episode is dominated by two main themes: the arpeggiated idea that opened the opera and a contrasting second theme of more regular tread, appearing as Falstaff replies to Caius's first accusation. The two themes are played out in an overtly developmental manner, with various comic allusions to sonata form, not least in the ineptly contrapuntal 'Amen' intoned by Pistol and Bardolph as Caius leaves and the 'sonata' comes to a close.

After some vain searching for funds, Falstaff lambasts his companions before celebrating his enormous belly in a suitably grandiose climax. Then, in a relatively stable musical episode, the central thread of the drama is first put forth: Falstaff reveals that he has amorous designs on both Alice Ford and Meg Page, the wives of rich townsfolk. But Pistol and Bardolph refuse to deliver his love letters, saying it is beneath their 'honour' to do so. Falstaff sends off his page with the letters and then, in the famous 'Onore' monologue, excoriates the traitors and their highflown ideals. The solo is typical of the opera as a whole, rapidly shifting in mood, full of ironic references, a veritable index of startling orchestral combinations and textures. As C major makes a late, triumphant return, Falstaff takes up a broom and drives his followers from the room.

ACT 1 Scene ii *The garden outside Ford's house* A scherzo-like introduction leads in Meg and Mistress Quickly, who meet Alice and Nannetta on the threshold of Alice's house. Meg and Alice discover that Falstaff has sent them identical letters, extracts from which they quote first to the mournful accompaniment of an english horn, later to a passionately lyrical phrase, undermined at the final cadence by mocking vocal trills. In an elaborate unaccompanied quartet, they pour scorn on the amorous knight and vow to revenge themselves on him. From the other side of the stage appears a male quintet (Fenton, Caius, Bardolph, Pistol and Ford) who, unaware of the ladies, superimpose their own ensemble. As the ladies fade into the background, Bardolph and Pistol warn Ford of Falstaff's designs; Ford vows to keep a close watch. The ladies return and the two groups, at the sight of each other, disperse, leaving Fenton and Nannetta together for the first of their brief love duets, 'Labbra di foco'. One of Boito's early ideas for the drama was to present the young lovers 'as one sprinkles sugar on a tart, to sprinkle the whole comedy with [their] love', and Verdi responded by weaving round them a musical world quite separate from the main body of the score: relaxed and lyrical, shot through with delicate chromaticism and soft orchestral textures. But the spell is soon broken: the ladies return and resolve to send Quickly to Falstaff as their go-between. Nannetta and Fenton snatch a further few moments; then the men reappear, Ford announcing that he will visit Falstaff in disguise to ascertain his intentions. The finale of the scene involves a masterly superimposition of the women's and men's ensembles. The ladies have the last word: a triumphantly derisive reprise of Falstaff's most passionate epistolary style.

ACT 2 Scene i   *The Garter Inn*   The opening of the act is extraordinary – even in the context of *Falstaff* – for the extravagant manner in which musical ideas match verbal tags: first as Pistol and Bardolph make elaborate, chest-beating penance before Falstaff; then as Mistress Quickly introduces herself with a low 'Reverenza!'; then as she expresses the amorous states of Alice and Meg with the phrase 'Povera donna!'; and finally as she makes an appointment for Falstaff with the former, 'dalle due alle tre' ('between two and three'). Quickly leaves, and Falstaff has time for a gleeful episode of self-congratulation, 'Va, vecchio John', before 'Mastro Fontana' (Ford in disguise) is shown in. In the ensuing duet, Fontana offers Falstaff money to seduce one Alice Ford (who will thus be made easier for Fontana to conquer); and Falstaff gleefully agrees, saying that he has already arranged an appointment 'between two and three'. The passage carries vague echoes of earlier 19th-century formal practice – perhaps particularly in the cabaletta-like close – but is more usefully seen as a kind of musical prose, in constant flux as the moods of the principals swing to and fro. Highlights include the magnificent orchestral depiction of the money Ford offers Falstaff; Ford's passionate declaration of his feelings for Alice (a hint of the deeply serious tone that will soon break through); and Falstaff's rousing conclusion in 'Te lo cornifico' ('I'll cuckold him for you'). As the knight goes off to pretty himself, Ford is left alone to brood on what he has heard (the impassioned arioso 'È sogno?'). For the first and only time, the opera swings for an extended period into the language of serious opera: to horn-calls (a pun on cuckoldry) and with tortured fragments of the preceding duet (in particular 'dalle due alle tre'), Ford contemplates what he believes is his wife's deception. However, no sooner has Verdi sealed the monologue with a stunning orchestral climax than there is yet another stylistic volte-face: to a delicate, trilling violin melody, Falstaff appears, tricked out in his finest clothes; the two men show exaggerated politeness before leaving the scene together to an orchestral reprise of 'Va, vecchio John'. Our knight, the orchestra seems to tell us, is winning the day.

ACT 2 Scene ii   *A room in Ford's house*   A bustling string introduction ushers in Alice and Meg. They are soon joined by Quickly, who gives a detailed narrative of her interview with Falstaff, replete with mocking repetitions of 'dalle due alle tre'. Realizing that the hour of assignation is almost upon them, the women hurry about their preparations, ushering in a large laundry basket; but the busy mood is interrupted by Nannetta, who tearfully reveals that Ford has ordered her to marry old Dr Caius. Alice will have none of this, and assures Nannetta of her support. Preparations then continue, with Alice directing operations and briefly coming to the fore with 'Gaie comari di Windsor!', one of the few, brief moments (at least before the final scene) in which Verdi even hints at a conventional solo aria. Alice then settles down to strum her lute, and is soon joined by Falstaff, who offers elaborate courtship with an ornamented song of Beckmesser-like awkwardness before celebrating his younger, nimbler self in the delightful vignette, 'Quand'ero paggio del Duca di Norfolk'.

However, just as the courtship reaches an intimate stage, Quickly rushes in to announce the imminent arrival of Meg Page. The music dives into a furious Allegro agitato, so beginning the first movement of a conventionally structured but highly complex concertato finale. This first section is in a near-constant state of manic energy: Falstaff hides behind a screen as Meg enters to announce the arrival of an insanely jealous Ford; Ford appears at the head of a band of followers, searches the laundry basket, then rushes off to seek his wife's lover elsewhere; Falstaff is then wedged painfully into the basket and covered with dirty clothes. A brief moment of calm ensues as Nannetta and Fenton meet and slip behind the screen for a few moments together, but very soon the energy is again released as the men reappear to continue their search. The music grinds to a halt as a loud kiss is heard behind the screen: the men are sure they have trapped their quarry, and the realization precipitates the second movement of the concertato, the Andante 'Se t'agguanto!'. In the traditional way, this movement forms a still centre during which all can reflect on their contrasting positions: the men cautiously prepare to pounce; the women vow to keep the game alive; Falstaff emits muffled cries from his suffocating confinement; and Nannetta and Fenton, oblivious to all, rise above the ensemble in lyrically expansive phrases. Eventually the spell is broken. The men overturn the screen, only to find Nannetta and Fenton, the latter angrily rebuked by Ford. But Bardolph seems to see Falstaff outside, and the men rush off again, allowing the women to summon their pages who – with a huge effort – hoist the basket up to the window. The men return just in time to see Falstaff tipped into the river below, and the act closes with a riotous fanfare of triumph.

ACT 3 Scene i *Outside the Garter Inn* As Boito remarked in a letter to Verdi, the problem in finding dramatic form for comic subjects was one of predictability: how to convince the audience that they should stay for the third act when the unravelling of the plot is already clear. In the case of *Falstaff* this problem is acute, as the protagonist's most clamorous punishment has already been inflicted by the close of Act 2. The startlingly original solution Boito and Verdi chose to this problem will be revealed in the second half of this act: but perhaps this first scene suffers slightly, the tempo of the opera winding down, its direction wavering. Falstaff's opening monologue is certainly the most fragmented passage in the opera, occasional reminiscences jostling with a series of violent changes as the knight bemoans his disgrace, calls for wine, and finally revives as the liquor tingles through his body to the accompaniment of a magnificent orchestral trill. The ensuing duet with Quickly repeats some of the motifs of their earlier encounter as Falstaff is again convinced, at first with some difficulty, of Alice's affection. A new assignation is made: Falstaff is to await his intended paramour at midnight under Herne's Oak in the Royal Park, disguised as the Black Huntsman. Quickly paints an evocative picture of the supernatural ambience and, as she leads Falstaff into the inn, the evocation is taken up by Alice, who has been observing the scene with Ford, Meg, Nannetta, Fenton and Caius. The scene then plays itself out in a relaxed, French-influenced musical setting, as the plotters decide on their disguises. Quickly overhears Ford and Caius, who are planning Caius's marriage to Nannetta that very night, and privately vows to stop them.

ACT 3 Scene ii *Windsor forest* Distant horn-calls introduce Fenton, whose extended solo immediately marks the departure taken in this final scene, which for the most part is structured in discrete units, without the rapid changes that characterize the remainder of the opera. And the delicate, nocturnal ambience serves further to make this final scene self-contained, separate in both formal and timbral terms from the main drama, thus sidestepping the danger of anticlimax that Boito had feared. That the scene begins with Fenton's extended sonnet, 'Dal labbro il canto', is also significant, because the delicate atmosphere established in intervals by the young lovers through the opera now becomes the dominant strain in the music.

Fenton is rudely interrupted by Alice, who provides him with a disguise before they rush off to take their positions. Falstaff appears and solemnly counts the 12 bells of midnight. He is joined by Alice, and a fleeting repetition of their earlier meeting ensues before Meg enters to warn of an approaching pack of witches. As Falstaff throws himself to the ground, fearing death if he sees these supernatural beings, Nannetta begins a delicate invocation that eventually flowers into 'Sul fil d'un soffio etesio', yet another aria suffused with the soft orchestral colours that characterize this scene. A sudden Prestissimo ushers in the rest of the cast, who begin tormenting

Falstaff in earnest. Their gleeful chorus, 'Pizzica, pizzica', later adorned with mock religious chanting, is halted only when Bardolph gets carried away and allows his hood to slip. Falstaff immediately recognizes him and bestows on him a generous torrent of abuse. Soon the entire deception is revealed, Falstaff assuming new stature in his philosophical acceptance of what has befallen him.

A gentle minuet introduces Caius and 'The Queen of the Fairies' (whom Caius thinks is Nannetta). They are joined by another couple and both pairs receive Ford's blessing. But with Ford's final words, the deception is revealed: 'The Queen of the Fairies' turns out to be Bardolph in disguise, and the other couple are – of course – Fenton and Nannetta. This time it is Ford's turn to admit defeat and (the minuet returning) he agrees to accept his daughter's marriage. Falstaff leads off the final ensemble, a comic fugue to the words 'Tutto nel mondo è burla' ('Everything in the world is a joke'). The ironic reference to an academic form, the polyphony and confusion of voices and, most of all, the constant, driving energy of the piece from a fitting end to Verdi's final opera.

*

Perhaps the most immediately obvious level of difference between *Falstaff* and all Verdi's previous operas lies in the music's tendency to respond in unprecedented detail to the verbal element of the drama. In much of the score, but especially in the great duets and monologues, the listener is bombarded by a stunning diversity of rhythms, orchestral textures, melodic motifs and harmonic devices. Passages that in earlier times would have furnished material for an entire number here crowd in on each other, shouldering themselves unceremoniously to the fore in bewildering succession. And a large number of these fresh ideas spring in a direct and literal way from the words. Such exaggerated literalism would be obtrusive in a tragic opera, in which the need for underlying emotional communication often overrides responses to individual words. But here, in the comic context, it furnishes an important means of filling the musical space with an endless variety of colours. And this is by no means the only level of diversification in the score, for it is clear that Verdi was fully aware of the opera's 'polyphonic' texture and was – on occasion – even prepared to interrupt the drama in order to enhance it. As he said in a letter to Boito discussing Fenton's sonnet in Act 3, 'as far as the drama goes we could do without it; but . . . the whole piece provides me with a new colour for the musical palette'.

These new aspects, possible only through the medium of comedy, served to stimulate Verdi's creative imagination to new levels of fecundity. In the midst of an increasingly fragmented aesthetic world, he was able to follow the whim of the moment, to gaze back serenely on past achievements and, as he said so many times in letters to Boito, simply to enjoy himself. Few would deny how richly Verdi deserved this final triumph, or how heartening a message *Falstaff* offers. The opera leaves us with a musical image that exactly reflects those famous photographs of Verdi in his last years: an old man, in black hat, with eyes that have lived through a lifetime of struggle, smiling out wisely at the world.

Glossary, Index of Role Names and Suggested Further Reading

Glossary

Act One of the main divisions of an opera, usually completing a part of the action and often having a climax of its own. The classical five-act division was adopted in early operas and common in serious French opera of the 17th and 18th centuries, but in Italian opera a three-act scheme was soon standard, later modified to two in *opera buffa*. From the late 18th century, operas were written in anything from one act to five, with three the most common; Wagner's ideal music drama was to consist of three acts.

Air French or English term for 'song' or 'aria'. In French opera of the 17th and 18th centuries it was applied both to unpretentious, brief pieces and to serious, extended monologues, comparable to arias in Italian opera.

Alto *See* Castrato; and Contralto

Apoggiatura (It.) A 'leaning note', normally one step above the note it precedes. Apoggiatura were normally introduced by performers, in recitativevs and arias in 18th century opera, to make the musical line conform to the natural inflection of the words an (in arias) to increase the expressiveness.

Aria (It.) A closed, lyrical piece for solo voice, the standard vehicle for expression on the part of an operatic character. Arias appear in the earliest operas. By the early 18th century they usually follow a da capa pattern (*ABA*); by Mozart's time they took various forms, among them the slow-fast type, sometimes called rondò. this remained popular in Italian opera during most of the 19th century (the 'cantabile-cabaletta' type); even longer forms, sometimes in four sections with interruptions to reflect changes of mood, appear in the operas of Donizetti and Verdi. The aria as a detachable unit became less popular later in the century; Wagner wrote none in his mature operas, nor Verdi in *Otello* or *Falstaff* ; in Puccini, too, an aria

is usually part of the dramatic texture and cannot readily be extracted. Some 20th-century composers (notably Stravinsky, in the neo-classical *Rake's Progress*) have revived the aria, but generally it has been favoured only where a formal or artificial element has been required.

Arietta (It.), **Ariette** (Fr.) A song, shorter and less elaborate than a fully developed aria or air.

Arioso (It.) 'Like an aria': a singing (as opposed to a declamatory) style of performance; a short passage in a regular tempo in the middle or at the end of a recitative; or a short aria.

Ballabile (It.: 'suitable for dancing') A movement intended for dancing; Verdi used the term in Act 3 of *Macbeth* for the song and dance of the witches.

Ballata (It.) A dance-song; Verdi used the term for 'Questa o quella', in *Rigoletto*.

Barcarolle A piece with a lilting rhythm suggesting the songs of Venetian gondoliers; the most famous operatic example is Act 3 of Offenbach's *Les contes d'Hoffmann*.

Baritone A male voice of moderately low pitch, normally in the range $A–f'$. The voice became important in opera in the late 18th century, particularly in Mozart's works, although the word 'baritone' was little used at this time ('bass' served for both types of low voice). Verdi used the baritone for a great variety of roles, including secondary heroic ones.

Bass The lowest male voice, normally in the range $F–e'$. The voice is used in operas of all periods, often for gods, figures of authority (a king, a priest, a father) and for villains and sinister characters. There are several subclasses of bass: the *basso buffo*

225

(in Italian comic opera), the *basso cantante* or French *basse-chantante* (for a more lyrical role) and the *basso profundo* (a heavy, deep, voice).

Bass-baritone A male voice combining the compass and other attributes of the bass and the baritone. It is particularly associated with Wagner, especially the roles of Wotan (the *Ring*) and Sachs (*Die Meistersinger*).

Breeches part [trouser role] Term for a man or boy's part sung by a woman. The central examples are Cherubino in *Le nozze di Figaro* and Oktavian in *Der Rosenkavalier*, but there are many more, among them Verdi's Oscar (Edgar) in *Un ballo in maschera*, Fyodor in *Boris Godunov*, Hänsel, and the Composer in *Ariadne auf Naxos*. In Baroque opera numerous male parts were written for women but, with the issue confused by castrato singers, casting was less sexually specific.

Brindisi A song inviting a company to raise their glasses and drink. There are examples in Donizetti's *Lucrezia Borgia*, Verdi's *La traviata* and *Otello* and Mascagni's *Cavelleria rusticana*.

Cabaletta (It.) Term for the concluding section, generally in a fairly rapid tempo and with mounting excitement, of an extended aria or duet, sometimes dramatically motivated by an interruption after the slower first part (the 'cantabile' or 'cavatina'). The most famous example is Violetta's 'Sempre libera degg'io' (the final section of 'Ah fors'è lui') in Act 1 of Verdi's *La traviata*.

Cadenza A virtuoso passage inserted in an aria, usually near the end, either improvised by the singer or, as in Verdi's later operas, written out by the composer.

Cantabile (It.) 'In a singing style': usually the first, slower part of a two-part aria or duet; it can also indicate an aria in slow or moderate tempo, with a broadly phased vocal line.

Canzone (It.) Term used in opera for items presented as songs, sung outside the dramatic action, for example Cherubino's 'Voi che spaete' in *Le nozze di Figaro* (although Mozart called it simply 'Arietta'). Verdi used it several times, notably for Desdemona's Willow Song in *Otello*.

Cavatina (It.) In 18th-century opera a short aria, without da capo, often an entrance aria. Mozart used the term three times in *Le nozze di Figaro*. Later examples are Rosina's 'Una voce poco fà' in Rossini's *Il barbiere di Siviglia* and Lady Macbeth's 'Vieni t'affretta' in Verdi's *Macbeth*. Cavatinas often concluded with a Cabaletta.

Coloratura Florid figuration or ornamentation. The term is usually applied to high-pitched florid writing, exemplified by such roles as the Queen of the Night in Mozart's *Die Zauberflöte*, Violetta in Verdi's *La traviata* or Zerbinetta in Strauss's *Ariadne auf Naxos*, as well as many roles by Rossini and other early 19th-century Italian composers. The term 'coloratura soprano' signifies a singer of high pitch, lightness and agility, appropriate to such roles.

Comic opera A musico-dramatic work of a light or amusing nature. The term may be applied equally to an Italian *opera buffa*, a French *opéra comique*, a German Singspiel, a Spanish zarzuela or an English opera of light character. It is also often applied to operetta or *opéra bouffe* and even musical comedy. Most non-Italian comic operas have spoken dialogue rather than continuous music.

Contralto (It.) A voice normally written for the range *g–e"*. In modern English the term denotes the lowest female voice, but the term could also denote a male falsetto singer or a castrato.

In opera, true contrato (as distinct from mezzo-soprano) roles are exceptional. They occurred in the 17th century for old women, almost invariably comic, but in the 18th century composers came to appreciate the deep female voice for dramatic purposes. In

Handel's operas several contralto roles stand in dramatic contrast to the prima donna, for example Cornelia in *Giulio Caesare*, a mature woman and a figure of tragic dignity. Rossini's important contralto (or mezzo) roles include Cinderella in *La Cenerentola*, Rosina in *Il barbiere di Siviglia* (original version), and the heroic part of Arsaces in *Semiramide*. In later opera, contraltos were repeatedly cast as a sorceress-like figure (Verdi's Azucena and Arvidson/Ulrica, Wagner's Ortrud) or an oracle (Wagner's Erda) and sometimes as an old women.

Dramma giocoso (It.) Term used in Italian librettos in the late 18th century for a comic opera, particularly for the type favoured by Carlo Goldoni and his followers in which character-types from the serious opera appeared alongside those traditional to comic opera. The *dramma giocoso* was not regarded as a distinct genre and the title was used interchangeably with others; Mozart's *Don Giovanni*, for example, is described on the libretto as a 'dramma giocoso' and on the scores an 'opera buffa'.

Dramma [drama] **per musica** [dramma musicale] (It.) 'Play for music': a phrase found on the title-page of many Italian librettos, referring to a text expressly written to be set by a composer.

Duet (It.) An ensemble for two singers. It was used in opera almost from the outset, often at the end of an act or when the principal lovers were united (or parted). Later the duet became merged in the general continuity of the music (Verdi, Puccini etc) or dissolved into a musical dialogue in which the voices no longer sang simultaneously (later Wagner, R. Strauss etc). The love duet had become characterized by singing in 3rds or 6ths, acquiring a mellifluous quality of sound appropriate to shared emotion. Often the voices are used singly at first and join together later, symbolizing the development described in the text.

Finale (It.) The concluding, continuously composed, section of an act of an opera.

The ensemble finale developed, at the beginning of the second half of the 18th century, largely through the changes wrought in comic opera by Carlo Goldoni (1707–93), who in his librettos made act finales longer, bringing in more singers and increasing the density of the plot.

Grand opéra A term used to signify both the Paris Opéra and the operas performed there. Later it tended to be applied more narrowly to the specially monumental works performed at the Opéra during its period of greatest magnificence, including Rossini's *Guillaume Tell* and several operas composed to librettos by Eugène Scribe by Meyerbeer and others during the 1830s (including *Les Hugenots*). The term also applies to operas by Donizetti, Gounod, Verdi and Massenet.

Interlude Music played or sung between the main parts of a work.

Key The quality of a musical passage or composition that causes it to be sensed as gravitating towards a particular note, called the keytone or the tonic.

Leitmotif (Ger. Leitmotiv) 'Leading motif': a theme, or other musical idea, that represents or symbolizes a person, object, place, idea, state of mind, supernatural force or some other ingredient in a dramatic work. It may recur unaltered, or it may be changed in rhythm, intervallic structure, tempo, harmony, orchestration or accompaniment, to signify dramatic development, and may be combined with other leitmotifs. The concept is particularly associated with Wagner, who used it as a basis for his musical structures, but the idea was older.

Libretto (It.) 'Small book': a printed book containing the words of an opera; by extension, the text itself. In the 17th and 18th centuries, when opera houses were lit, librettos were often read during performances; when an opera was given in a language other than that of the audience, librettos were bilingual, with parallel texts on opposite pages.

Melisma A passage of florid writing in which several notes are sung in the same syllable.

Melodrama A kind of drama, or a technique used within a drama, in which the action is carried forward by the protagonist speaking in the pauses of, or during, orchestral passages, similar in style to those in operatic accompanied recitative. Its invention is usually dated to J.-J. Rousseau's *Pygmalion* (*c*1762). Georg Benda was its chief exponent in Germany; Mozart, influenced by him, wrote melodrama sections in his *Zaide*, Beethoven used melodrama sections in the dungeon scene of *Fidelio*; Weber used it, notably in *Der Freischütz*, Most 19th-century composers of opera have used it as a dramatic device, for example Verdi, for letter scenes in *Macbeth* and *La traviata*, and Smetana in *The Two Widows*. It has been much used by 20th-century composers, among them Puccini, Strauss, Berg, Britten and Henze.

Melodramma (It.) Term for a dramatic text written to be set to music (*see* Dramma per musica), or the resultant opera. It does not mean Melodrama. Verdi's second opera, *Un giorno di regno*, with a libretto by Felice Romani, was termed a *melodramma giocoso*; the term reappeared on *I masnadieri* and *Macbeth*, as well as *Rigoletto*, *Un ballo in maschera* and the revised *Simon Boccanegra*, but it is hard to attach any special significance to it as terms were used interchangeably.

Mezzo-soprano Term for a voice, usually female, normally written for within the range $a–f\sharp''$. The distinction between the florid soprano and the weightier mezzo-soprano became common only towards the mid-18th century. The castrato Senesino, for whom Handel composed was described as having a 'penetrating, clear, even, and pleasant deep soprano voice (mezzo Soprano)'. The distinction was more keenly sensed in the 19th century, although the mezzo-soprano range was often extended as high as a $b\flat''$. Mezzo-sopranos with an extended upper range tackled the lower of two soprano roles in such operas as Bellini's *Norma* (Adagisa) and Donizetti's *Anna Bolena* (Jane Seymour). Both sopranos and mezzo-sopranos sing many of Wagner's roles.

The mezzo-soprano was often assigned a Breeches part in the era immediately after the demise of the Castrato, such as Arsace's in *Semiramide*; at all periods they have taken adolescent roles such as Cherubino (*Le nozze di Figaro*) or Oktavian (*Der Rosenkavalier*). The traditional casting however is as a nurse or confidante (e.g. Brangäne in *tristan und Isolde*, Suzuki in *Madama Butterfly*) or as the mature married woman (e.g. Herodias in Strauss's *Salome*). Saint-Saëns's Delilah is an exception to the general rule that the principal female role (particularly the beautiful maiden) is a soprano.

Modulation The movement out of one key into another as a continuous musical process. It is particularly used in opera as a device to suggest a change of mood.

Motif A short musical idea, melodic, rhythmic, or harmonic (or any combination of those).

Music drama, Musical drama The term 'Musical drama' was used by Handel for *Hercules* (1745), to distinguish it from opera and Sacred Drama. In more recent usage, the meanings attached to 'music drama' derive from the ideas formulated in Wagner's *Oper und Drama*; it is applied to his operas and to others in which the musical, verbal and scenic elements cohere to serve one dramatic end. In 1869, Verdi distinguished between opera of the old sort and the *dramma musicale* that he believed his *La forza del destino* to be. Current theatrical practice tends to qualify this unity by performing music dramas with the original music and words but freshly invented scenic elements.

Number opera Term for an opera consisting of individual sections or 'number' which can be detached from the whole, as distinct from an opera consisting of continuous music. It applies to the various forms of 18th-century opera and to some 19th-century grand operas. Under Wagner's influence the number opera became unfashionable, and neither his operas nor those of late Verdi, Puccini and the *verismo* school can be so called. Some notable works can be considered number operas, such as Berg's *Wozzeck* and Stravinsky's deliberately archaic *The Rake's Progress*.

Opera buffa (It.) 'Comic opera': a term commonly used to signify Italian comic opera, principally of the 18th century, with recitative rather than spoken dialogue. Though now applied generically, it was one of the several such terms used in the 18th century.

Ostinato (It.) Term used to refer to the repetition of a musical pattern many times over; the Ground bass is a form of *ostinato* used in early opera.

Overture A piece of orchestral music designed to precede a dramatic work. By the mid-18th century the Italian type prevailed and the first movement had become longer and more elaborate; there was a tendency to drop the second and the third movements. In serious opera there was sometimes an effort to set the mood of the coming drama as in Gluck's *Alceste* and Mozart's *Idomeneo*; the famous preface to *Alceste* emphasizes the importance of this. In Mozart's *Don Giovanni*, *Così fan Tutte* and *Die Zauberflöte* the overture quotes musical ideas from the opera. Between 1790 and 1820, there was usually a slow introduction. The notion of tying the overture to the opera in mood and theme was developed in France and also appealed to the German Romantics. Beethoven made powerful use of dramatic motifs in his *Leonore* overtures while in Weber's *Der Freischütz* and *Euryanthe* overtures almost every theme reappears in the drama. Composers of French grand opera tended to expand the overture. For Bellini, Donizetti and Verdi the short prelude was an alternative, and it

became normal in Italian opera after the mid-century. Wagner, in the *Ring*, preferred a 'prelude' fully integrated into the drama, as did Richard Strauss amd Puccini, whose prelude to *Tosca* consists simply of three chords (associated with a particular character). In comic operas and operettas the independent overtures lasted longer; the structure based on the themes from the drama became a medly of tunes. The 'medley' or 'potpourri' overture used by Auber, Gounod, Thomas, Offenbach and Sullivan can still be traced in musical-comedy overtures.

Parlando, Parlante (It.) 'Speaking': a direction requiring a singer to use a manner approximating to speech.

Pezzo concertato (It.) 'Piece in concerted style': a section within a finale in Italian 19th-century opera in which several characters express divergent emotions simultaneously, as it were a 'multiple soliloquy'. It is usually in slow tempo and is sometimes called 'largo concertato'.

Preghiera (It: 'prayer') a number common in 19th-century opera in which a character prays for divine assistance in his or her plight. Moses's 'Dal tuo stellato soglio' in Rossini's *Mosè in Egito* (1818) is perhaps the best-known *preghiera* actually so titled; Desdemona's 'Ave Maria' in Verdi's *Otello* is a late example of the traditional gentle *preghiera*.

Prelude *see* Overture

Prima donna (It.) 'First lady': the principal female singer in an opera or on the roster of an opera company, almost always a soprano. The expression came into use around the mid-17th century, with the opening of public opera houses in Venice, where the ability of a leading lady to attract audiences became important. Singers who became prima donnas insisted on keeping that title; when conflicts arose, manegerial ingenuity devised such expressions as 'altra prima donna', 'prima donna assoluta' and even 'prima donna assoluta e sola'.

Some prima donnas made it a point of their status to be difficult. Adelina Patti (1843–1919), at the height of her career, stipulated that her name appear on posters in letters at least one-third larger than those used for other singers' names and that she be excused from rehearsals. The need to meet a prima donna's demands shaped many librettos and scores, particularly because her status was reflected in the number and character of the arias allotted to her.

Prologue   The introductory scene to a dramatic work, in which the author explains, either directly or indirectly, the context and meaning of the work to follow. In early opera, an allegorical prologue may pay homage to the author's patron. Prologues were a usual feature in early Baroque opera; in the late 18th century and the early 19th they were rare. Wagner's *Das Rheingold* may be seen as a prologue to the *Ring* since it represents the background to the plot. There are significant prologues to Gounod's *Roméo et Juliette*, Boito's *Mefistofele* and Leoncavallo's *Pagliacci* (the last modelled on those of ancient drama and with an exposition of the theory of *verismo*). In the 20th century various kinds of literary prologue have preceded operas, as in Stravinsky's *Oedipus rex*, Prokofiev's *Love for Three Oranges* and Berg's *Lulu*.

Quartet   An ensemble for four singers. Quartets appear as early as the 17th century; Cavalli's *Calisto* ends with one and A. Scarlatti wrote several. There are quartets in Handel's *Radamisto* and *Partenope*. They appear in many *opéras comiques*. In *opera buffa* of the Classical era, when ensembles are sometimes used to further the dramatic action, quartets sometimes occupy that role: examples are the Act 2 finale of Mozart's *Die Entführung aus dem Serail*, where the sequence of sections shows the consolidation of the relationships between the two pairs of lovers, and in Act 1 of his *Don Giovanni*, where 'Non ti fidar' draws together the dramatic threads. The quartet in the last act of *Idomeneo* is however more a series

of statements by the characters of their emotional positions, as is the quartet for the 'wedding' toast in the finale of *Così fan tutte*. Another canonic quartet is 'Mir ist so wunderbar' from Beethoven's *Fidelio*. Verdi wrote a quartet in *Otello*, but his best-known example is the one from *Rigoletto*, an inspired piece of simultaneous portrayal of feeling.

Quintet   An ensemble for five singers. Quintets, except within ensemble finales, are rare in the operatic repertory. Notable exceptions are the two in Mozart's *Così fan tutte*. The only substantial ensemble in the sense of a number where the characters sing simultaneously in Wagner's late operas is the famous quintet in *Die Meistersinger von Nürnberg*, a rare moment in his operas where the dramatic action is suspended an the characters take emotional stock.

Rataplan   Term used onomatopoeically for a type of chorus based on the martial life, with flourishes of drums, fanfare-like figures etc.

Recitative   A type of vocal writing which follows closely the natural rhythem and accentuation of speech, not necessarily governed by a regular tempo or organized in a specific form. It derived from the development in the late 16th century of a declamatory narrative style with harmonic support, a wide melodic range and emotionally charged treatment of words. During the 17th century, recitative came to be the vehicle for dialogue, providing a connecting link between arias; the trailing off before the cadence (representing the singers being overcome with emotion), leaving the accompaniment to provide the closure, became a convention, as did the addition of an apoggiatura at any cadence point to follow the natural inflection of Italian words.

By the late 17th century a more rapid, even delivery had developed, a trend carried further in *opera buffa* of the 18th century. Recitative was sung in a free, conversational manner. Plain or simple recitative, accompanied only by Continuo, is known as *recitativo semplice* or *recitativo secco* (or simply *secco*), to distinguish it from accompanied or orchestral recitative (*recitativo accompagnato*, *stromentato* or *obbligato*), which in the 18th century grew increasingly important for dramatic junctures. In France, the language demanded a different style, slower-moving, more lyrical and more flexible.

Recitative with keyboard accompaniment fell out of use early in the 19th century. Recitative-like declamation, however, remained an essential means of expression. Even late in the 19th century, when written operas with spoken dialogue were given in large houses where speech was not acceptable (like the Paris Opéra), recitatives were supplied by house composers or hacks (or the composer himself, for example Gounod with *Faust*) to replace dialogue: the most famous example is Guiraud's long-used set of recitatives for Bizet's *Carmen*. With the more continuous textures favoured in the 20th century, the concept of recitative disappeared (as it did in Wagner's mature works), to be replaced by other kinds of representation of speech. *Sprechgesang* may be seen as an Expressionist equivalent of recitative.

Rescue opera Term used for a type of opera, popular in France after the 1789 Revolution, in which the hero or heroine is delivered at the last moment either from the cruelty of a tyrant or from some natural catastrophe, not by a *deus ex machina* but by heroic human endeavour. It reflected the secular idealism of the age and often carried a social message. Some rescue operas were based on contemporary real-life incidents, among them Gaveaux's *Léonore, ou l'amour conjugal* (1798) and Cherubini's *Les deux journées* (1800), both to librettos by J. N. Bouilly. The former was the source of Beethoven's *Fidelio*.

Romance Term used in 18th- and 19th-century opera for a ballad-like type of strophic song. It suited the sentimentalism of *opéra comique*, and in Germany was used in Singspiel, notably by Mozart

(Pedrillo's 'Im Mohrenland' in *Die Entführung aus dem Serail*) and later Weber ('Nero, dem Kettenbund' in *Der Freischütz*); Italian examples include several by Verdi, notably Manrico's 'Deserto sulla terra' (*Il trovatore*) and Radamès's 'Celeste Aida' (*Aida*).

Scena (It.), **Scène** (Fr.) Term used to mean (1) the stage (e.g. 'sulla scena', on the stage; 'derrière la scène', behind the stage), (2) the scene represented on the stage, (3) a division of an act (*see* Scene). In Italian opera it also means an episode with no formal construction but made up of diverse elements. The 'Scena e duetto' is a typical unit in opera of the Rossinian period. A *scena* of a particularly dramatic character, often (though not invariably) for a single character, may be described as a 'gran scena', e.g. 'Gran scena del sonnambulismo' in Verdi's *Macbeth*.

Scene (1) The location of an opera, or an act or part of an act of an opera; by extension, any part of an opera in one location. (2) In earlier usage, a scene was a section of an act culminating in an aria (or occasionally an ensemble); any substantial (in some operas, any at all) change in the characters on the stage was reckoned a change of scene, and the scenes were numbered accordingly.

Septet An ensemble for seven singers. Septets are rare in the operatic repertory; a famous example is 'Par une telle nuit', from Berlioz's *Les troyens*, based on a text from Shakespeare's 'On such a night as this' (*The Merchant of Venice*).

Set piece An aria or other numbers clearly demarcated from its context.

Soprano (It.) The highest female voice, normally written for within the range $c'-a''$; the word is also applied to a boy's treble voice and in the 17th and 18th centuries to a castrato of high range. The soprano voice was used for expressive roles in the earliest operas. During the Baroque period it was found to be suited to brilliant vocal display, and when a singer achieved fame it was usually because of an ability to perform elaborate music with precision as well as beauty. The heroine's role was sung by the most skilful soprano, the prima donna; to her were assigned the greatest number of arias and the most difficult and expressively wide-ranging music. The highest note usually required was *a* and little merit was placed on the capacity to sing higher.

The development of the different categories of the soprano voice belongs to the 19th century, strongly foreshadowed in the variety of roles and styles found in Mozart's operas (although type-casting was not at all rigid: the singer of Susanna in 1789 created Fiordiligi the next year). It was a consequence of the divergence of national operatic traditions and the rise of a consolidated repertory. Italian sopranos of the age of Rossini and Bellini developed a coloratura style and the ability to sustain a long lyrical line (the coloratura soprano and the lyric soprano); later, in Verdi's time, with larger opera houses and orchestras, the more dramatic *spinto* and *lirico spirito* appeared. In Germany the dramatic or heroic soprano was already foreshadowed in Beethoven's Leonore and Weber's Agathe; Wagner's Brünnhilde, demanding great power and brilliance, was the climax of this development. French *grand opéra* developed its own style of lyric-dramatic soprano. The operetta too produced a light, agile voice of its own.

Spinto (It.) 'Pushed': term for a lyric voice, usually soprano or tenor, that is able to sound powerful and incisive at dramatic climaxes. The full expression is 'lirico spinto'. The term is also used to describe roles that require voices of this character, for example Mimì in Puccini's *La bohème* and Alfredo in Verdi's *La traviata*.

Stretta, Stretto (It.) Term used to indicate a faster tempo at the climactic concluding section of a piece. It is common in Italian opera: examples include the end of the Act 2 finale of Mozart's *Le nozze di Figaro* and Violetta's aria at the end of Act 1 of Verdi's *La traviata*.

Strophic Term for a song or an aria in which all stanzas of the text are set to the same music. The term 'strophic variations' is used of songs where the melody is varied from verse to verse while the bass remains unchanged or virtually so. The form was popular in early 17th-century Italy; 'Possente spirito', sung by Monteverdi's Orpheus, is an example, and Cavalli occasionally used the form.

Tempo d'attaco (It.) Term used in Italian opera of the 19th century for the fast movement of a duet (or an aria) following the recitative.

Tempo di mezzo (It.) 'Middle movement': term used in Italian 19th-century opera for a fast transitional passage seperating the two principal sections of an aria (such as the Cantabile and the Cabaletta).

Tenor The highest natural male voice, normally written for within the range *c–a'*. Although the tenor voice was valued in early opera – a tenor, Francesco Rasi (1574– after 1620), sang Monteverdi's Orpheus (1607) – heroic roles in middle and late Baroque opera were assigned to the castrato. Tenors took minor roles, such as the old man (sometimes with comic overtones), the lighthearted confidant, the mischievous schemer or the messenger, or even a travesty role of the old nurse. By the 1720s, important roles were occasionally given to tenors, and by the Classical era the voice was more regularly used in central roles. Such roles as Mozart's Bassilio, Ottavio, Ferrando and Titus – comic, docile lover, more virile lover, benevolent monarch – define the scope of the voice at this period.

A creation of the early 19th century was the *tenore di grazia*, a light, high voice moving smoothly into falsetto up to *d''*, called for by many Rossini roles. With the increasing size of opera houses, and the changes in musical style, the *tenore di forza* was called for. The tendency continued as, with Verdi's operas, the *tenore robusto* developed. For the German heroic tenor roles of the 19th century, especially Wagner's, a more weighty, durable type was needed, the Heldentenor. The lighter tenor continued to be cultivated for the more lyrical French roles. Many of the great tenors of the 20th century have been Italians, and made their names in Italian music, from Enrico Caruso (1873–1921) to Luciano Pavarotti; to these the Spaniard Plácido Domingo should be added.

Terzet, Trio An ensemble for three singers. Terzets or trios have been used throughout the history of opera. there is an example in Monteverdi's *L'incoronazione di Poppea*; Handel used the form several times, notably in *Tamerlano*, *Orlando*, and *Alcina*, and Gluck wrote examples in the closing scenes of his Italian reform operas. Mozart's include three (one in *Don Giovanni*, two in *La clemenza di Tito*) which are akin to arias with comments from two subsidiary characters. There are two in Weber's *Der Freischütz* and several for very high tenors

in Rossini's serious operas. The form was much used by the Romantics, among them Verdi, who wrote three examples in *Un ballo in maschera*.

Tonal Term used for music in a particular key, or a pitch centre to which the music naturally gravitates. The use of tonalities, or the interplay of keys, can be an important dramatic weapon in the opera composer's armoury.

Trio *see* Terzet

Vaudeville final (Fr.) Placed at the end of an act or play, the *vaudeville final* reassembled on stage all the important characters and required each to sing one or more verses of a vaudeville, usually with a choral refrain. This style was common in French opera and *opéra comique*. The influence of the *vaudeville final* may be seen in other genres, and continued into later periods, as in Gluck's *Orfeo*, Mozart's *Die Entführung aus dem Serail*, Rossini's *Il barbiere di Siviglia*, Verdi's *Falstaff*, Ravel's *L'heure espagnole* and Stravinsky's *The Rake's Progress*.

Index of role names

Index of role names

Suggested further reading

The New Grove Dictionary of Opera, edited by Stanley Sadie (London and New York, 1992)

*

CATALOGUES

C. Hopkinson: *A Bibliography of the Works of Giuseppe Verdi, 1813–1901*, i (New York, 1973) [vocal and instrumental works excluding operas]; ii (New York, 1978) [operas]

M. Chusid: *A Catalog of Verdi's Operas* (Hackensack, NJ, 1974)

LETTERS AND DOCUMENTS

M. Conati: *Interviste e incontri con Verdi* (Milan, 1980; English translation as *Interviews and Encounters with Verdi*, 1984)

M. Conati and M. Medici, eds: *The Verdi-Boito correspondence* (English translation, W. Weaver; Chicago, 1994)

BIOGRAPHY, LIFE AND WORKS

F. Toye: *Guiseppe Verdi: his Life and Works* (London, 1931)

F. Walker: *The Man Verdi* (London, 1962)

W. Weaver: *Verdi: a Documentary Study* (London, 1977)

W. Weaver and M. Chusid, eds: *The Verdi Companion* (New York, 1979)

M. Mila: *L'arte di Verdi* (Turin, 1980)

D.R.B. Kimbell: *Verdi in the Age of Italian Romanticism* (Cambridge, 1981)

A. Porter: 'Giuseppe Verdi', *The New Grove Masters of Italian Opera*, ed. S. Sadie (London, 1983)

J. Rosselli: *The Opera Industry in Italy from Cimarosa to Verdi: the Role of the Impresario* (Cambridge, 1984)

J. Budden: *Verdi* (London, 1985)

C. Osborne: *Verdi: a Life in the Theatre* (New York, 1987)

G. Martin: *Aspects of Verdi* (New York, 1988)

R. Parker: *Studies in Early Verdi 1832–1844: New Information and Perspectives on the Milanese Musical Milieu and the Operas from 'Oberto' to 'Ernani'* (New York, 1989)

M.J. Philips-Matz: *Verdi, a biography* (Oxford, 1993)

ANNALS

T. Kaufman: *Verdi and his Major Contemporaries: a Selected Chronology of Performances with Casts* (New York, 1990)

MUSICAL STUDIES

C. Osborne: *The Complete Operas of Verdi* (London, 1969)

J. Budden: *The Operas of Verdi*, i: *From Oberto to Rigoletto* (London, 1973); ii: *From Il trovatore to La forza del destino* (London, 1978); iii: *From Don Carlos to Falstaff* (London, 1981)

G. Edwards and R. Edwards: *The Verdi baritone studies in the development of dramatic character* (Bloomington, 1994)

P. Petrobelli: *Music in the theater: essays on Verdi and other composers* (Princeton, NJ, 1994)

M. Chusid, ed.: *Verdi's middle period, 1849–1859: source studies, analysis, and performance practice* (Chicago, 1997)

G. de Van: *Verdi's theatre creating drama through music* (English translation, G. Roberts; Chicago, 1998)

OPERAS

D. Rosen and A. Porter, eds: *Verdi's 'Macbeth': a Sourcebook* (New York, 1984)

N. John, ed.: *Macbeth* (London, 1990); *Rigoletto* (London, 1982); *Il trovatore* (London, 1983); *La traviata* (London, 1981); *Simon Boccanegra* (London, 1985); *Un ballo in maschera* (London, 1990); *The Force of Destiny* (London, 1983); *Don Carlos* (London, 1992); *Aida* (London, 1980); *Otello* (London, 1981); *Falstaff* (London, 1982) [ENO opera guides]

H. Busch: *Verdi's 'Aida': the History of an Opera in Letters and Documents* (Minneapolis, 1978)

J.A. Hepokoski: *Giuseppe Verdi: Otello* (Cambridge, 1987)

H. Busch: *Verdi's 'Otello' and 'Simon Boccanegra' (revised version) in Letters and Documents* (Oxford, 1988)

J.A. Hepokoski: *Giuseppe Verdi: Falstaff* (Cambridge, 1983)